effective group discussion

third edition

effective group discussion

john k brilhart

University of Nebraska at Omaha

wcb

WM. C. BROWN COMPANY PUBLISHERS
Dubuque, Iowa

Copyright © 1967, 1974, 1978 by Wm. C. Brown Company Publishers

Library of Congress Catalog Card Number 77—83020

ISBN 0—697—04154—9

Fifth Printing, 1981

Printed in the United States of America

57134

Contents

Preface

Effective Group Discussion began as a short, practical book intended for use as one of several print sources in a basic speech communication course. However, it was used extensively as the text in beginning and intermediate courses in small group communication, largely because of the strong emphasis on practical "how to" techniques. The second edition enjoyed wide adoption in discussion and small group communication courses, maintaining the practical emphasis with considerably greater underpinning from the research and theoretical literature. This third edition retains the clear dedication to the practical and useable: it has been written for the person interested in becoming a more effective participant and leader in small group discussions of all types. Like its predecessor editions, it should be useful to more than the student in "speech" courses: instructors in group dynamics, education, continuing education, business administration, and community leadership should be able to use it. Leaders should find it an even more helpful reference source than were the previous two editions.

I believe strongly that to understand any field of study or any complex phenomenon (such as the small group) one must acquire the specialized vocabulary of the field; one does not acquire jargon for its own sake, but as a tool for observing, understanding, and predicting. To this end I have tried to help the student of small groups develop a mastery of the terminology by including, for the first time, a list of definitions of "key concepts" at the end of each chapter. Combined, these lists make a core glossary.

The chapters are written so that after the first two, each is relatively independent of the others. Thus, they can be studied in almost any order desired by an instructor, and they can be used as a reference source without having to read it all to understand a technique presented in Chapter 8. I usually assign students to skim the entire book when beginning a course, then deal with each section in detail via discussions, demonstrations, and the exercises presented at the end of each chapter.

The number and types of exercises have been increased greatly over the second edition. I believe that a course in small group communication must be largely experiential rather than a study of concepts and theory in the abstract. I debated long with myself over whether to write a separate "instructor's manual," and decided against it for two reasons: (1) I believe the instructor must not be manipulative, playing tricks or games with the students, the instructor being the only one who knows the objective of an exercise or activity; and (2) I believe students learn best when they participate in the selection of goals and activities. To this end, the "instructor's manual" has been largely incorporated into the text and exercises. All I would add in a separate instructor's guide is a pool of examination questions and a schedule/syllabus. But it is my experience that the questions others write often do not work well for me, and the questions based on new text could not be item analyzed before publication. The schedule for a course is implied in the very structure of the book and exercises, though numerous variations in chapter sequence and activities are possible.

This third edition, like its predecessors, was written for students, not for faculty scholars. Repetition is consciously present. Many examples are included from personal experience to offset the limited experience of some freshmen. Figures are designed to clarify rather than to entertain. In revising, I have reviewed most of the research and theory literature, and selected that which I felt could be applied with a reasonable level of confidence. Much of the research is too circumscribed in design, locale, and subjects to make any valid generalizations to the groups with which people in the world of everyday affairs are involved. A theory of leadership and group dynamics is provided, bolstered by research. And I have tried to provide a rationale, as thoroughly grounded in research as possible, for most group procedures and techniques. But much that I advise is based on what I find happening in the many councils, committees, boards, and classroom groups in which I have been involved.

Thus, much that is new in this edition is highly practical. For example, I have gone into detail on parliamentary procedure in committees, because I have found this to be a critical issue in the many faculty committees on which I serve. I have included thorough coverage of the Nominal Group Technique because at times I have found it helpful in very real working groups. I find no conflict between the encounter techniques of the human potential movement and the rational problem-solving procedures of Kepner and Tregoe; to me these are complementary, not contradictory. Both have an important place in this book.

In the areas of problem solving, decision making, and leadership I focus on what has been found to produce optimal outcomes (including on the "bottom line") rather than describing how the average (but possibly ineffective and untrained) group functions. Thus, I remain largely "prescriptive" rather than "descriptive" of the average (and too often mediocre). The reflective thinking pattern is still being applied to all sorts of problems by many writers in the area of group communication despite numerous studies by Maier, Delbecq, Larson, Kepner and Tregoe, and Brilhart which demonstrated that it has severe limitations as a prescriptive guide for problem solving. Studies of decision emergence and phases in field groups tell us little about how to function *optimally* in groups, just as the antileader stress of some "group dynamics" enthusiasts never could work in the real-world group.

More space than before has been devoted to learning discussions of various types. These are often overlooked by colleagues with an almost total problem-solving focus. Yet this book is well suited to the course devoted just to problem-solving discussion. But it has far more.

While revising this book I have been reminded anew of my indebtedness to many teachers, both in and out of the classroom, who interested me in discussion, group dynamics, creative thinking, and human growth. I offer special thanks to J. Donald Phillips, Elton S. Carter, Sidney J. Parnes, Frances Whaley, Kenneth Hance, and acquaintances associated with the National Training Laboratories. My fellow participants in encounter groups, training laboratories, and innumerable committees and councils have made indirect contributions. I deeply appreciate the advice and support of fellow instructors of small group communication courses. Perhaps most of all my own students, both undergraduate and graduate, have helped me to evaluate and improve *Effective Group Discussion*.

J.K.B.

1

Discussion and Small Groups in Today's World

In our complex, organized society every person is a participant in many small groups. For most of us, much of each day is spent interacting in small groups. An adequate description of any modern organization will reveal many separate but interdependent work groups, task forces, teams, committees, councils, and the like—and meeting upon meeting in the schedule. The higher one goes in any organizational hierarchy, the more time the person spends in group discussions.

At this point, stop reading for a minute and list the small groups (3 to as many as 20 people) in which you participated even briefly during the past week. ... How many did you list? Is it like mine, with Committee C, Committee III, Communication 101 staff, graduate teaching assistants, beagle club board, three graduate committees, communication task group, gourmet club, and several informal discussions among clusters of students and faculty members? Even if the number for you was lower, wait a few years! Consider the following excerpts from actual discussion groups.

A subcommittee of the Graduate Council Committee on Faculty and Student Affairs had just met to do its work. The chairman spoke first:

> "Well, group, we've been given a charge to come up with two alternative plans, each with graduate faculty ranks and criteria for them, to present to the next Council meeting. I propose that we begin by examining the purpose of designating ranks among graduate faculty, how we came to get this assignment, and then design possible plans and discuss the merits of each until we reach a decision."

> "Well, okay Ward; but I've given this a lot of thought and I think we ought to come up with a plan that will encourage the Council to keep our present two ranks."

1

"So do I, frankly. But I think we have to do an honest job of devising a workable three-rank plan, also."

"Yeah. Let's face it. The purpose of graduate faculty membership and ranks, as I see it, is not to reward faculty or provide a basis for administrators to give pay raises and tenure, but to provide graduate students at each level with the best possible teaching and research guidance."

"Are we all agreed on that point of view? [signs of agreement from all present] Okay, I'll write that down to include in our report. Now, what? . . ."

The five students selected at random from the enrollment in a discussion course were required to develop a task force report on any issue they chose to tackle. The end products would include both a formal written report and an oral presentation to the class.

"Hey, you guys, tell you what we should do. Let's look into filmmaking and how it should be taught on our campus. We've got a lousy film program."

"Well, maybe that's a possibility. But I don't know anything about it. I'd like to work on how to make prostitution legal in our state, like it is in Nevada."

"Yeah, man, I dig you."

"You guys cut it out! What did Dr. Brilhart want when he assigned us this dumb job? Uh, you know, what will get us a good grade from the old boy?"

"Okay, good, so we'll go with the film thing, for I heard the department would like to establish a better film program. Mr. Knox said so in my movie class. Joe, what we oughta do is. . . ."

After dessert the family was talking around the table about a complaint Bev had lodged against her junior high school history teacher:

"Bev, how did your history class go today?"

"Oh, heck, Mom, Mr. Stoner said he didn't care what the Supreme Court had said, he felt we all ought to be reading our Bibles and going to church every Sunday."

"He did? Wait a minute. Just exactly what did he say?"

"Well, Dad, as best I can recall it. . . ."

The scene was the office of the vice-president in charge of research. Also present were the vice-president in charge of sales, the chief actuary, the executive vice-president, and two staff actuaries.

"You say your latest figures show a loss of $68,300 per year for the past three years on policy H-279?"

"Yes, and it's getting worse this year. Last year we actually put out $75,300 more on that line of policies than we took in."

"Joe, we can't go on like this. I know your boys like this policy because it is a good seller, but we're in business to make a profit."

All of the above are typical discussion situations. Each discussion type represented here is going on in hundreds of places across the country right now. And these are only a few of the types of situations and groups from which discussions emerge. Of all types of sustained direct oral communication, none is more common or important to our way of life than discussion. Yet when we study or talk about speech communication, we are often inclined to focus on the more glamorous but far less frequent process of public speaking—one person doing most of the talking with many persons more or less listening. It is in the process of *shared* talking and listening by two or more people that most of our communication through the spoken word is achieved. Discussion, a give-and-take process, is the medium and the context for the cooperative effort which makes group life of any sort possible. Indeed, discussion emerges almost every time people with a common interest come together.

Much of the decision making and planning in large organizations today is far too complex for one or two persons to handle successfully. Small groups gathered for the purposes of advising, inventing, and problem solving have become a way of life. Managers with extensive responsibility find it necessary, not just helpful, to consult frequently with advisory groups. In other than basic production work, the schedules for the majority of people list meeting after meeting.

Indeed, discussion groups are all around us. Each unit in a modern business, although controlled by policies set by groups above it, is responsible for solving its own problems as they arise. Small groups of representatives from basic work units must coordinate the efforts of their various departments at all levels—discussions, discussions! What is said here of business is just as true of governmental agencies and legislative bodies. Both state and federal legislative bodies are replete with study committees, investigative groups, hearing and bill-considering committees, etc. A clue to the real work and power of any legislator is the committee posts held. A look at his work calendar will reveal far more time spent in small group discussion than in parliamentary sessions of the entire legislature.

In formal education, small group discussion has become a way of life in classrooms at all levels. "Open classrooms" have children clustered in small groups in various "resource centers" all over a large open area. Many secondary schools are using some form of modular scheduling or learning packs—designs which involve extensive and intensive interaction among students. In colleges, while lecturing continues, more and more student time is spent in direct interaction in small groups, often subdivisions of a large class. At the graduate level, most classes proceed as learning seminars involving, primarily, a specialized process of group discussion.

Despite attacks from without and incompetent facilitators within, the encounter group has become a standard tool in the study of group processes, improvement of interpersonal communication, clarification and enrichment of self-concept, development of management skills, and personality growth. Much current mental and social health work (therapy) utilizes group discussion to assist people in relating more satisfactorily with others. The interacting group can be a powerful tool for change and growth in personality.

In sum, no one person in the world today lives apart from small group communication; many of us spend a large proportion of our time engaged in discussion. As Patton and Giffin wrote,

> *The small group is an individual's defense against the dehumanizing aspects of a mass society.* The progress of mankind poses a severe threat to our individualism. As societal complexity increases, so does the necessity that people work cooperatively to survive and attain personal goals. . . . Since the individual today is experiencing a growing dependency on groups of all descriptions, it is important that people be familiar with the dynamics of group interaction. Once a person has acquired an understanding of the nature of groups, the bases of their development, and their interrelationships with individuals and other groups he has the basis for prediction and control.[1]

In short, for personal well-being, successful participation in organizational life, and self-protection, we need to understand small groups and how to participate effectively in them.

But many discussions are ineffectual, frustrating, and time wasting. Communication in small groups is at best slow, redundant, and inefficient. Meetings are frequently characterized by the satirical definition of a committee as "a group that wastes hours and keeps minutes." This sentiment was clearly indicated when the chancellor of the university where I teach was applauded loudly for saying, "One thing I feel is needed immediately is a drastic reduction in the number of standing committees. This faculty is being meetinged to death." An excellent General Electric Corporation training film on conference leadership takes its title from the disgusted remark of a supervisor who, on being called to attend another problem-solving discussion, says, "That's all I need—a conference!"

If small groups have such a bad name in some parts why do we continue to depend on them? First, because they are *more effective problem solvers in the long run* than are individuals. Group members can see the blind spots and biases in each other's thinking, eliminating many faulty solutions and leaving as a remainder an idea that is better than any one member alone could devise. For many of the decisions we must make there is no "correct answer at the back of the book"; only the judgment of our peers arrived at through consensus can guide us in choosing among alternatives. Second, participation in work planning or problem solving has been proven to be a great motivator of effort. People work harder and better when they have helped decide what to do. No plan of action is good if the people who must carry it out don't like it and work

---

1. Bobby R. Patton and Kim Giffin, *Problem-Solving Group Interaction* (New York: Harper & Row, Publishers, 1973), p. 6.

halfheartedly. A long line of investigations has shown that groups are powerful persuaders of their members, leading to more personal change than study, lectures, or a one-to-one pitch. Third, participation with others in shared enterprise is a fundamental human need, called the "need for belonging" or "affiliation." Even our self-concepts and personalities are largely formed by interaction in small groups.

Although participants in all too many meetings are feeling frustrated by the lack of progress, waste of time, and chaos, it need not be so. They leave other meetings feeling that a great deal has been accomplished, that they are closer to their colleagues and very satisfied, as indicated by remarks such as: "I really look forward to our meetings—our discussions go someplace." For example, I recently met with several people to explore goals and strategies for achieving equal opportunity in higher education. We had a very enjoyable time, and got a great deal of planning accomplished. We cycled between serious work and just "rapping" for fun. Each time we got off the problem, the chairman would say something like, "Hey, group, it's my task orientation again—let's see if we can finish this plan," and back to serious work we would go. The work done, summarized, and checked by all with a detailed course of action and assignments agreed upon, we relaxed and socialized for another hour, disclosing bits of our private selves, supporting each other as persons, laughing, and building the trust on which our concerted efforts would hinge.

What makes the difference between effective and ineffective discussions, between participant satisfaction and disgust? What makes for efficient and inefficient committees? That's what this book is about. We will extract the usable ideas from laboratory and field research germane to making discussions more productive. And we will explore the implications of research on small group leadership from many settings. But before we go any further, some definition of "discussion" is needed.

DISCUSSION: A DEFINITION

"Discussion," like many words, is used in numerous ways. Even we textbook writers don't define it in exactly the same way. In this book, *discussion* refers to *a small group of people talking with each other face to face in order to achieve some interdependent goal, such as increased understanding, coordination of efforts, or a solution to a shared problem.* This seemingly simple definition implies several characteristics of group discussion:

1. *Cooperation is paramount to discussion.* There may be disagreement and argument during a discussion, but all members of a discussion group must cooperate in the search for a group product that will be as satisfactory as possible to all. Argument should become a way of testing the soundness of ideas rather than a way of winning. A predominantly competitive relation-

ship in which someone must win and someone must lose precludes discussion.

2. *Interaction occurs continuously.* Interaction is defined as "mutual or reciprocal influence between two or more systems," indicating that each member is influencing each other member and in turn is being influenced by each other member.[2] The members are constantly reacting, adapting, and modifying their behavior in response to each other. No one can engage in discussion with prepared speeches. Nor can he leave the discussion unchanged by the interaction. In common terms, discussion entails give and take.

3. *A group exists,* rather than a simple collection of people. The most commonly mentioned characteristic of a group is members with interdependent objectives. Each member has some feeling of need which she hopes to satisfy wholly or in part through discussion. In addition, any group has some shared values and norms.[3]

4. *Speech is the primary medium of communication.* Words and vocal characteristics are the major means by which members interact, although they will also interact through movement, posture and position, gesture and facial expression, and touch and writing.

5. *Interpersonal perception.* All the above characteristics indicate that members must, to some degree, be aware of the presence, actions, and reactions of each other. A frequently cited definition of *small group* is that "each member receives some impression or perception of each other member distinct enough so that he can . . . give some reaction to each of the others as individual persons, even though it be only to recall that the other was present."[4]

Each of these characteristics will be elaborated on in subsequent chapters.

DISCUSSION AND OTHER SPEECH CONTEXTS

Probably you have already been introduced to a diagram of the process of human communication which attempted to explain in graphic form the dynamic process by which perceptions and reactions to one's environment are encoded, transmitted, received, and decoded. All face-to-face speech communication depends primarily upon the media of light and sound waves using verbal, vocal, and

2. Horace B. and Ava C. English, *A Comprehensive Dictionary of Psychological and Psychoanalytical Terms* (New York: Longman's, Green and Company, 1958), p. 270.

3. Colvis R. Shepherd, *Small Groups* (San Francisco: Chandler Publishing Company, 1964), p. 5.

4. Robert F. Bales, *Interaction Process Analysis* (Reading, Mass.: Addison-Wesley Publishing Company, 1950), p. 33.

visible signals. In various types of speech contexts, these three kinds of signals may vary in importance. But in all contexts, interpersonal speech *communication* entails both speaking and listening. Other sensory modalities such as touch and smell may play a part in small group communication.

Balance and Direction of Speaking and Listening

Discussion and other types of interpersonal speech communication such as conversation and interviewing require that each participant assume relatively equal responsibility to speak and listen. This is not to say that all members of a group will speak and listen in equal amounts, but all are equally *responsible* to listen and to speak. The primary source of communicative acts in a discussion will constantly change, with other participants being secondary sources for the moment. Each participant will be primarily a listener, then primarily a speaker, again a listener, and so on.

Public speaking and most broadcasting differ from discussion in that the primary source of communicative acts, the speaker, is constant throughout. Some modification occurs in a forum period, but this is usually classified as a form of discussion. Lecture-discussion, the situation in which a teacher speaks with limited comments and questions from students, is a hybridization of public speaking and discussion.

In contrast to most public speaking and virtually all broadcast speaking, a discussant can be asked immediately to clarify or justify a statement. A breach of honesty, ambiguous statements, seeking selfish ends instead of group good, a lack of evidence, or faulty reasoning can be challenged immediately. The immediacy of response and the degree of reciprocal influence is potentially much greater in discussion groups than in public communication contexts.

Attitude Differences: Discussion vs. Debate or Persuasion

Dialectic, the "search for truth" (in the sense of the best possible answer), since Aristotle has been considered to be a counterpart of rhetoric (the science and art of influencing others through speech or writing). Discussion, in most instances, is a form of group dialectic. People who have made up their minds cannot honestly engage in a decision-making or problem-solving discussion. They can only seek to persuade others of the rightness of their prior positions by practicing persuasion; they cannot engage in dialectic. In discussion, attempting to persuade others is a very important process, but must be reciprocated—willingness to be persuaded by others, in a search for the best possible answers. Even learning discussions are blocked by the out-and-out persuader; the intent of discussants must be to share, to explore differing conceptions and to foster mutual understandings out of which common values, images, and actions can emerge among equals. In this regard, debate and persuasion are diametrically opposed to discussion. If one is not interested in understanding and exploring opinions, values, and ways of doing things different from his own, he cannot engage in learning discussions, and if he has reached unalterable conclusions he cannot engage in decision-making discussions—only "pseudodiscussions." Such a participant will either subvert other participants, stymie group progress, or be excluded from the group after much friction and loss of time. To join a discussion group with one's mind closed on the issues facing the group, unable to suspend judgment and undergo the process of cognitive dissonance, is no less than a breach of morality. It demands of others what one is not willing or able to do himself—change position.

This is not to say that argumentation has no place in discussions, that no one should take a strong stand, or that "giving in" is advised. Careful weighing of evidence, evaluation of all reasoning, detecting and testing assumptions, and constructive "debating" of different points of view can contribute greatly to the quality of group decisions. Open and honest conflict is a sign of cohesiveness and stability in a group; concealing differences of opinion and negative feelings indicates a lack of unity. Conflict over ideas and decisions reflects real concern and involvement. The best forge for testing ideas is to bring in all contrary evidence and arguments. Decisions based on avoidance of conflict or contrary evidence, or consisting of vague statements and platitudes, do not work; the details of solutions are not settled and the problem continues. Rigid adherence, conformity for its own sake, and dogmatic rejection of information or reasoning are to be avoided.

Skills in Discussion and Public Address

There appears to be no necessary relationship between overall skill in public speaking and effectiveness as a discussant. You have probably observed that some instructors who are excellent lecturers are very poor at stimulating or leading class discussions. The opposite also occurs. I remember a professor who was very skilled at conducting a seminar discussion with stimulating guidance, clarification of student comments, and enlightening comments. As a lecturer he rambled, spoke to himself, and often ran out of content before the end of the period. Students had to struggle to stay awake. It's said that Jefferson and Washington were excellent in informal discussion, but neither made much of a mark as a public speaker. But Lincoln and Kennedy were outstanding in both conference and public speaking.

The reason is simple: Some of the skills essential to each type of speech situation are different. The detailed skills of organizing a speech are not needed for the short impromptu remarks of discussants. Strategy and stylistic devices of use to public speakers may be detrimental to developing the trust needed in a small group. The overly forceful participant may be perceived as a manipulator of the group, and so resisted. Appropriate behavior depends on an understanding of differing circumstances and role flexibility. To help you develop such an understanding, the next section of this chapter concerns different types of groups and discussions.

TYPES OF DISCUSSIONS

Discussions can be classified along a number of dimensions. In order to accurately describe a given discussion, one must classify it into at least two categories: public or private and problem solving or enlightenment. In each of these dichotomies there are several types of discussions. It is important for you to establish an image of the general characteristics of each major type of discussion so that you can communicate about discussions with your classmates and instructor.

Public or Private

Any discussion which is conducted primarily for the benefit of an audience can be classified as a *public* discussion. One which takes place primarily in order for the participants to reach an agreement, solve a problem, or obtain learning will be classified as *private*. Interested nonparticipants observe many private discussions such as meetings of city councils, legislative committees, and other public agencies, but unless the meeting was planned primarily for the purpose of communication with nongroup members (e.g., a *hearing*) the discussion would be classified as private. Thus it can be seen that all problem-solving discussions would be classified as private, whereas learning discussions can be either public or private. However, a public discussion may be organized *as if* it were problem-solving in nature, usually to convince an audience that the group's decision is the best alternative, or it may be organized to present several possible alternatives for audience decision.

Private Discussion Groups

Small groups, usually from three to twenty people, exist for many purposes and have their origins in many sources. The student of discussion needs a simplified scheme for thinking about small groups that will help him observe, analyze, and talk about the groups with which he will come into contact. The classification of private groups provided here is only one of many to be found, but has proven practical for many students.

PRIMARY OR PSYCHE GROUPS

These are groups of people who are together for the human need of affiliation rather than to accomplish some specific purpose. All are long-term groups. Examples include the family, the gang which regularly shares cokes in a student center, four girls who eat lunch and often attend movies together, two or three couples who often dine and bowl together, friends who share most coffee breaks, and college professors who regularly drop into each other's offices for a chat. Such groups *may* take on specific tasks and often make decisions, but more often they provide personal support, chat about a variety of topics, "let off steam," and generally enjoy each other. Their talk will often be disorganized and informal—for talk is not the means to an end so much as the end in itself, a part of human companionship.

Figure 1.1. A typical psyche group enjoys a casual conversation.

THERAPY AND ENCOUNTER GROUPS

These are groups which have come together to study group interaction, overcome personality problems, grow as individuals from the feedback and support of others—to engage in personal learning and growth. Members of such groups do not choose each other. They usually have some authority figure present, such as psychiatrist, therapist, transaction analyst, facilitator, or trainer. No *group* product is sought, but each member needs the presence of others to accomplish personal aims. Such groups are highly artificial and have a limited term of existence. At times your class in speech, discussion, or group dynamics may become this sort of group. It is formed in much the same way as an encounter group: several people with a desire to learn for individual reasons but needing others for such learning to occur, come together under the guidance of an authority figure probably called the "instructor."

Figure 1.2. An encounter group helps members with personal problems.

STUDY OR LEARNING GROUPS

These groups are similar to encounter and therapy groups to the extent that they are formed as a medium for the learning and growth of the participants. If you are reading this book for a course concerned with small group discussion, your class may be organized into several learning groups. Such groups, rather than seeking growth in the personality as the primary end (although that may be one objective), primarily meet to understand a subject more thoroughly by pooling their knowledge, perceptions, and beliefs. While they are exchanging information the participants also gain practice in speaking, listening, critical thinking, and other communication skills.

I hope you have participated in learning groups in such courses as literature, social science, and philosophy. I have had the pleasure of being in innumerable such groups. As a breeder and trainer of hounds, I have learned an immense amount from discussions with friends while driving to field trials for our dogs. Much of my appreciation of painting came from extensive discussions with others of what we saw in paintings. On my campus, posters advertise the Women's Resource Center, inviting any interested person to drop in for "rap" sessions to explore feelings, beliefs, and values about sex roles in our society. Such learning groups, formal or informal, sponsored or spontaneous, with or without designated leaders, are ubiquitous.

COMMITTEES

These are groups of people who have been given an assignment by a parent organization or some person in authority. A committee may be formed to investigate and report findings, to recommend a course of action for the parent group, to formulate policies, or to plan and carry out some action. All such tasks require discussion among the members. Boards, councils, and staffs are special types of committees. For example, the board of directors is often called an executive committee. Such groups represent a larger organization, often with very extensive power to make and execute policy.

Committees are usually classified as either *ad hoc* or *standing*. The *ad hoc* or special committee has a defined task to perform, and when that has been accomplished it goes out of existence. Such groups may have one, few, or many meetings. Recently I have served on *ad hoc* committees to evaluate credentials of job applicants, to select a library for a club, to draft a constitution, to hear a student appeal, and to evaluate a scholarship program. Standing committees continue indefinitely even though the membership may change periodically. Such groups are usually given a definite scope of responsibility by their parent organization, usually described in the constitution or bylaws. Every organization has them.

CONFERENCE

This term is widely used to refer to almost any type of face-to-face communication; for example, a secretary will often say that her boss is "in conference" when he is talking with other persons in his office. At times "conference" is used to refer to a large gathering of persons who hear speeches, study various topics, and perhaps engage in small group discussions.

Figure 1.3. A business conference.

In this book, *conference* will be used to refer to a meeting of representatives from two or more other groups; since every large organization contains within it many small functioning groups, conferences are very important for coordination within and among organizations. The conferees communicate information from one group to another, perhaps coordinating their efforts. Intergroup conflicts and competition must be mediated to work out a solution acceptable to all groups represented. For example, representatives of various charitable organizations meet to coordinate the efforts of their respective groups and to exchange information and ideas. The various crew heads, designers, and directors must confer periodically to plan and coordinate the efforts of the many people involved in producing a play. Conferences between delegates of the Senate and House of Representatives attempt to resolve differences in legislation bearing on the same issue. Representatives of business and labor meet to decide on wages, working conditions, and fringe benefits. Conferences are frequently held with representatives from the various campuses in a university system to resolve differences in policies, coordinate academic programs, etc. Such conferees must often report their decisions for approval by the groups they represented.

Public Discussion Groups

All public discussions are planned for the enlightenment and influencing of a listening audience. Hence, every public discussion is a "show," and may have the elements of showmanship and detailed planning needed for efficiency and heightened impact. At the same time, spontaneity and the dynamic emergence characteristic of all discussions must be present. To bring about such a balance takes careful selection of members, preparation, and a special style of moderating.

A *panel* is a type of public discussion in which several participants, guided by a designated moderator, interact directly with one another in a relatively spontaneous way for the benefit of an audience. The participants should be knowledgeable and articulate representatives of varying points of view bearing on a question of public interest. Although panel members need an agreed-upon outline of questions to follow, the speaking should be impromptu and relatively informal, with direct responses to each other's remarks. Panel discussion provides an excellent format for presenting programs to relatively small audiences, such as a class. Your instructor may assign groups in your class to prepare and present panels. Public television and educational radio stations carry many panel discussions. The lively interchange can make for intellectually stimulating listening and viewing.

A *public interview* may be conducted by one or more interviewers of one or more interviewees at a time. "Meet the Press" and "Issues and Answers" are well-known interview programs on both radio and television which you may have witnessed. So-called "press conferences" are interviews conducted by news correspondents with spokesmen of major institutions and organizations; presidential news conferences are common examples. Interviewers and interviewees may agree in advance on a list of major questions or topics to be discussed, or the show may be entirely spontaneous. The interviewer's responsibility is to represent the audience by asking questions she thinks they would most want or need to have answered. Obviously, the interviewee is selected because of a special role or position in society.

A *forum* refers most often to a period of time when the audience to a panel discussion, lecture, film, or other presentation is invited to ask questions or express opinions. This term is also used to refer to a discussion held by a large gathering of people, such as a hearing on a proposed change in zoning laws or a public hall meeting in which a political official or administrator goes before all interested people to discuss with them any of their concerns about the office or agency he represents. Mayors, legislators, county commissioners, and other officials schedule "town hall" forums in many communities.

A *symposium* consists of a series of brief public speeches on a single major problem or topic, with each speaker selected because of his position, point of view, or expertise. Although some writers still insist on classifying symposia as discussions, there is no direct interaction among the speakers; each prepares his remarks carefully; and there is little direct reference, if any, by the speakers to what the others have said. Hence it is not discussion, and will not be considered further in this book.

Frequently programs for public meetings contain a number of phases, some discussion and some not. Thus we may have a brief symposium in which each participant talks for several minutes, followed by a panel discussion, followed by a forum period.

Problem Solving or Enlightenment

The result sought by a discussion group is either a solution to a problem shared by the group, or individual enlightenment and growth. *Many* decisions must be made during the course of a full-fledged problem-solving discussion, and even an enlightenment group must make many decisions about such matters as procedures to follow, issues to discuss, and whose personal problem to tackle next. A learning group (enlightenment) may sound like a problem-solving group, but such a group does not intend to take any collective action nor even make recommendations; the purpose is the development of understandings and beliefs by members of the group. To illustrate, a college class in criminal justice may discuss what the law should be governing prostitution, but it will take no action *as a group.* However, if the class were to decide to send a recommendation to the state legislature, then it would become a problem-solving group.

The *advisory group* is a special type of problem-solving group. Such a group lacks the authority to make a binding decision, yet it must produce a decision and plan of action to recommend to some person or organization which has the authority to make the final decision and act on it.

In summary, any discussion which is to result in a *group* product should be classified as a problem-solving discussion, and any discussion which is to result only in *individual* learnings should be classified as an enlightenment discussion.

Many other words have been used to refer to variations in discussion formats and groups. We could talk about colloquiums, committee hearings, workshops, and so forth. However, all of these are modifications of types of discussion already described. The important dimensions for describing any group discussion are the primary purpose of the group, whether or not the meeting is for the sake of the participants or an audience, and when the group is discussing a problem, whether or not it has power to decide or only to advise. The essence of all discussion is a group of people with an interdependent purpose to be achieved (at least in part) by direct and cooperative speech communication.

Key Concepts

Jargon for its own sake is abominable!—or so I feel. People often build walls between each other by using esoteric words when commonly used ones would be as precise and communicate far more effectively. Using jargon to impress or as a form of one-upmanship (I know more big words than you so I'm better than you) does not belong in any cooperative relationship. But just as strongly as I believe that, I also believe that you cannot comprehend any field of study until you acquire its terminology with comprehension of how the jargon is used in the field. As psycholinguists have demonstrated, our words determine what we can perceive and think about; they help create the reality we experience. So in order to make it easier for you to learn the special terminology of the field of small group communication, discussion, and group dynamics, a glossary is included at the end of each chapter. In it is a list of key terms introduced in the chapter with a brief special definition of each. Memorizing these is not enough. You will need to *use* the words correctly in observing and classifying behavior of people in small groups; the words must refer to events which are not words, but human behavior and things.

Committee—small group of people given an assigned task or responsibility by a larger group (parent organization) or person with authority.
> *ad hoc* or special—given a specific task to perform, and goes out of existence when this job is completed.
> standing—continues indefinitely with an area of responsibility which may include many tasks.

Conference—discussion by representatives from two or more groups in order to find ways to coordinate efforts, reduce conflict, etc.

Discussion—a small group of people talking with each other face to face in order to achieve some interdependent goal.

Enlightenment or learning discussion—discussion for the purpose of individual members' enlightenment or growth.

Forum—large audience interacting verbally, usually following some presentation.

Group—two or more people with interdependent objectives, shared norms and values, who interact.

Interaction—mutual influence by two or more people via communication process.

Panel—small group interacting informally for benefit of listening audience.

Private discussion—conducted so participants can reach some agreement, solve a problem, or learn.

Problem-solving discussion—conducted to clarify and solve a problem, ending with agreement on a plan of action to be taken.

Public discussion—conducted before an audience for enlightenment and influence of that audience.

Public interview—one or more interviewers asking questions of one or more respondents for benefit of listening audience.

Symposium—series of brief public speeches on a single major problem or topic, with no direct interaction among speakers.

Exercises

1. Keep a journal on your experiences in small groups, with at least an entry for each class meeting. Date each entry, writing it as soon as convenient following each class or small group meeting. Present descriptions of what happened in small groups of which you were a member, evaluations of each class session, principles or guidelines which you formulate about how to participate in small groups, insights into your personal behavior as a small group member, etc. As much as possible, use the special jargon of small group communication. Make your entries concise, but clear and thorough. Be completely honest, frank, and open; no one but you and your instructor will ever see the journal unless you show it to someone. Below is a response form which your instructor may use to react to your journal entries.

RESPONSE TO JOURNAL ENTRIES

   1. COMPLETENESS:

   _____ Descriptive account missing
   _____ Personal reactions missing
   _____ Evaluation of class missing
   _____ Lack of use of language and concepts of small group theory
   _____ Entries lack thoroughness
   _____ Fairly complete
   _____ Complete and thorough

   2. DEPTH OF ENTRIES:

   _____ Superficial and sketchy
   _____ Shows very limited insight
   _____ Shows *some* insight
   _____ Shows good insight
   _____ Shows excellent insight

3. PARTICULAR NEEDS TO RESOLVE:

_____ Provide regular dated entries
_____ Provide lists of those in group
_____ Provide clearer exposition of events
_____ Include evaluation of each class
_____ Report applications in groups out of class
_____ Report insights into yourself as discussant and small group leader
_____ Clearer distinction between *what happened* and *your* feelings
_____ Clearer and more thorough exposition of your feelings and personal reactions
_____ More depth of analysis and description of discussions
_____ Formulate principles, concepts, generalizations, about groups based on observations and analyses

Student: _____

2. This exercise is designed to help reduce tensions and barriers among people who do not know each other. If your class is small, the instructor will seat you in a circle, then conduct the activity. In a larger class or group, divide into groups of about 8-12 members, designate one person in each such circle to ask the questions, and proceed.

Breaking Boundaries: A Structured Conversation

Instructions: Read each question, asking each person to answer *briefly* without explanation, honestly, with the *first response that comes to mind.* Point out a different person to begin responses to each new question. Go around the circle clockwise, as quickly as possible. Everyone (including the questioner) is to answer every question.

1. Who do you think is the most important person who has lived in the last few years?
2. What is the best movie you've ever seen?
3. What means more to you than anything else?
4. What is the ugliest thing you know?
5. What TV program do you most enjoy?
6. If you could be an animal other than human, what would it be?
7. How do you select your friends?
8. What is the most important thing that guides your life?
9. How many children make up an ideal family?
10. What is your favorite sport?
11. What is your biggest worry?
12. What is the most beautiful thing you have seen?
13. What do you think people like most in you? Least?
14. When do you feel best?
15. What one day in your life have you enjoyed the most?

Synthesis set of questions:
1. What person in the group did you learn about most?
2. Who do you think was most honest?

3. What image did you want to project to other members of the group?
4. What answer surprised you the most?
5. Who pays the most attention to what is going on?
6. Who enjoys life the most?
7. Which person is most like you? Least like you?
8. What answer from another person most pleased you?
9. How do you now feel about the group?

3. For one week keep a list of all the small groups in which you actively participate during the week. See if you can devise some system for classifying these groups. Then make a list of all the small groups of which you consider yourself a member but in which you were not active during the week. Compare your lists with those of other members of your class. What do you conclude?

2
An Orientation to Small Group Processes

No doubt you have been puzzled about why some groups are very successful and others fail miserably. You leave one discussion group feeling very satisfied, and then leave another feeling equally frustrated. In one discussion you may be pleased with the fine job you did; you may be quite disappointed with your participation in the next discussion.

The jokes and complaints about committees seem endless, indicating that much of our discussing is less than effective. "A camel is a horse designed by a committee" goes one saying—and too often we have little or no idea of why one group comes up with a mangy camel while another produces a trim thoroughbred. Understanding the dynamic processes of small groups is a *must* if we are to make our discussion effective and satisfying. The overall goal of this chapter is to present a schema for analyzing, evaluating, and improving any discussion group of which you happen to be a member.

Despite the fact that we all learned to speak and listen as small children, we cannot just do what comes naturally and be effective participants in discussions. Consider the hobby of bass fishing, a highly stylized form of human activity. You must learn the characteristics of bass behavior, cover, feeding, and movement. It takes a lot of study, observation, and practice to become one of the ten percent of bass fishermen and women who catch ninety percent of the bass. Group discussion is a far more stylized and complicated form of human activity, and infinitely more important, than fishing. It will take much study, observation, analysis, theorizing, and practice if you are to be a truly valuable member of the wide variety of discussion groups in which you will find yourself. It will not be particularly easy to develop the participant-observer perspective you will need. Such a perspective will make it possible for you to actively participate in the *content* of a group discussion while you also observe its *processes,* and thus adjust your behavior to what is needed by the group. More specifically, as a result of reading, study, and discussion of this chapter you should:

1. Understand the concept "group," and be able to distinguish between small groups and collections of people.
2. Be able to detect the presence or absence of a clear group purpose, and help any group find goals when these are missing.
3. Acquire a set of terms and definitions concerning group structure, and with them be able to describe the roles, relationships, and communication patterns in working groups.
4. Understand the concept "norm" and be able to describe (in writing, if asked to do so) the norms of a discussion group.
5. Understand the role "fantasy chains" play in the development of a group, and recognize them when they occur in discussions which you observe.
6. Appreciate the importance of high cohesiveness to effective discussion, and be able to state the conditions which produce cohesiveness in small groups.
7. Understand the importance of group size, and determine the appropriate size for several types of discussion groups.
8. Be able to describe the phases in a group's life, and recognize them in a group which you observe.
9. Be able to distinguish between primary and secondary tension, and describe the causes of each type.
10. Develop a model of effective discussion groups, and be able to apply it as a participant-observer.

"GROUP" AND "DISCUSSION GROUP" DEFINED

When defining group discussion in Chapter 1, it was necessary to mention many of the major characteristics of groups. In order to communicate clearly with such a loosely used term as *group,* it is necessary to develop a construct definition.

The word *group* has been used to refer to many kinds of phenomena: A collection of items (such as trees or numbers); a large organization (such as an insurance company, the people who attend a football game, or the members of a religious denomination); two or more people having anything in common (such as standing at the same corner while waiting for a bus). In the phrase *group discussion,* we will use the term *group* in a much more restricted sense; it will refer to a specific and definite set of characteristics.

A discussion group has at least the following characteristics:

1. A sufficiently small number of people so that each will be aware of and have some reaction to each other (from 2 to rarely more than 20).

2. A mutually interdependent purpose in which the success of each person is contingent upon the success of the others in achieving this goal.
3. Each person has a sense of belonging or membership, identifying himself with the other members of the group.
4. Oral interaction (not all of the interaction will be oral, but a significant characteristic of a discussion group is reciprocal influence exercised by talking).
5. Behavior based on norms, values, and procedures accepted by all members.

Group, in this sense, refers to what is often called a "pattern property" or nonadditive dimension. "Groupness" emerges from the relationships among the people involved, just as "cubeness" emerges from the image of a set of planes, intersects, and angles in specific relationships to each other. One can draw a cube with twelve lines (try it), but only if they are assembled in a definite way. Any other arrangement of the lines gives something other than a cube. Likewise, one can have a collection or set of people without having a group or a discussion group. A robber and three policemen may interact orally, but they do not constitute a group (lacking an interdependent purpose, shared norms, and procedures). Bridge players may or may not constitute a group, depending on whether or not they have, as primary, the promotively interdependent purpose of entertainment and enjoying each other's company. A "promotively interdependent purpose" exists when all members succeed or fail together. The success of each is dependent upon the success of all. Each member promotes the success of the others.

Half a century ago the question of whether or not there was such a phenomenon as a "group mind" aroused strong controversy, which can still be heard in some quarters.[1] Today the idea is generally accepted that a small group develops characteristics different from a sum of the characteristics and personalities of its members. Kurt Lewin, the "father" of group dynamics, wrote about "group atmosphere." Cartwright referred to the emotional dimensions of a group. Cattell developed the term "syntality" to refer to this complex of group attributes, the group "personality."[2] Such a concept is necessary if you are to build a model of effective group discussion. In analyzing a project group in your class, a committee, or any other discussion group, you will need to consider the syntality dimensions and dynamics of the group as well as the members of the group

---

1. For the author's position on this issue, see John K. Brilhart, "Fostering Group Thinking," *Today's Speech* 8 (April, 1960), pp. 9-11, 19.

2. Kurt Lewin, *Resolving Social Conflicts* (New York: Harper, 1948); Dorwin Cartwright, "Emotional Dimensions of Group Life," in *International Symposium on Feelings and Emotions,* M.L. Reymert, ed. (New York: Harper & Row, 1950); R.B. Cattell, "New Concepts of Measuring Leadership," in *Group Dynamics,* D. Cartwright and A. Zander, eds. (Evanston, Ill.: Row, Peterson and Co., 1956).

as unique personalities. Rensis Likert and associates, while studying what made large organizations productive, found that managers needed to think of work units as groups or teams, and manage them as a group to get optimal levels of production.[3]

PURPOSE AND SOURCE OF THE GROUP

Is there an interdependent purpose for the group and is it clearly understood by all members? Frequently group members do not understand why they have been selected for membership in a committee, or the purpose of a group they belong to voluntarily. The writer has frequently asked each member of a discussion group to write down the purpose of the discussion, only to find that each person had a decidedly different idea about the group purpose and problem. Until there is a common goal, progress is impossible except toward establishing a definite objective. When a purpose acceptable to all members has been identified, progress can be made and satisfaction achieved. While different members may have different personal objectives, these must contribute to the group's overall objective if the group is to be truly effective. People who place a high value on the purpose of the group will work diligently; people who perceive that the group is making progress will remain satisfied, loyal, and diligent.

A recent experience made me even more aware of the importance of clear goals which are seen as important by all members of a group. I was appointed to a special committee to evaluate and make recommendations to the administration of our university. At our first several meetings no one seemed to know what we were to accomplish or why *we* had been picked to serve on the committee. We met only because we felt we had to, but our meetings were apathetic in the extreme and we accomplished nothing. After several months we finally determined what we were expected to produce, and that it was very important. Some initial investigating showed us why each of us was needed on the committee, and then our meetings came to life. In a relatively short time we produced a well-documented report and set of recommendations, for which we have received much praise.

Sometimes a group will be ostensibly working for one purpose, but actually working toward another. Many discussion groups (such as standing committees) lose sight of their original reason for being, yet go on discussing aimlessly. Such lack of purpose results in inefficiency, dissatisfaction, member loss, and decay of the group. Groups can be compared to other living organisms in this regard. All forms of life are formed of similar elements organized in some specific fashion. When the organism has begun to decay, it sooner or later must die. Then its elements break apart and are gradually incorporated into other organisms. In the

3. Rensis Likert, *New Patterns of Management* (New York: McGraw-Hill, 1961).

same way that we keep our environment clean, satisfying, and productive by hastening recycling processes and not overloading the ecoconversion systems, so we need to help small groups that have served their purpose either adopt new objectives or end rapidly so they do not become a drain on society. How many "friendship" groups have you known that went stumbling along although most of the positive feelings for each other were gone? How many marriages retain form without life, meaning, or satisfaction of the partners' needs? How many functionless committees, councils, etc., do you know that limp along, draining far more energy than their productivity warrants? Each of us can strike a blow for conservation of the social environment by helping such groups die quickly and with grace.

Confusion of group purpose may also result from *hidden agendas*. This refers to an objective of an individual member (or a subgroup of members) which is different from the avowed group purpose. For example, one member may be seeking attention in order to get elected to an office. Another may need much response and affection, and may find ways to get it at the expense of the group as a whole. A member of an intercampus committee—which was assigned to develop a formula for equitable funding of all campuses of a state university system—found something wrong with every idea anyone presented. Finally, he admitted that his real purpose was to keep the present arrangement by which his campus received more money per student than did the other campuses. Hidden agendas like this one result from what is commonly called a "conflict of interest." Hidden agendas may or may not be at variance with the group purpose, but we must be on watch for evidence of them in behaviors which are detrimental to the group purpose. If detected, harmful hidden agendas can usually be dealt with by bringing them to the attention of the group.

Every group exists within the setting of some *external system*, which consists of the physical, technical, and social environment. The very forces which led to the forming of the group are a part of this external system as are the values, beliefs, norms of conduct, and restrictions placed on the group and its members. Successful small groups are continuously aware of changes in their environment. For example, a basketball team needs to scout the style of play and the strengths and weaknesses of its opponents, and adapt. To stick to a game plan that is not working is a failure to adjust to a changing external system. Especially important as a part of the small group's external system, is any "parent" group of which it is a part, and to which it must report. Large organizations, such as corporations and government bureaucracies, consist at one level of many small groups, interacting within themselves and among each other.

The *area of freedom* (scope of authority, power) of a discussion group is defined by such a parent group, especially in the case of a committee, commission, board, task force, or production group. If the area of freedom (and its concomitant limits) is not kept clearly in mind, trouble is inevitable and the group will waste much time. The author has seen members of a religious study-discussion group try to convert other members to a particular faith, whereas the purpose defined by the parent organization was for members to understand the similarities and differences among religions. These proselytizing members were highly unpopular and a definite handicap to the group. Advisory committees which think they have reached a final decision frequently express anger and generate needless conflict when an administrator or parent body does not follow their advice.

Very recently I was involved in a major conflict between a committee which heard faculty appeals to decisions made by a dean. We committee members thought the bylaws of our Board of Regents granted us the power to overturn the administrator's decisions, but the dean believed that we had no power but to *recommend* that he change his decisions. A great deal of professor time was spent trying to resolve this conflict over our area of freedom. For a period of time we refused to consider any appeals. Finally, the dean agreed to abide by our decision on any appeal to his previous decision, and once again we began to function. In short, it is vital that a group be constantly aware of the limits on its authority.

Answers to the following questions may help to clarify the area of freedom of discussion groups to which you belong:

Is this a group which was assigned to produce a suggestion for a larger parent organization or administrator, or has it power to make a final decision and to act?

Is it a group seeking only to understand a variety of points of view on a given topic, or is it a group which should reach a decision to which all members are expected to subscribe?

Often a discussant can render great service to his group by inquiring about the group purpose, whether or not the other members understand that purpose and feel it is worthwhile. If the answer is unclear or negative, action can be taken to change, clarify, or terminate group activity. If members are dissatisfied with their group, either the group purpose, individual purpose, or group membership should be changed. People working on what they feel is insignificant or against their individual objectives work poorly at best.

TIME

A few researchers have studied how human groups change through time, going through a series of phases. Single-meeting groups have been compared with groups which have numerous discussions over a period of weeks or months. The time variable is definitely interrelated with the types of roles members take, the distribution of power and prestige among members, the efficiency of the group's procedures, and the rigidity of the group. Mortensen, for example, found evidence indicating that appointing someone as "leader" of a one-meeting group helped the group begin interaction and made for effective discussion, but that in a group having several meetings such a designated leader would have to demonstrate abilities expected of a leader or be displaced—a process expensive of time, unity, efficiency, and good human relations.[4]

The point is that *time* is an important factor in understanding any group, whether one is considering phases in problem-solving discussion or the emergence of a definite structure of relationships among members.

Single-meeting groups differ from most committees and other types of groups which meet for several or more discussions. The one-meeting group has no chance to develop a history, regular procedures and rituals, or extensive norms and values. Except for previous contacts with other participants in different group contexts, there is little basis on which to predict each other's behavior. There is no future for the group, no need to build cohesiveness. Models of group emergence have little relevance. An assigned leader will usually be accepted willingly unless he is totally incompetent. With little time to spare, members usually accept the designated discussion leader's statements about the purpose and procedures for the meeting. If the leader has an agenda or outline to follow, the group will likely do so with gratitude.

When members know that they will be meeting numerous times, they will take much more time to get organized and will move through a series of phases in the life history of the group. First comes a *period of orientation* during which the group will not readily follow any outline for problem solving. Even though it may appear that the discussion is about facts of a problem, objectives, and possible alternatives, the real agenda item will be the development of a group structure: roles for members (especially, who will be our primary leader?), norms to govern behavior, shared values, general procedures for decision making and problem solving, who will interact with whom and in what ways, shared objectives, and so forth. This period of time may seem like aimless milling around to an untrained observer. But after such relational issues have been resolved to some degree, the group will go into a *work* phase characterized by much compiling of information, suggesting of courses of action, and more or less open conflict until decisions emerge. Depending on the degree to which the group achieved a stable structure of roles, norms, and procedures, there may be continual cycling between serious work and problems of interpersonal relations, with the group seeming to have to begin anew at many meetings. Or it may move forward from problem to problem with great dispatch, spending little time on matters of value, procedure, roles, and interpersonal relations.

Invariably there will be some cycling through time between matters of work to be done and group maintenance (socioemotional relationships). Every

4. David C. Mortensen, "Should the Discussion Group Have an Assigned Leader?" *Speech Teacher* 15 (1966), pp. 34-41.

problem-solving group has both task and social dimensions to be dealt with through discussion; these are virtually the same in an encounter group. By 1950 Bales had factored all group member behaviors as being primarily concerned with either task or socioemotional matters.[5] Tuckman found issues of group task and structure both continuing to occupy the group during its period of development. These are not totally separable, but the emphasis will shift from social relations to task, as a group becomes more clearly organized through time.[6]

The tension experienced by members also varies through time, dependent upon handling of both social and task issues. When one feels tense, she may be irritable, ill at ease, and generally uncomfortable. Muscles are tightened in the face, neck, abdomen, hands, and even in the feet and legs. Headaches may develop if tension is not dealt with. Depending on the source, Bormann has labelled the two types of tension as *primary* and *secondary.*

Primary tension is his name for

> the social unease and stiffness that accompanies getting acquainted. . . . The earmarks of primary tension are extreme politeness, apparent boredom or tiredness, and considerable sighing and yawning. When members show primary tension, they speak softly and tentatively. Frequently they can think of nothing to say, and many long pauses result.[7]

Members who are extremely affected by primary tension may pull back from the circle of others, look away from the group, or even read. Most such persons are apprehensive about meeting new people, afraid of not being accepted, and have a negative self-concept. Thus, what appears like a lack of interest may not be that at all. Various ways of helping persons who experience very high levels of primary tension have been developed and may be available from your instructor or school. For instance, systematic desensitization may reduce communication apprehension, as may assertiveness training and personal therapies such as gestalt therapy and transactional analysis. I have many case studies showing that participation in cooperative task and learning groups as part of a small group communication course helped many students who had experienced excessive primary tension; they fell well within the range of normal by the end of the course.

Members of one-meeting groups cannot afford the time needed to get well acquainted with each other, but groups that will meet often may be wise to do so. Groups failing to do so, talking only about their work and the problems confronting them, often continue to be plagued by shyness, reticence, apparent

---

5. Robert F. Bales, *Interaction Process Analysis* (Reading, Mass.: Addison-Wesley Publishing Company, 1950).

6. Bruce W. Tuckman, "Developmental Sequences in Small Groups," *Psychological Bulletin* 63 (1965), pp. 384-399.

7. Earnest G. Bormann, *Discussion and Group Methods: Theory and Practice,* 2nd ed. (New York: Harper & Row, Publishers, 1975), pp. 181-182.

apathy, absenteeism, and inability to reach decisions based on open and honest confrontation of ideas and beliefs. Very early in the life of a continuing group it pays to deal directly with primary tensions: take time to talk about who each person is, ask each other questions, air differences in feelings and backgrounds, chat about hobbies and interests, maybe even have a social hour or party. Don't expect members of a continuing group to get to work on the agenda at the very start of each new meeting, either. Even groups with considerable history experience some amount of primary tension at the start of each meeting. Members need to confirm where they stand with each other, to reaffirm their relationships, and that each is accepted as a unique individual. Thus a brief period of "ventilation," chitchat, or small talk is needed before getting down to work, often before the meeting is "called to order" by a designated leader.

Secondary tension results from differences among members as they try to accomplish their goals. People in a small group differ over their perception of a problem, over procedures for working as a group, over values of relative importance and goodness, over alternative means for achieving goals, and over who should do what for the group. The signs of tension from such conflicts are quite different from those of primary tension. Voices get loud and strained. There may be long pauses, followed by two or more people trying to talk at once. Members twist and fidget in their seats, bang on the table, wave their arms, or even get up and pace around the room.

Every group must develop norms and procedures for reducing secondary tension. Once it is under control, a decision will usually emerge quickly, be confirmed by the group, and details of implementation will be worked out rapidly. Throughout its history a group will cycle from periods of high to low tension among members, and periods of high to low harmony and productivity in accomplishing the work of the group. Figure 2.1 represents such cycling in a

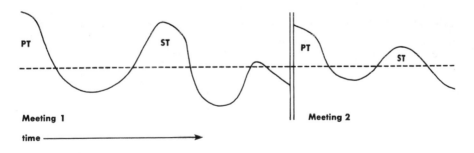

Key: PT—primary tension
      ST—secondary tension
- - - - level of tension, above which group is inefficient

Figure 2.1. The **tension cycle** in a hypothetical problem-solving group.

hypothetical group. Above the dotted line are the periods of high productivity, while periods of high tension are below the dotted line. Some groups try to ignore secondary tensions because dealing with them is often very difficult, uncomfortable, or even painful. A group may dodge the issue of a clash over values or means to a goal.

> They leave the touchy area of human relations and return to the safe area of doing the job. The problem, however, never goes away, and if ignored or dodged will continue to . . . impede their progress. Facing up to secondary tensions realistically is the best way to release them.[8]

This may mean discussing how members feel about each other, joking, and openly discussing each other's behavior, roles, and norms. It may take conciliating, compromising, or other techniques for resolving conflicts and disagreements. Some degree of tension is helpful, of course. Just as the individual is not productive when totally relaxed or hypertense, so with the group. Learning to maintain a productive level of tension, developing tension-reliever roles, and procedures for handling tension are keys to effective group discussion.

STRUCTURE OF ROLES AND BEHAVIORAL FUNCTIONS

The term *structure* is used here to refer to a complex of ordered and interrelated parts, forming some perceived whole or object. A group (the whole) consists of people (parts) who are related to one another in many ways (complex order, interrelationships). Each person in a discussion group holds a definite position in relation to each other person. This position, however, will be related to the purpose of the group and the work the member is able to do toward achieving group purposes. For example, the position of a skilled woodworker would be very different in a group organized to design and build a cabin when compared to his position in a group planning a boy's club to combat juvenile delinquency.

Some discussion groups have certain appointed or elected posts. For example, most committees have a designated chairperson who is responsible for such duties as calling meetings, planning agendas, coordinating the work of other committee members, and making reports to the parent organization. A committee may also have a designated secretary or recorder. Study-discussion groups invariably have a designated leader (or leaders) responsible for initiating and organizing the discussions; such groups may also have a host who supplies light refreshments. A board of directors will usually consist of the president, the treasurer, the secretary, and other officers of the parent organization, each of whom has certain definite functions to perform for the board as well as for the parent body.

For a group to be effective, a stable set of roles or division of labor must

8. *Ibid.*, p. 190.

emerge, with each member having certain types of functions or tasks in the group which she can be predicted to perform. This is not to say that everyone plays a totally different role from everyone else, or that two or more members may not often perform the same sorts of functions, but that each has developed a unique set of skills which, taken together, provide for all the group's needs in discussing and doing its work. Ideally, members have considerable flexibility, and each can perform a wide variety of needed tasks. But an effective long-term group always develops specialists, people who can be counted on to behave in certain ways and to take the lead when their skills are needed. Perhaps the all-around discussant would be one who is so sensitive and versatile that he can diagnose what each group needs from him, and perform those things—but, no human being can be all things, so we tend to seek role profiles suited both to our strengths and limitations and to the needs of each group. In a course concerned with small group communication you have an excellent laboratory for developing new behaviors.

The role a member plays in a group is not determined by that person alone, nor can it be predicted accurately from roles she had in previous groups. The role a person has varies from group to group. For a minute think of several different small groups to which you have belonged—I bet you behaved very differently in some of these groups. You probably have noticed, also, that in some groups your role changed considerably through time as you changed, as new persons joined the group, and as the problems facing the group changed. A major principle of small group theory is this: *the role of each member of a group is worked out by interaction between the member and the rest of the group.* Hence the role structure is unique to each group I have never seen any two groups in which the roles were even close to the same, anymore than they are in any two plays (it is from dramatic theory that we borrow the concept of role). What seems to happen is this: a member of a discussion group does something. If others respond favorably, he is likely to do this sort of thing again, a response to previous positive reinforcement. Soon that type of behavior is a part of his role. If other members reject the behavior or do not respond favorably (negative reinforcement), the person will not be likely to act that way again. Gradually, from this pattern of selective reinforcement, a fairly stable set of roles emerges in the group, and members come to expect each other to behave in some ways and not in others. Of course a member who has been reinforced for proposing new ideas may not always be able to do so as the problems change, and members who have not previously been initiators of ideas may suddenly have experience leading them to try idea initiating. If positively reinforced, a new facet has been added to their roles. Roles do change somewhat.

In the study of member behaviors and roles, group researchers and theorists have developed numerous classification systems, all of them oversimplified. Each such set of roles or behaviors has some limited uses and inadequacies. For

example, the most commonly cited is the "task" and "socioemotional" categories already referred to. But every communicative act in a group discussion has
both content (task) and relationship (social) implications. If a member says,
"Betty, why don't you get us some coffee?" she is both suggesting a task for
Betty to perform *and* that she has a right to expect Betty to do what she asks
(relationship). If I suggest that two members who are talking past each other in
an excited argument about two different solutions (secondary tension being
manifested) should listen more carefully, my statement although focused on
their way of relating to each other, may also have a direct bearing on the task
achievement of the group. And it not only implies a procedure for them to
follow, but also that my role in relation to them is such that I have a right to
suggest changes in their behavior. Every act in a discussion, then, can be viewed
as having both a *task* and a *relational* aspect, probably with greater impact in one
area than in the other. As shown in Figure 2.2, an act could have much impact
on both dimensions, much on one and little on the other, much on both, or little
on either.

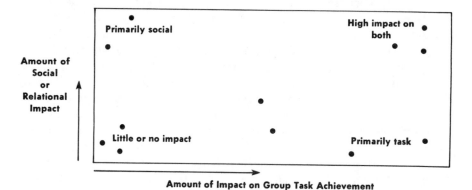

Figure 2.2. Two major dimensions of the impact of discussant behaviors.

What follows is a partial list of functions which members of small groups
perform during discussions. You may find this list helpful in the analysis of small
group communication behavior, provided you keep in mind that a single speech
or statement may perform two or more of these functions at once, and that an
individual's role in a small group will be an amalgam of several of these functions, with varying amounts of each. Thus one person might be described as
having the role of initiator, information giver, information seeker, evaluator,
recorder, gatekeeper, and tension reliever, as indicated in Figure 2.3.

Initiating and orienting—proposing goals, plans of action, or activities; prodding group to greater activity; defining position of group in relation to external structure or goal.

Information giving—offering facts and information, evidence, personal experience, and knowledge pertinent to the group task.

Information seeking—asking other members for information; requesting relevant evidence.

Opinion giving—stating beliefs, values, interpretations, and judgments.

Opinion seeking—asking other members for their opinions.

Clarifying and elaborating—interpreting issues; clarifying ambiguous statements; developing an idea previously expressed by giving examples, illustrations, and explanations.

Dramatizing nontask or even deviant commenting that evokes fantasies about other persons and places than the present, including joking, storytelling, suggesting indirectly.

Coordinating—showing relationships between or among ideas; integrating two or more solutions into one; summarizing or reviewing what has been said, pulling it all together; suggesting teamwork.

Evaluating—testing information and ideas; proposing or applying criteria; considering costs, practicality, difficulties, or outcomes of ideas.

Consensus testing—asking if group has reached a decision acceptable to all; suggesting that agreement may have been reached.

Suggesting procedure—suggesting an agenda of issues, outline, problem-solving pattern, or special technique; proposing some procedure or sequence to follow.

Recording—keeping group records on chalkboard or paper; preparing reports and minutes; serving as group memory.

Supporting—agreeing, praising, indicating warmth and solidarity with others.

Harmonizing—attempting to reconcile disagreements; pointing out common ground of values and beliefs; suggesting compromises; conciliating an angry person; reducing secondary tension.

Gatekeeping—encouraging others to speak; helping another to get the floor; stopping a dominant member from cutting off a comment by a less assertive member.

Tension relieving—introducing strangers, and helping them to feel at ease; reducing status differences; encouraging informality.

Norming—suggesting standards of behavior for members; challenging unproductive ways of behaving in group; giving negative response when another violates a group norm.

These and many other types of behavior are needed to develop a collection of people into a group, coordinate their efforts, and achieve interdependent goals.

Some behaviors, springing from personal needs at variance with the best interest of the group (hidden agendas), also occur during discussions. Among these behaviors which may characterize the roles of some members are:

Blocking—preventing progress toward group goals by constantly raising objections, repeatedly bringing up the same topic or issue after the group has considered it and rejected it. (It is not blocking to keep raising an idea or topic the group has not really listened to or considered.)

Attacking—attacking the competence of another, name-calling, impugning the motive of another instead of describing own feelings; joking at expense of another; attempting to destroy "face" of another.

Recognition seeking—boasting, calling attention to one's own expertise or experience when it is not necessary to establish credibility or relevant to group task; relating irrelevant experiences; game-playing to elicit sympathy or pity.

Horseplaying—making tangential jokes; engaging in horseplay that takes the group away from serious work or maintenance behavior.

Dominating—giving orders; interrupting and cutting off; flattering to get own way; insisting on own way.

Advocating—playing the advocate for the interests of a different group, thus acting as its representative, apologist, or advocate counter to the best interests or consensus of the current group.

Withdrawing—avoiding important differences; refusing to cope with conflicts; refusing to take a stand; covering up feelings; giving no response to comments of others.

The list of self-oriented behaviors could be expanded greatly. The important thing is to notice whether a member seems to be trying to contribute to the group, takes no responsibility for it, or seems to be manipulating or using others for strictly selfish goals. Benne and Sheats developed a very early list of "roles."[9] Your instructor may want you to examine this list or others like it. The important point is that every behavior has some impact on the group, primarily in helping achieve goals, develop procedures, enhance cohesiveness and teamwork, or self-enhancing at the expense of the goals, relationships, and procedures which make for effective group discussion.

9. Kenneth D. Benne and Paul Sheats, "Functional Roles of Group Members," *Journal of Social Issues* 4 (1948), pp. 41-49.

Initiating and orienting	Information giving
	Opinion giving
Information giving	Opinion seeking
Information seeking	
Opinion giving	Coordinating
Evaluating	
	Consensus testing
Suggesting procedures	Tension relieving
Norming	
Dramatizing	Gatekeeping

Figure 2.3. Roles of 2 hypothetical group members, as composites of behavioral functions.

NETWORKS OF COMMUNICATION

Concomitant with the development of somewhat specialized roles in a group is the development of a communication network. The phrase "communication network" refers to a pattern of message flow or "linkages" of who actually speaks to whom in discussions. A member who opens a meeting may find the others expecting him to initiate discussion on a new topic or at subsequent meetings. A person who speaks frequently will find others looking (literally) to him or her for some comment on each new issue or when there is a lag in conversation. Infrequent verbal participants will themselves be more and more overlooked, and the comments they do make ignored.

Most of the so-called "network" studies of communication in task groups seem to be largely irrelevant to discussion groups in natural (as opposed to laboratory) settings. People passing notes through holes in plywood partitions (typical in the network studies) to solve contrived problems imposed on them do not interact any more like people in discussion groups than do baboons in a zoo interact like baboons in natural clans in a forest or veldt.

Many types of networks have been identified, but the "permissible" as well as the actually used channels must be looked at in any group to fully understand its structure. Hopefully, the democratic group has an "all-channel" network in which all participants are free to comment on a one-to-one basis with all others, and to the group as a whole (see Figure 2.4). A "wheel" network is to be

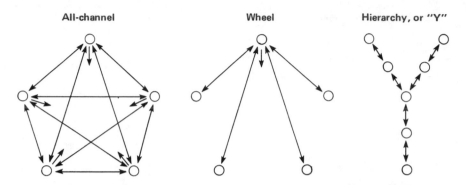

Figure 2.4. Communication networks.

avoided in which all comments are directed toward one central person ("leader") who alone may speak to the group as a whole or to any individual in it. A "Y," or hierarchical network, occurs when an autocratic leader has "lieutenants" with whom he interacts directly, and who in turn talk to subordinates. The persons at the ends of the Y rarely if ever interact directly with the leader. In both wheel and Y networks the central person is usually very satisfied with his participation and status, but the peripheral members tend to find little satisfaction in participation in the group. Also to be deplored is the breakdown of group communication which is indicated by two or more "private" conversations going on between pairs of individuals at the same time. The all-channel network permits rapid communication without having to get clearance from a central gatekeeping authority; everyone is free to say what he wants while it is pertinent and fresh in mind. Communication flows freely from person to person. At least half of the comments are addressed to the group as a whole, and all group members can hear and attend to all one-to-one or one-to-few comments. Free feedback of questions and responses is thus encouraged. Many studies have shown morale to be highest when all channels are open, and some have indicated superior problem solving on complex tasks by groups with such networks compared to more restricted networks of flow of communication. You are well advised to see that departures from an all-channel flow are very brief.

Who talks to whom, and how often each member speaks in a face-to-face small group is related to such other characteristics of the group as members' personalities, external system, spread of knowledge among members, goal and type of immediate task, discussion skills, time, sex, and status. As a baseline for studying the communication flow among groups of from three to five members,

Bostrom constructed a model of the interactive possibilities in theoretically "structureless" groups. To illustrate, consider a four-person group with members A, B, C, and D. Each can speak to each other singly, to each possible combination of two persons, or to all three other members—a total of twenty-eight initiating interactions. For an eight-person group, the possibilities are 1,056! In our hypothetical group of four members, the ratio of one-to-one messages as compared to one-to-group would theoretically be 3/1. However, the interaction behaviors Bostrom found in his groups were not distributed at all like this. First, most comments in groups of four or five members were addressed to either one person or the group as a whole (roughly 95%). As group size increased from three to four to five, the percentage of one-to-one comments increased steadily from 46.8 to 58.2 to 64.7. Conversely, the percentage of messages addressed to the rest of the group as a whole decreased. High-ranking senders also tended to be high-ranking receivers of comments. Persons named as "leaders" by fellow discussants were high on all these indexes of communicative interaction. Persons named as "good discussants" were ranked above others as senders but not as receivers. Satisfaction with one's own participation was found to be correlated with rank as sender but not as receiver.[10]

We can draw some important conclusions from these findings. Your satisfaction with a discussion and your influence in the group will both be enhanced by being above average in frequency of speaking. A wheel or Y network forces some members into a position of low sending, and hence low satisfaction. As the group size increases, it becomes more and more likely that remarks will be addressed to one other person rather than to the entire group, thus restricting the flow and making it increasingly hard to get the floor if one is not a very active participant. Finally, to have a functional all-channel network will take some conscious effort on the part of group members.

Appointment of a discussion leader tends to focus the flow of communication. Mortensen found that it was concentrated heavily from the start around members who were assigned positions as "leaders," even if these leaders were incapable of maintaining their positions.[11] As a group develops definite role structure, more and more restrictions on the flow of communication also tend to develop. As the skills of various members are more or less needed from phase to phase of a discussion (problem analysis, evaluation of ideas, decision making, etc.), the individuals will vary in their frequency of participation, altering the communicative network.

10. Robert N. Bostrom, "Patterns of Communicative Interaction in Small Groups," *Speech Monographs* 37 (1970), pp. 257-263.

11. C. David Mortensen, "Should the Discussion Group Have an Assigned Leader," *Speech Teacher* 15 (1966), pp. 34-41.

STATUS

Status refers to the relative importance of each member and his or her prestige. As group roles emerge, each person is placed on a sort of "ladder" or "pecking order" within the group. Thus, status is closely associated with position in a communication network. Researchers have found that high-status members talk more often than do low-status members, that highs communicate more often with each other than with lows, and that lows tend to address their comments to people higher in status than themselves rather than to members of equal or lower status.[12] Discussants tend to interrupt and ignore the comments of low-status persons far more often than those of highs. However, the status heirarchy of a small group is not inflexible; it may change through time as members make contributions to the group's goals, and roles change. Most people find satisfaction in the psychological rewards that come from high status: being admired, responded to, supported, and liked. We spend much time and effort acquiring the symbols of high status—big automobiles, tailored clothing, houses in exclusive neighborhoods, trophies, and titles.

When a small group is first developing, status will often be ascribed on the basis of each member's position in the society external to the small group, guided by such benchmarks as wealth, education, work, personal fame, or position in the parent organization of a committee. For example, a committee comprised of a college dean, a professor of biology, an English instructor, two seniors, and two sophomores would initially have that order of ascribed status. But status is *earned* or achieved in the small working group based on each member's perceived contributions to the group's goals, so that order would likely change drastically as functional roles emerged.

Sex has an unpredictable impact on status and roles in a group today, depending on the beliefs and values of the members. A decade ago one could predict that in a mixed sex group a male would almost always emerge as leader, and that the status of females would on the average be lower than the status of males. As Bormann and Bormann say, some men ". . . tend to resist the leadership of a woman, no matter how capable . . ." and some women will refuse ". . . as a matter of principle to follow any plans suggested by a man."[13] When the discussion group mirrors the struggle between the sexes for position in society at large, this hidden agenda item will interfere with productive work. Further complications arise when sexual attraction occurs between members of a small group, as many case studies by my students attest.

---

12. J.I. Hurwitz, A.F. Zander, and B. Hymovitch, "Some Effects of Power on the Relations Among Group Members," in *Group Dynamics: Research and Theory,* 3rd ed., D. Cartwright and A. Zander, ed. (New York: Harper & Row, Publishers, 1968), pp. 291-297.

13. Earnest G. Bormann and Nancy C. Bormann, *Effective Small Group Communication,* 2nd ed. (Minneapolis: Burgess Publishing Company, 1976), p. 52.

Most small groups establish two or three levels of status in their hierarchy. This does not mean that lower status members are not judged to be of value, or that they are unhappy in the group. Cohesive groups value the contributions of each member, and every member knows it. High is not necessarily better, just more influential. Case studies of student groups often contain such comments as this: "Every member of our group played a vital role. Jim, our leader, was most important in the success of our project, but even quiet Norman made a vital contribution with his careful research and by arranging a place where we could meet. He could always be counted on to do his part. I would not change a member of this group even if I could."

NORMS

Every group develops *norms*. These are rules of conduct, standards of participation, or expectations of how members should behave. They are not regulations imposed by a head person with power to punish, but guidelines that all or most members accept implicitly. Norms both guide and regulate behavior of group members. They determine how and to whom members speak, how they dress, where and how they sit, what they talk about, what language may be used, and so on. Such group norms may or may not be stated openly, but they can be detected by an observer. A norm can most clearly be written as a "may," "should," or "should not" statement. Practice in formulating them in the form shown in the examples which follow should help you to perceive norms in a small group.

Two general types of norms develop as a group culture emerges: (1) those governing the specialized role of each member; and (2) those which apply to all members. Members share in the expectation that both types of norms will be complied with.

Some examples of role-specific norms are:

"The leader should prepare and distribute an agenda in advance of each meeting."

"The leader should summarize from time to time, but other members may do so if the leader does not when a summary is needed."

"Mary may play the critical tester of all ideas, asking for evidence, pointing out logical fallacies, and otherwise evaluating."

"Mike should tell a joke to relieve secondary tension when the climate gets stressful from an argument over different points of view."

Some examples of typical norms which would apply to every member of a small group are:

"Each speaker should relate his comment to what has been said previously during the discussion." (productive)

"Discussants should avoid challenging the President's opinions." (counterproductive)

"Members should keep quiet if they have not read the assignment for this week." (largely productive)

"Members should arrive on time." (productive)

"People in this group should all be addressed on a first name basis." (productive)

"Slang is acceptable in this group." (productive)

"It is acceptable to talk about whatever you want." (usually counterproductive)

The existence of a group norm will be revealed by two types of phenomena: (1) behavioral patterns that are repeatedly enacted or avoided; and (2) some sort of punishment or sanction taken against a member who deviates from the norm. For example, others may frown, fail to respond, comment negatively about the behavior, or even scold the violator—"let's stick to the issues and not go blaming one another." Every norm has some impact on a group's productivity and member satisfaction. The norms that are counterproductive or reduce satisfaction need to be changed.

Perhaps a few examples of norms will help you to understand them better. These are stated as "do's" and "don'ts." Taking the trouble to formulate norms in this way often helps to clarify their nature and function. Evidence that these norms were in force in many groups has been observed by this writer.

Conformity to procedural norms is essential if members are to work together. Discussants are usually inclined to conform to the procedural norms of the group.[14] Any violation of the norms may mean that the norm is not understood by the violator or he disagrees with it. If procedural norms are clearly understood but still violated by one or more members, this should be called to the attention of the group and some action should be taken. Continued violation means the member feels the norm is somehow detrimental.

The degree to which a member will conform to group norms (both procedural and opinion norms) depends on his evaluation of the group and his status in it. The more a person prizes membership in a group, the more he will conform; the higher his status, the more he will conform.

During the developmental stage of a new small group, norms are developed rapidly, often without the members realizing what is occurring. The first meeting is quite important in establishing norms, especially the first few minutes. At that time, behaviors which are typical of primary tension can become norms if the tension is not released early—speaking softly, being extremely polite, avoiding questioning the sources of another's information, or even opinionated and dogmatic ways of stating beliefs can become norms if not challenged.

---

14. Do not confuse conformity in procedure with conformity in thinking. While conformity in procedure is necessary, unthinking conformity to majority opinion can be very damaging both to group products and to individual personality.

In order to clarify and possibly change the norms of a discussion group, first study their effects. Group awareness of harmful effects can lead to change. A participant should try to discover answers to the following questions if she senses that something is wrong that may be due to a counterproductive norm:

1. What regularities of behavior can be seen? (For example, who talks to whom? How do the people talk? Where do they sit? To what degree do they ask for evidence supporting a position? How are ideas evaluated?)

2. What seem to be the practical effects of each of these modes of behaving? (For example, are ideas going untested? Are some members' ideas accepted uncritically while others' ideas are ignored or rejected? Do members always sit in the same positions? Is there much evidence of frustration?)

3. What happens when a member deviates from a norm? Is this deviant behavior punished in some way?

Once you have formulated the norm you believe to be detrimental to the group, state it to the members, describe the evidence of its existence, and suggest that it be replaced by a different norm or pattern of behavior. The group will likely discuss this problem for a few minutes, and decide to make the change. Even if this is done by consensus, members may still need reminders of the new norm for some time to come until it has become largely habituated.

Norms are based on the shared values—beliefs of what is relatively good or bad, productive or unproductive. Values are often explored and developed in what appear to be tangents to a group's discussion topic, in sequences of comments which are called "fantasy chains." The process of group dramatizing or fantasy chaining was first described by Bales in 1970.[15] Bales claimed that all fantasy chaining relates to "unconscious meanings" or needs of one or more participants. Hence such fantasies have great power to motivate discussants. Usually several people participate in a group fantasy chain, but not necessarily all members. Consider how this process occurs. Quite often the group seems at a loss for what to say or do. Talking peters out, or perhaps there is an awkward tenseness due to conflict among members. Suddenly someone says something which appears to be off the subject, a tangent about persons in some other time and place.

> Interaction speeds up, a pitch of excitement is heard in the voices; often there is some conflict or an edge of hostility. The volume of sound often goes up as the group begins the chain association. Many signs of interest are seen among those who do not participate verbally. Restless . . . movements increase as people try to find a way to get into the conversation. New images and

15. Robert F. Bales, *Personality and Interpersonal Behavior* (New York: Holt, Rinehart and Winston, Inc., 1970), pp. 105-108, 136-155.

reported events may be rapidly injected, but apparently somehow on the same theme, psychologically . . . for some period—a minute or two, sometimes much longer.[16]

The fantasy is manifestly about persons and events outside the group, that could have occurred in another time (past or future) and another place. At the same time, on a different level, the talk mirrors indirectly the problems of the group at the moment, such as fears, dislikes, loves, jealousies, tense relations between members, relations with other groups, unverbalized hidden agendas, etc.

Fantasy chains can easily be detected by an observer watching for them by noting sudden changes of pace, levels of excitement, and a sort of electric tension in the air. To interpret the fantasy, Bales suggested that the observer look for a sudden insight into what is going on in the group that has not been openly discussed. Systematic analysis will not work. Through fantasy chains a group establishes a new realm of social reality for its members, a myth that becomes the truth, a sense of unity in a group involved in some dramatic conflict, with shared values and interests.

COHESIVENESS

The degree of cohesiveness in a small group is related to every other syntality characteristic of the group such as productivity, openness and completeness of communication, objectives of the group, procedures, and so on. "Cohesiveness" refers to the "stick togetherness," or member attraction to the group. High cohesiveness and high morale of members are closely associated; if members perceive the group to be meeting their goals and participation to be personally satisfying, their attraction and loyalty to the group will be high. The higher the cohesiveness of the group, the greater control over member behaviors the group as a whole will be able to exert.

A high degree of cohesiveness is associated with a high degree of ability to cope effectively with unusual problems, and to work as a team in meeting emergencies. Production groups, if highly cohesive, *can* produce more than low cohesive groups, but may not do so if the members are being influenced by intragroup norms for less production. High cohesiveness is associated with the group's ability to get members to conform to the majority or high-status members' desires. Janis has pointed out that conformity in many problem-solving groups contributes to very low-quality decisions, the result of "groupthink" which allows for no disagreement with beliefs of high-status members.[17] Deviance from the beliefs of high-status members or the majority may be put down

---

16. *Ibid.*, p. 138.
17. Irving L. Janis, *Victims of Groupthink* (Boston: Houghton Mifflin Company, 1973).

so powerfully that a person holding valid information which negates those be-liefs even begins to doubt his own information. As such groups continue through time they become very predictable, less creative, less able to use novel ideas—the "nuts" are silenced or even put out. The very people who could contribute most to the quality of solutions by pointing out fallacious thinking find the group less and less attractive while the cohesiveness among the majority is growing. Thus we have a dilemma of how to maintain a productive degree of creativity and critical thinking while at the same time maintaining a high degree of cohesiveness essential to high potential, personal satisfaction, and loyalty. Specific techniques will be presented later, especially for designated leaders. *Awareness of the prob-lem* is the point here.

However, we do know that a group that accomplishes its objectives, provides members with satisfaction in their participation, offers prestige in belonging, and is successful in competing with other groups, has high attractiveness to its mem-bers. This knowledge can be used to offset the strains produced by uncertainty, risk, and deferment of judgment necessary to achieve high-quality work. We also know that cohesiveness is fostered by the degree to which members know and like each other as persons, their frequency of interaction, and the amount of influence exerted by each on the group. Interestingly, open disagreeing has been shown to be more frequent in high-cohesive groups than in low-cohesive groups. A climate of trust in which each member feels secure permits expressions of disagreement on issues, facts, and ideas—provided the disagreement is aimed at arriving at high-quality solutions. But if high-status members resist disagreement as a personal affront, then whatever cohesiveness is achieved by other means will be at the expense of low-quality decision making—"groupthink." Highly success-ful and cohesive groups tend to first get well acquainted and interested in each other as persons. They accept the need for secondary tension generated by disagreements, and find ways to reduce these tensions by giving priority to evidence, rational thinking, and compromise. After decisions have been reached, such groups restate the value of the group and of each of its members. Members can be heard saying such things as: "I'm proud of our group, we really thresh out ideas until we arrive at the best, and then we team up." "Even if I disagreed with you, Joe, I'm glad you spoke up. We disagreed openly and honestly, and I learned a lot from you. I like that."

In order to enhance cohesiveness, Bormann and Bormann suggest that a group should consciously do the following:

1. Develop a strong identity as a group and a group tradition or history. This can be done by developing nicknames for the group, insignia of member-ship, referring to past events with pride and pleasure, ceremonies and rituals, and emphasizing the high quality of accomplishments.

2. Stress teamwork, and give credit to the group. Avoid talking about what you did personally for the group, especially if you are the designated

leader. Volunteering to do things for the group, and emphasizing how important the group is to you will help get members feeling closer to each other.

3. Recognize contributions to the group goal by members, thus rewarding individual members from *within* the group. Low-status members especially need reward and praise from other group members, and *not* criticism, if they are to develop the loyalty which will make them more productive and dependable.

4. Show human concern for the people who make up the group, providing warmth, affection, and direct attention to personal tensions and problems which members indicate. As soon as personal needs are dealt with, however, the group should get back to the group task.

5. Support both disagreement and agreement, which basically means working for a norm of open expression of disagreement or support for ideas. Highly cohesive groups show more disagreement; open conflict needs to be encouraged, not repressed. When the conflicts are settled, signs of solidarity such as joking, laughing together, compliments to people who supported rejected ideas which helped build a better group solution, and comments such as "Let's get behind this" are needed.

6. Help the group set clear and attainable goals, which also provide enough of a challenge to yield a sense of pride in group achievement. Continuing groups which fail to reach their objectives tend to display lowered cohesiveness and may even break up. On the other hand, beating a high school team would not enhance the cohesiveness of a college soccer squad.[18]

GROUP SIZE

The number of persons forming a group is a major determinant of what happens during discussions. A person needs to be flexible in adjusting to groups of different sizes. As group size increases, the complexity increases rapidly; the number of interpersonal relationships increases geometrically as the number of members increases arithmetically.

Increased size means less opportunity for the average participant to speak and to influence others. In student learning groups, increased size results in lower satisfaction with the discussion.[19] Frustration increases with group size. In larger groups, the less forceful and less confident discussants speak less, while the more forceful tend to occupy an even greater proportion of the time. There is a

18. Adapted from Earnest G. Bormann and Nancy C. Bormann, *Effective Small Group Communication,* 2nd ed. (Minneapolis: Burgess Publishing Company, 1976), pp. 70-76.

19. James A. Schellenberg, "Group Size as a Factor in Success of Academic Discussion Groups," *Journal of Educational Psychology* 33 (1959), pp. 73-79.

Figure 2.5. Small and large groups are different.

tendency for one central person to do a proportionately greater amount of talking.[20] Also speeches tend to be longer, often including several points not particularly pertinent to the issue of the moment.

20. E.F. Stephan and E.G. Mishler, "The Distribution of Participation in Small Groups," *American Sociological Review* 17 (1952), pp. 598-608.

As group size increases, more centralized control of procedures is both expected and needed. Leadership roles become more specialized and formal. Great demands are made on designated leaders to keep order, to keep the discussion organized, and to control the flow of ideas. Large groups usually rely on formal rules of parliamentary procedure, with the general rule being that the larger the group the more the "rules of order" need to be detailed and followed rigorously. Sometimes, however, small committees (contrary to the advice of even Henry Robert) use much of the formidable panoply of parliamentary law. The effect of main motions, seconding, points of order, tabling, etc., is primarily to delay, obfuscate, and frustrate meetings. The members less knowledgeable of the table of motions will likely participate little for fear of making errors. Even formal committees of legislative bodies are advised to have only minimal procedural controls.[21]

Other effects commonly occurring when group size increases include greater difficulty in establishing criteria or values, more time reaching a decision, lowering of cohesiveness (attraction to the group), and a tendency for cliques to develop within the group.[22] Small wonder, then, that students who have become proficient in discussing in groups of five to seven people often flounder in confusion when the class as a whole tries to engage in discussion with the same sort of informality and loose structure used in smaller groups.

How large should a discussion group be? The answer depends in a large part on the purpose of the group and its organizational setting. As early as 1927, Smith demonstrated that groups of three were more efficient in solving problems with "easy" solutions than groups of six members, but groups of six were more efficient with problems requiring that a number of solutions be considered and poor ones promptly rejected.[23] Slater found that experimental problem-solving discussion groups of four to six members were most satisfying to the participants, whereas groups larger than six were felt to encourage too much personal aggressiveness, inconsiderateness, competitiveness, centralization, or disorganization into cliques. Participants in groups of less than four reported being too tense and too constrained to express their attitudes and feelings openly.[24] Groups with even numbers of members tend to have more trouble reaching agreement than do odd numbered groups. Studies of committees have shown the most *common* sizes to be five, seven, and nine.[25]

21. For more detail, see Henry L. Ewbank, Jr., *Meeting Management* (Dubuque: Wm. C. Brown Company Publishers, 1968), pp. 29-37, Chapter 8.

22. See bibliography for research sources which support these generalizations.

23. E.B. Smith, "Some Psychological Aspects of Committee Work," *Journal of Abnormal and Social Psychology* 11 (1927), pp. 348-368, 437-464.

24. Philip E. Slater, "Contrasting Correlates of Group Size," *Sociometry* 21 (1958), pp. 129-139.

25. Clovis R. Shepherd, *Small Groups* (San Francisco: Chandler Publishing Company, 1964), p. 4.

Keeping the results of such studies in mind, and that maximum personal involvement is essential for high productivity and efficient use of human beings, the group should be large enough to accomplish its goals and at the same time insure members of satisfaction through opportunity for frequent participation. Thelen's "principle of individual challenge in the least-sized groups" is applicable. Thelen declared that to secure maximum motivation and quality performance, we should establish the *"smallest groups in which it is possible to have represented at a functional level all the social and achievement skills required for the particular required activity."*[26]

Other factors being taken care of, the ideal task-oriented discussion group seems to be five, which is small enough to promote an all-channel network and to permit informality and ease in reaching decisions, yet large enough to bring the many types of information and varied points of view needed for wise decisions. For learning groups, the size may range from as few as three to as many as fifteen or more. If the purpose is to encourage individual questioning and thinking, choose a small group. If the purpose is to expose participants to as many points of view as possible, a larger group is better.

A MODEL OF THE EFFECTIVE DISCUSSION GROUP

A basic objective of this book, and possibly of the course for which it may be a text, is to help you become a skilled *participant-observer* in discussion groups. The participant-observer is a person who is a regular member of the group, engaging actively in its deliberations, but who at the same time is observing, evaluating, and adapting to its processes and procedures. In terms of role, the participant-observer directs part of his attention to task functions and part to maintenance functions, trying always to be aware of what the group needs at the moment. Then he or she can supply the needed information, ideas, and actions, or seek them from other group members.

Being able to maintain a balanced perspective on the processes of a discussion group while actively participating calls for a general image or "model" of the ideally productive group. As you engage in discussion, you can develop the details of your own model by drawing tentative concepts about what behaviors and procedures are most helpful for specific purposes under specific conditions. Any serious student of the discussion process and self-as-discussant will need to review analytically and critically virtually every discussion and his role in it, seeing what tentative generalizations about the group's process he can derive as guidance for future group participation. Indeed, in classroom discussions this is a "must." Teachers of small group communication who do not use such learning

---

26. Herbert A. Thelen, *Dynamics of Groups at Work* (Chicago: University of Chicago Press, 1954), p. 187.

activities as fishbowl discussion, process feedback, and analytical discussion leading to generalizations about group interaction, are certainly missing one of the greatest of all inductive teaching-learning procedures available.

As a beginning model or "image" for studying problem-solving discussion (and to some degree learning discussion), the following summary of this chapter is presented.

1. *The group's purpose is clearly defined and accepted by all members.* There is adequate perspective on the external structure, including an understanding of the area of freedom. The group makes constant adaptations to the changes in conditions facing it. All members give the group goal priority over personal goals or needs not in harmony with the group objectives.

2. *Roles of members are relatively stable, mutually understood, and accepted by all members.* Each finds satisfaction of personal needs/motives in her role. Although there is sufficient role definition to permit members to predict each other's behavior, there is also sufficient flexibility to permit anyone to make any needed contribution to the task or group maintenance. The leadership position has been settled in the minds of all members, and the leader has a group-centered orientation. Leadership functions are optimally shared by all members.

3. *Cohesiveness is high,* with each member having a strong sense of identification with the group, commitment, and responsibility. Teamwork is evidenced by sharing of rewards, mutual support, and consensus decisions. A high degree of informality, openness, and trust exists (low primary tension), and the group has developed procedures for overcoming secondary tensions.

4. *The principle of least group size is exemplified,* with a number sufficiently small for all to be active participants, yet large enough to supply the variety of backgrounds and knowledge or skills needed to produce quality work.

5. *The flow of communicative interaction reveals an all-channel network,* with a high proportion of remarks directed to all members, and few cliques or dialogues.

6. *Norms and the values underlying them are understood and adhered to,* or else openly discussed and changed when found not to be productive. The group has a culture of beliefs, values, and standards which encourage thorough searching for and testing of facts and ideas, open conflict over the merits of ideas, and displays of affection, support, and solidarity.

7. *Procedures and thought patterns of effective problem solving and decision making are understood and used by the group.* Members insist that the best possible thinking and problem-solving patterns be followed; they keep the discussion orderly and organized most of the time.

The major group variables which affect the quality of discussion have been presented in this chapter. In the rest of this book we will explore a number of these in depth, and consider specific techniques which should help you to bring groups of which you are a member into congruence with this model.

Bibliography

Bales, Robert F., *Personality and Interpersonal Behavior,* New York: Holt, Rinehart and Winston, Inc., 1970.

Bormann, Earnest G., *Discussion and Group Methods: Theory and Practice,* 2nd ed., New York: Harper & Row, Publishers, 1975.

Cathcart, Robert S., and Samovar, Larry A. (eds.), *Small Group Communication: A Reader,* 2nd ed., Dubuque: Wm. C. Brown Company Publishers, 1975.

Collins, Barry E., and Guetzkow, Harold, *A Social Psychology of Group Processes for Decision-Making,* New York: John Wiley & Sons, Inc., 1964.

Fisher, B. Aubrey, *Small Group Decision Making: Communication and the Group Process,* New York: McGraw-Hill Book Company, 1974.

Golembiewski, Robert T., *The Small Group. An Analysis of Research Concepts and Operations,* Chicago: The University of Chicago Press, 1962.

Hare, A. Paul, *Handbook of Small Group Research,* New York: The Free Press of Glencoe, 1962.

Shaw, Marvin E., *Group Dynamics: The Psychology of Small Group Behavior,* 2nd ed., New York: McGraw-Hill Book Company, 1976.

Key Concepts

Area of freedom—scope of authority or power, defining limits within which a group may take action.

Behavioral function—any act or behavior of a member of a small group; the total set of behavior functions by a member determines that member's role.

Cohesiveness—a term referring to the degree of attraction members feel for the group, their sense of unity and commitment.

Discussion group—small number of people with sense of belonging to each other, interdependent purpose, and shared norms who interact orally while face to face.

External system—the field in which a group consists.

Fantasy chain—a series of statements by members of a discussion group in which they dramatize a story about other persons in other places and times, in order to create a social reality, norms, and shared values.

Hidden agenda—a purpose or motive of a member, subgroup, or entire small group different from the expressed purpose of the group; often in conflict with the group goal.

Interaction—reciprocal influence among members of group, mediated via communication, primarily talking.

Interdependent goal—a group goal such that the achievement of it by one member is dependent upon achievement by all.

Long-term group—a continuing group which has several or more meetings through time, permitting development of a history, culture, explicit roles, and elaborated norms and procedures.

Network of communication—a model or diagram of the flow of messages within a small group, revealing who may talk to whom.

Norm—a rule of conduct or guideline for behavior of members of a group; may be stated openly, or implied by patterns of behavior.

Parent group—a larger group which has established a committee or subgroup with a definite assigned area of freedom and responsibility.

Principle of least-sized groups—formulated by Thelen, states that a group should be no larger than necessary to include all needed information, skills, etc., within the members.

Primary tension—social unease which occurs when members of a new group first meet or at beginning of meetings of a long-term group.

Role—pattern of behavior displayed by, expected, and permitted of a member of a small group.

Secondary tension—tension and discomfort experienced by members of a group from conflict over values, points of view, and alternative solutions.

Social or maintenance behaviors—member acts which primarily serve to reduce tensions, increase solidarity, and facilitate teamwork rather than accomplishing the work of the group.

Status—position of a member in the hierarchy of influence and power within a small group, a corollary of prestige; may be attributed on basis of personal characteristics, but must be earned on basis of performance in a continuing group.

Task behaviors—acts of members which primarily contribute to doing the work and accomplishing the goals of a group.

Exercises

1.   Divide your class into two groups of from ten to fifteen each, depending on the size. Select a topic or problem for discussion, and begin discussion simultaneously in the two large groups. Then, after fifteen minutes, divide each group into two smaller groups. After fifteen minutes divide again into four groups of two to four members each. Then after fifteen minutes, go back into the two large groups. Each student should now write a list of the differences he observed in the different size groups and the differences in personal feelings he experienced in the groups of differing sizes. Complete the following scales:

   a.   I most preferred participating in the group of _____ members;
        I least preferred participating in the group of _____ members.
   b.   I felt most satisfied with my participation in the group of _____ members;
        least satisfied in the group of _____ .
   c.   I felt that the content of the discussion was best in the group of _____ ; worst in the group of _____ members.

   Now discuss your papers and answers to these scales as a class and see what general conclusions you can come to as a class. Record these in full sentence form as tentative generalizations about small group discussion.

2. You and two or three classmates should observe the same group discussion and *independently* write out all the norms you could observe at work in the group. Make brief notes of what you noticed as evidence of each norm. Indicate if you think the norm was goal productive with a (+), had no effect on productivity with a (0), or counterproductive with a (−). Write the norms as rules of conduct using the following form:

    General norm—"Members of this group (should, should not, or may) _____ ."
    Role-specific norm—"(The leader, the secretary, Mary, etc.) should (or should not) _____ ."

    In the evidence column put descriptions of behavior you actually observed, such as what was done regularly and accepted, or behavior that was given negative reinforcement.

Norm	Evidence of the Norm	Impact

3. Observe a group with several of your classmates. Using a list of group functions as a guide, list the functions each member performs, and how often each member performs each function. Then describe the overall role taken by each member in a brief paragraph. Compare your findings with those of your fellow observers.

4. First, make a list of at least ten small groups in which you have been an active member during the past year (your instructor may wish to change this time span). Then, in a single sentence, describe the role you had in each group. Compare your list with the lists of three to five classmates. What do you discover about a person's roles in different groups?

5. Choose a problem for discussion. After about fifteen minutes of discussion in a group of four to seven members, each member should write out (independently) the: (a) problem; (b) goals; (c) important facts and opinions. Compare papers. What can you conclude?

6. Diagram the flow of communication in a discussion group you observe, using the form shown on page 245. Be sure to record how many times each person speaks and to whom. What is the proportion of the total statements made by each member? What sort of communication network exists in the group?

7. Divide the class into groups of six or seven members each, and put each group in a separate room or corner of the large classroom. Form different networks by seating the members as shown on page 50. Except in the all-channel network, members should talk only in a whisper to each other so no one else can overhear. Speak only to persons indicated for your network. Your instructor will give you a simple problem to solve. Keep track of how long it takes you to solve the problem (everyone must agree to the

solution). Then rate your personal satisfaction with your participation in the group on a scale of 7 to 1, with 7 meaning "very satisfied" and 1 meaning "very dissatisfied." Your instructor will record each participant's satisfaction rating on the board on a diagram of your group's network, as well as the time it took the group to solve the problem. What do you learn from this exercise?

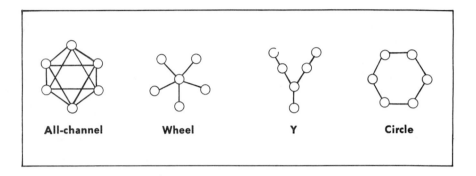

All-channel **Wheel** **Y** **Circle**

8. Each member of the class should read the following case, then select his candidates. Next divide into groups of five to six members each. Each group must then reach a consensus decision (accepted by all members as the best choice they can agree upon). If you have trouble agreeing, be sure to discuss the values or criteria on which your choices are based. You may need to decide on criteria acceptable to all before going over the list of choices.

Now answer the following questions in a brief paper:

1. What most hindered you in reaching decisions?
2. What most helped you to reach a decision?
3. Who were the most influential members of your group, and why?

Meet again in your small group, and draw up a list of guidelines for making decisions efficiently by consensus. Have a spokesman report the guidelines formulated by each group. These may be compiled, duplicated, and given to each class member.

Next have each group select a representative to a conference. The conferees should meet in the center of the room, with the other members of each conferee's group seated together just behind the conferee. The conferees are to arrive at a final selection of two persons to be served by the kidney machine. Members of each group may discuss quietly among themselves, and if they decide they want to give instructions to their representative, they may do so by sending the representative a note. The conferees may at any time request a recess so that they may consult with the groups they represent; any recess must be approved by all conferees. A recess may last no more than three minutes.

After the conference has proceeded for about 15 minutes, have the conferees describe how they feel. Then send them to a private room where they may confer without observers. They must arrive at a decision within

20 minutes. While they confer, the rest of the class should engage in some other activity. As soon as the conferees have reached a decision, have them report any differences in what they felt while discussing with observers and while discussing in private. Then have each conferee explain the outcome of the conference to the group which he or she represented. What conclusions can you draw from this exercise about conducting conferences and about relationships between representatives and the groups they speak for?

9. Tape record a discussion of the Kidney Machine case. Then listen to the recording, and see if you can identify each fantasy chain that occurred. Note the point in time (or in feet on the recorder's indicator) at which the fantasy began. What is the manifest content of each fantasy? What has it to do with the emergence of values or standards for judging applicants for the machine? With relationships among members of the group? With members' roles? With the emergence of a group from a collection of people assigned to come to a decision? Discuss your findings with several other persons who have analyzed the same recorded discussion, and write out any conclusions you can agree on about the importance of fantasy chains in group formation, structure, and work.

As an alternative, your instructor may provide a video recording of a discussion for analysis and discussion as above.

THE KIDNEY MACHINE DECISION

The year is 1974.

Memorial Hospital in Memphis has a newly developed, world-famous kidney machine. It can preserve the lives of people suffering from a rare kidney disease which until just a few years ago was always fatal. Only a few can benefit from kidney transplant operations; finding a matching donor often takes far longer than the person can remain alive, and more often no matching donor is ever found. For those who can get on it, the machine can maintain life indefinitely. Unfortunately, this machine is very expensive; only one exists in the entire Memphis area. People who have the disease must come to the hospital once a week and remain on the machine for twenty hours. This means that only eight people can be helped by it, though many more need its assistance to remain alive.

Foundations have been working to raise money to help such sufferers. One foundation pays all costs for using the machine, so it costs nothing to the recipient. Another is trying to raise enough funds to buy another machine.

The physicians of the Memorial Hospital staff can make an accurate prognosis of who will benefit from the machine, and they have a long list of people hoping to get on the machine who would benefit. The decision as to who gets on the machine (and so lives) and who does not is thus not a medical one. Memorial Hospital has appointed a voluntary panel of people like ourselves to decide who shall be given this help when any vacancy opens up. Panelists are given a biographical profile of each candidate, plus a psychiatrist's report which evaluates the personality of the applicants. The psychiatrist conducts an extensive interview with each prospective beneficiary. The panel members study the reports, then meet to discuss the people nominated and make a decision by consensus (not vote). The panel meets in private, decides, and reports. They never meet the applicants nor see any pictures of them. The panelists are all strangers who see each other only when they meet as a group.

The panel is guided by the following guidelines:

1. People between twenty-five and forty seem to have the best promise of a relatively normal life when served by the machine.

2. People served by the machine often show considerable emotional distress. Some patients become very sullen and resentful of their dependence on the machine. A few have become very hostile and nasty to the doctors and nurses who serve them, realizing the ego-investment these professionals have in successful treatment.

3. Income or wealth is not a factor.

Your assignment is to study the information provided about ten current medically-approved applicants, and select the two who are to benefit from vacancies on the machine schedule. Write down your choice, then meet with your small group and develop a way to make a decision. The group will select two persons by consensus, then write a report justifying these persons as the beneficiaries. Then the entire class may meet to select two recipients, or each group may select a representative to meet in a conference before the rest of the class to make the final decision. Following the writing of your personal analysis and report, the class will probably discuss the group processes.

JAMES B. Caucasian, age 39. Holds M.D. degree, teaches and does research in medical school. Wife, 37. Son, age 15, in high school. Son, age 13, in junior high. Daughter, age 11, in elementary school. Son, age 5, mentally retarded. Family income is $62,000 per year, entirely from earnings of James B.

Psychiatrist's report: James B. is working on a team in cancer research in which he seems highly involved. He asserts that he is on the brink of a "major breakthrough in cancer treatment." Colleagues report him to be a brilliant investigator, but somewhat hard to work with as he is volatile and impatient with others.

He and his wife have talked a lot about divorce, but they are keeping the marriage intact in the interest of the children. Parents apparently have little contact with each other. James B. is too busy, what with his work, Little League, Ecology League, Rotary, and activities of the John Birch Society (he is alleged to be working to oppose welfare medical programs). His wife is active in various charitable groups and the Junior League.

Professionally, James has received numerous honors. The American Medical Association named him one of the ten most outstanding medical researchers in the United States. He has published about twenty research articles in prestigious medical journals. He appears very dedicated to his work, and would be likely to remain productive if able to continue it. He appears very anxious to be selected for treatment by the kidney machine.

MARETHA W. Age 24. Black female. Occupation is outreach worker in a neighborhood community social service center. Divorced, with no children. Holds B.A. in Social Work. Income is $5,500 per year.

Psychiatrist's report: Maretha W. is a dedicated Black activist, using the name Selima X. She is in an auxiliary to the Black Panthers. She directs literacy training for young adults in her community, and spends much time trying to develop ethnic pride in Black children. She talked at length about her goals for her people and seems selfless in her ambitions. She is a passionate leader; although frankly hostile to whites as a class, her attitudes should permit her to deal openly and honestly with the white populace. She claims she trusts completely a few white people who work in the community center. She talked favorably of Black Nationalism, but seems realistic.

She appears almost paranoid about her kidney disease, as if it were some kind of plot against her. She protested that the psychiatrist was white, twice refusing to be interviewed, and only agreed to be interviewed when a black psychologist agreed to also participate in the interview. She cross-examined the psychiatrist about his attitudes on racial questions before she was willing to answer any questions.

CHARLES G. Caucasian, age 30. Self-employed owner of a public relations firm and a free-lance writer. Wife, age 21, employed as nightclub entertainer. No children. B.S. degree in chemical engineering from famous university. Family income: approximately $1,000,000 per year, of which wife earns about $60,000.

Psychiatrist's report: Charles G. is a tough entrepreneur. After graduation from college, he started out as a human relations consultant to business firms, then rapidly built a public relations business into one of the largest in the entire South. He devotes much time to community problems, and presently serves as chairman of the state campaign against air and water pollution. Commercials he wrote and produced in this role are shown on TV stations all over the state.

Charles G. appears very proud of his wife's success as a singer in a local nightclub. They met in Las Vegas, and were married within three days. They are planning a retreat home in the mountains of East Tennessee. Charles is also proud of his wife's work in fund raising for black colleges and ghetto action projects.

Mr. G. is regarded by his competitors as highly ethical and skillful. He declared that if he is permitted to live he knows that he will be able to do "something that will make a real contribution to this city." He intends to make this region a model of air and water pollution control for the rest of the country to emulate. He said that whether or not he is chosen he will con- tribute a sum equal to the cost of his care to one of the kidney machine foundations and will give free assistance to the foundations in fund raising.

HENRY L. Caucasian, age 30. Insurance actuary. Wife, 29, is employed as secre- tary in the same company as Henry L. Son, age 6, in first grade. The L's also support and care for Mrs. L's mother, who is bedridden. Holds B.B.A. from state university. Family income is $18,000 per year, $5,500 from wife, $600 social security for mother, and balance earned by Henry L.

Psychiatrist's report: Mr. L. seems very distressed about his role in life, describing in vivid detail his distaste for a nine-to-five job in a large insurance firm. He talked at length about his dreams of being a creative writer of short stories and poetry, and showed some of his writing to the psychiatrist. The writing indicated considerable inner disturbance. Mr. L. is writing a daily journal of his reactions, hoping it can be published after his death and the proceeds given as a financial stake to his wife. He is very concerned that there is no one else to help her. He became very heated in a discussion of the plight of the middle class citizen, with no one concerned about his welfare while the government serves the very rich or taxes the middle class to waste funds on "People who don't want to work and who eat up funds of people who care to get ahead."

Mr. L. is very active in the work of a politicized Protestant church and worked in the last campaign for George Wallace. He says he turned to Wallace in desperation because the "country needs his kind of leadership." If allowed to live, Mr. L. says he plans to run for major office and make some big changes in the country.

NATHAN R. Caucasian, age 37. Rabbi for largest synagogue in the region. Holds B.A. and D.D. from Union Theological Seminary. Wife is 34, not employed. Two children, a boy of 9 and girl of 7. Family unit appears strong. Wife is active in women's groups of the congregation and teaches in Hebrew school. She and children spent last summer in Israel (she is Israeli by birth) while Rabbi R. enrolled in graduate school of the local university. When Rabbi R. came to his present congregation eight years ago, it had 50 families. It now has 520, and recently dedicated a new synagogue which he helped design and for which he led the fund drive. Congregation regards him highly as spiritual leader, organizer, and builder. Recently gave him a life contract.

Psychiatrist's report: Mr. R. appears to be a self-reliant, rather austere man who takes his illness as a matter of fact, expressing a fatalistic acceptance of it. He asked questions about the other applicants, and expressed a desire to see that those most "worth saving" be chosen. He suggested that people presently on the machine participate in the selection panel: "The people would have insight into the kind of person who would give the most in return for the gift of life." Rabbi R. appears exceptionally stable.

RICARDO M. Chicano, age 24. Occupied as dock hand. Illiterate in English. Mrs. M. is 18, unemployed. Daughter five months old. Neither parent has any formal schooling. Family income, approximately $3,400 per year. Mr. M. moved to the area six months ago, just before the baby was to be born. Before that, both parents had worked as migrant farm laborers. With the birth of the child he found a steady job.

Psychiatrist's report: Mr. M. hopes that he will be able to work for a long time, at least "til the baby is grown." But he is very pessimistic about the future, since he is unlearned and, in his opinion, not able to learn. When the suggestion was made that he enroll in the basic literacy program run by the Memphis Public Schools, he showed no interest. He appeared equally uninterested in acquiring vocational training for a semiskilled job. He is very difficult to understand, a very limited command of spoken English. He asked numerous questions about charitable and welfare resources for his wife and child in the case of his death. He believes that someone like him has little or no chance of being picked to get the services of the machine. He does appear devoted to his family, but to be little concerned about anything else.

LANA Y. Caucasian, female, age 34. Occupation, housewife. Husband, 38, works as bartender. Children include son, age 15, in high school. Son, age 13, in junior high. Daughter, age 10, in elementary school. Daughter, age 9, in elementary school. Son, age 6, in first grade. And son, age 2. Now about 5 months pregnant. Both she and husband have high school diplomas. Family income of $12,000 per year earned entirely by husband.

Psychiatrist's report: Mrs. Y. says that her goal is to be "an ideal Catholic mother." She is strongly against the women's liberation movement. She seems totally devoted to her children, and gives no indication of interests or activities outside her family and church. She enrolled last year in a painting course, but dropped out when it "took too much time away from the kids."

She is taking her illness badly, spending much time in bed although the physician's report indicates that this is not necessary. She has persuaded her mother-in-law to move in and help care for the children. She has great fears about how the family could get along without her. Attempts to get information about her relationships with children and mother-in-law were thwarted: Mrs. Y was unwilling to have a case worker conduct an in-the-home interview with the family. The grandmother is not very strong, so it would probably create great hardship for the family if she dies.

MERLIN F. Caucasian, male, age 19. Student in local university, a junior in philosophy. Father, 44, owns a small men's apparel store; mother has been dead four years. A sister of 14 is in junior high school, and a brother of 10 is in elementary school. No income. Father's income approximately $23,000. Merlin has been involved in several political-social demonstrations, and was jailed once for his participation in an anti-Nixon demonstration. Has excellent academic record, with a 3.92 average.

Psychiatrist's report: Mr. F. appears to be a very sincere young activist, a pacifist, deeply upset about the Watergate scandals. He expressed deep concerns about the plight of man, problems of inner-city residents, and the dilemmas of the Mid-East and Vietnam. He hopes to work for a graduate degree in philosophy and to work with young people. However, he also stated that his father wants him to become a lawyer, and his mother had encouraged him to become a physician. Obviously, he is somewhat undecided about a career. He is engaged to a fellow student, whose father would like Merlin to shift into business administration and then join his company after graduation from college.

Mr. F. spends little time in the company of his father. He shows almost no interest in his brother or sister. Warmth and a sense of humor are not his strong points! For example, he said: "Dying now may be better than living, considering the mess the country and the world are in." Immediately thereafter he said: "It would not be fair if I were denied my chance to do something for the world. I hope this doesn't sound arrogant, but maybe I'll find the solution to man's social ills. I'd hate to die before I find out."

His professors characterize him as a superb student, one who could readily earn any degree. They like to work with him because of his intellect, but all characterize him as a bit pompous and humorless.

WILLIE L. Black, male, age 31. Occupation, auto mechanic, but mostly just lubricates cars and changes oil. Withdrew from school in sixth grade, but later took vocational training with the local Manpower center. Wife, age 25, employed as legal secretary and has business school education. Son, age 5, in kindergarten. Family income $12,000, of which Mr. L. contributes $4,500 and Mrs. L. $7,500. Mr. L. is currently enrolled in night school, hoping to get enough skill and knowledge to open his own garage. His employer doubts his capacity to be little more than a "grease monkey." Mr. L. is involved in community betterment work, particularly with young people, and helps direct a recreation program at the community center. He is also a leader in his church, and the minister calls him "a good Christian and a good family man."

Psychiatrist's report: Mr. L. does not seem to realize the seriousness of his disease, or that the decision of the panel will be crucial to his survival. He appears to be a man of thorough personal integrity, exceptionally honest. His intelligence appears limited, and it is unlikely he will rise much above his present position. He shows a touch of resentment about his wife's superior position and professional skills. There is the potential for serious family trouble between he and his wife, but it does not appear to be a problem at the moment. He is apolitical and uninvolved in any sort of movement to promote the status of Black Americans. He stated: "I just want to make a good living and be a good neighbor."

ELIZABETH G. Caucasian, female, age 31. Executive secretary to president of large commercial enterprise. Holds B.S. in secretarial science with special training in legal stenography and computer operation. Single. Salary $18,000 per year. Miss G. is considered indispensible by her boss, and has a reputation for efficiency, intelligence, and dedication. She is a devoted professional, yet well liked by fellow employees for her personal warmth. She is active in charitable work, teaches on weekends in a Head-Start program in a ghetto neighborhood. She is currently directing a community chorus in a production of Handel's "Messiah," in which she also will be a soprano soloist.

Psychiatrist's report: Although she appears to be a very dedicated professional, Miss G. is a warm and loving person. She indicated that she has never been very interested in marriage. She dated while in high school, but has had no personal relationships with men since then. She acknowledged two brief lesbian relationships, but said they were not really satisfying. The latest was several years ago. She appears very emotionally stable, and well adjusted to her disease; she shows no fear of dying. She has willed her body to the medical school. She said she would be willing to withdraw her application for a place on the kidney machine in order to reduce the "terrible judgment facing the panel."

3

Communication in the Small Group

The success of any small group is dependent on the quality of communication among its members. We can communicate in ways that make for cooperation or competition, trust or defensiveness, satisfaction or frustration. Misunderstanding, deception, and "gaps" between people of different backgrounds and cultures concern us all. Dissatisfaction with committee meetings, task groups, social gatherings, classes, and our families all indicate serious inadequacies in small group communication. Although we need to understand how we humans communicate, such knowledge is useless unless we put it into personal practice. Much of our ability to discuss constructively depends on how we feel about ourselves and others—accepting them as unique individuals from whom we can learn and with whom we have much in common if we seek it out, or as wrong because different, to be feared and controlled, the enemy.

This chapter could appropriately be entitled "Participating Constructively in the Small Group," "How to be a Positive Influence in Discussion," or "Exerting Leadership." These terms and topics are inseparable; the effective participant exerts leadership (influence that helps a group achieve goals) through communicative behavior. In a very real sense, you need to know the whole of discussion processes and techniques before you can understand any part well. It will pay you to read this book through before studying any part of it in detail.

The focus in this chapter will be on the process of interpersonal communication, the attitudes of a constructive discussant which underlie his communication, specific types of communicative acts which facilitate or impede group achievement, and specific skills in listening, encoding verbally and nonverbally, formulating questions, and keeping records. As a result of studying the chapter, you should:

1. Be able to diagram and explain the process of communication in a small discussion group.
2. Understand the importance of nonverbal signals in small group communication, and learn to observe closely such cues as facial expressions, seating arrangements, posture, movements and gestures, dress, vocal characteristics, and physical setting.
3. Desire to have all initiated remarks responded to, and to respond to all remarks sent to you.
4. Understand how to communicate your feelings and concepts descriptively without invoking defenses in another, and be able to reduce defensive reactions in yourself.
5. Recognize the degree to which members of a group feel cooperative or competitive toward each other from how they state opinions and suggestions.
6. Be able to recognize and correct a variety of linguistic miscommunicative acts when they occur, including bypassing, ambiguous and vague statements, stigmatizing, name-calling, using clichés, and allness.
7. Be able to distinguish between meaningful and nonsense questions, and between open-ended and closed questions.
8. Be able to describe the function and importance of each of the types of questions which are subject to discussion, and ask each type when appropriate during a discussion.
9. Be able to write a resolution, report, or minutes of a small group meeting.

THE INTERPERSONAL COMMUNICATION PROCESS

Interpersonal communication refers to the entire transactional process by which the person evokes meaning and response in another. Human communication may be intentional, accidental, or both; it may be primarily verbal, nonverbal, or both; it may be complementary, crossed, or ulterior.[1] Leaving aside the aspect of moral responsibility in communicating, *intentional* communication attempts are effective to the degree that the receiver responds in the way intended by the sender (in transactional analysis terms, from the appropriate ego state). Even though the speaker may want to be perceived as calm and confident, a twisted pencil, a twitching lip, and an edge in the voice would reveal uncertainty and strain. The intention may be that you understand how to arrange a group for discussion in a TV studio, but your understanding may produce fouled-up arrangements. The speaker may be looking for personal support, but

---

1. For a lucid explanation of these three types of transactions, as presented in transactional analysis of communication, see Muriel James and Dorothy Jongeward, *Born to Win* (Reading, Mass.: Addison-Wesley Publishing Company, 1971).

get a rational analysis of an idea. As the topics, issues, and problems discussed become more complex and abstract, or as deeper levels of emotion are tapped, the likelihood of miscommunication from crossed or ulterior transactions increases rapidly. Since discussants do not deal with the purely factual or the cut-and-dried, the probability of misunderstanding among them is great.

Your understanding of how communication occurs as a transactional process should be facilitated by careful study of the diagram in Figure 3.1, in which the interpersonal communication process among members of a three-person group is represented. The diagram, like all diagrams, is static and so cannot adequately represent a dynamic process which has no separately definable parts. Furthermore, the process involves so many components or forces that they could not possibly be represented unless we had a diagram of such size and complexity that it could not be included in a book, or if it were, it would be virtually undecipherable. Figure 3.1 represents a simplified representation of some of what goes on. But this should be enough to help you describe the physical/psychological process of communication within a small group. On the right half of the page is located a large circle in which there are three small circles, made with dotted lines. The three small circles represent three members of a small group. The large outer circle represents the external structure or "context" of the group. The three persons are identified by the letters A, B, and C. Sitting face to face in close proximity, they have many channels through which signals may pass among them. Each is sending and receiving signals of many types, though it seems to be virtually impossible to receive and decode verbal signals (words) while at the same time sending them. Thus for all practical purposes one cannot listen to the verbal messages of another in the group while either thinking of his own message (verbal signals sent and received inside the same nervous system) or sending such signals. But while members A and B are listening to C, they will inevitably be sending many nonverbal signals to which C may respond.

To understand the diagram more fully, consider member A for a moment (represented by the large dotted circle on the left half of the page). The inner circle "IP" represents the information processor of the central nervous system with its programmed logic, languages, values, and norms from reference groups, enculturated ways of operating, unique biology, complexity, sensitivity, and so forth. The next circle or layer is shown with a dotted line, because these are not really separate in action. Here are represented the needs, desires, self-concepts, and other similar forces driving the person. The next outer level of this diagram represents the culture shared with the others at the moment, the role(s) of A, his status as he perceives it in the group—in short, his relationship to B and C as perceived by A. The left half of the circle represents the input process by which information comes into the central information processor of the person through various sensory organs and afferent nerves. Included are the obvious senses of hearing, sight, touch, smell, and kinesthesia; but we have many other senses,

INTERPERSONAL COMMUNICATION IN A THREE-PERSON GROUP

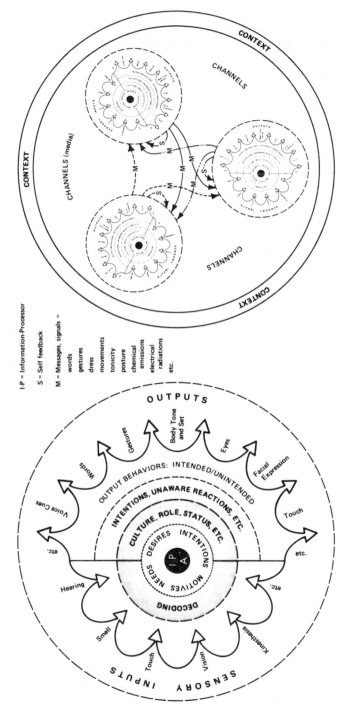

I-P = Information-Processor

S = Self feedback

M = Messages, signals =

words
gestures
dress
movements
tonicity
posture
chemical
emissions
electrical
radiations
etc.

Figure 3.1.

according to current scientists possibly as many as twenty or twenty-five, which we know very little about, but may well explain what is commonly called intuition and ESP. The right half of the outer shell represents the output behaviors of A—all he does which can be perceived through the sensory inputs of B and C. Here are represented all muscular activity (gestures, posture, tension, facial expressions, and so on), sound waves (vocal cues, including words, sound of the voice, coughs, grunts, etc.), touch, chemical emissions (odors, perspiration), electrical emissions, and *any* perceivable behavior. Now refer again to the right half of Figure 3.1 representing the three-person group. Obviously, not all that a person emits can be detected by other members in this three-member group, and not all that can be detected will be perceived and/or interpreted. And what is perceived will be at various levels, from a highly conscious level to a subliminal level where the receiver is not even conscious that he has responded to cues from another member (for example, we may tense up in response to the muscular tensions of another member, and not be conscious of this communicative response at the time). The arrows in the communication channels represent the flow of signals and the process of "feedback." Thus the shortest arrow (S) represents the perception of member A to his own outputs, perhaps correcting some pronunciation error he has perceived ("That only costs tin cents—I mean ten cents"). The arrows between persons (M) indicate that all the time signals are going from each member to each other member. Ideally, as the focus of attention shifts from member A as *primary* message encoder (usually speaker of the moment) to member B, B is responding in a complementary fashion to what A has said and done. If communication in this small group is free and relatively unrestricted, all members are responding openly all the time to the signals of others, and even while A is speaking he is getting feedback responses from B and C, indicating their interest, understanding, confusion, agreement, disagreement, or other reactions. This process is going on continuously, an ever changing flux of mutual influence and response. At the verbal level, usually A speaks, then B, then C but all behave constantly, and all cues emitted are potentially communicative in that members may perceive and respond to them. For simplification of understanding, we often speak or write as if first one member begins to communicate, then another, and so on—but in reality all are actively communicating to some degree all the time. Interpersonal communication occurs in each instance where there is any perception by a discussant of cues from another. Thus Figure 3.1 represents *interaction* or reciprocal influence among the members of a small group.

NONVERBAL COMMUNICATION IN THE SMALL GROUP

A large percentage of what goes on in a small group is nonverbal. Much of our analysis of the process of discussion is of the verbal communication. This is needed, but to ignore the nonverbal is to overlook what is often most significant in group interaction. Birdwhistle has estimated that of all that goes on between people, sixty-five percent of meaning is the result of nonverbal signals.[2] Mehrabian put the percentage of meaning derived from nonverbal cues during face-to-face interaction as high as ninety-three percent.[3]

Four implications of communicating via nonverbal signals are especially important to understanding what goes on during small group discussion:

1. You cannot *not* communicate. Nonverbal cues go out from you constantly; you cannot stop them. Even if sitting relatively immobile and impassive, that behavior will be seen and responded to by others, possibly with distrust, dislike, worry about what you are up to or what is wrong with you. Another way to put it is that in a group "nothing never happens."

2. Many nonverbal cues are highly ambiguous, even more so than words. For instance, a smile can mean friendship, support, disdain, gloating, a private reverie, or just about anything.

3. In any case where the words signal one attitude or meaning to a perceiver and the nonverbal cues signal another, the priority in determining the meaning of the sender will be given to the nonverbals. Thus if you say "I'm interested in that idea" in a flat tone while looking away from the previous speaker, he is almost certain to believe that you do not care.

4. Feelings, emotions, how we see our relationships to others, and our self-concepts—these are the primary "content" to which our nonverbal cues relate. That these can rarely be concealed from sensitive group members has been shown by reading numerous case studies of project groups from discussion classes. Integrity or sincerity is the only means to reducing tension from the "mixed" messages which result when one attempts to deceive, bluff, or play manipulative games with people in a group.

Within a few seconds after you enter a group you are ready to pass judgments on the other members. You are ready to predict which members will be friends, which will be hard workers, and which trouble-makers. But if someone dared to ask how you made these judgments, you would probably be hard-put to provide an articulate answer. Is it the clothes they wore? The shape and smell of their bodies? How they combed their hair? Maybe it's the way they sat, or where they sat, or how they moved their bodies when they turned to look at you? . . . It's possible that the shape, size, color, or decorations of the room "turned you off."[4]

2. Ray L. Birdwhistle, Lecture at Nebraska Psychiatric Institute, Omaha, Nebraska, May 11, 1972.

3. Albert Mehrabian, *Nonverbal Communication* (Chicago: Aldine-Atherton, Inc., 1972).

4. Lawrence R. Rosenfeld, *Now That We're All Here: Relations in Small Groups* (Columbus, O.: Charles E. Merrill Publishing Company, 1976), p. 31.

Unfortunately, relatively little research has been done on nonverbal communication within small groups. Most of what we know has come from the study of two-person situations. But its importance is so great that we need to extrapolate it to small group communication.[5] The nonverbal cues are usually the best indicators of the socioemotional development of a group. The greater the group members' degree of sensitivity to nonverbals of gesture, intonation, posture, movement, setting, seating arrangement, distances among members, eye direction and movement, and so on, the greater the probability of effective communication and the clearing out of ulterior motives, concealment, and problems of morale.

There are many ways of classifying types of nonverbal signals and signs. None is totally adequate, but to sharpen your perceptions, if indeed they need sharpening, here are a few types of cues that are sources of interaction among group members.

Dress and Accessories—How we dress and adorn ourselves suggests much about our self concepts, moods, and attitudes toward others. Aiken found correlations exist between women who like decoration in dress and such traits as conformity, sociability, and nonintellectualism whereas comfort in dress correlated with controlled extroversion. Conformity in dress correlated with conformity in general and submissiveness. Economy in dress correlated with intelligence and efficiency.[6] The results might be different today, and certainly would vary from culture to culture as the values of the cultures differed, but clothing definitely indicates personality characteristics, emotional states, and personal relationships. It also affects our ability to influence others. For example, Lefkowitz and associates found pedestrians more likely to follow a well-dressed person who violated a "wait" signal than a poorly dressed one.[7] For better or worse, we ignore the impact of our adornment in small groups at the peril of being less effective than desired.

Smoking has become a major issue in many groups. Nonsmokers, especially those who have unpleasant physical reactions, often respond very negatively to smokers who light up without at least asking if anyone minds. Even if no one says anything, negative nonverbal reactions can be seen. If you smoke, it will pay to ask if anyone objects before you light up in a group meeting, and even then to watch for any negative signs.

5. For a scholarly book summarizing most of the findings on nonverbal communication, see Mark L. Knapp, *Nonverbal Communication in Human Interaction* (New York: Holt, Rinehart and Winston, 1972); for a popularized presentation, see Julian Fast, *Body Language* (New York: M. Evans and Company, 1970).

6. L. Aiken, "Relationships of Dress to Selected Measures of Personality in Undergraduate Women," *Journal of Social Psychology* 59 (1963), pp. 119-128.

7. M. Lefkowitz, R. Blake, and J. Mouton, "Status Factors in Pedestrian Violation of Traffic Signals," *Journal of Abnormal and Social Psychology* 51 (1955), pp. 704-706.

Facial Expression—Facial expression is vital in interpersonal communication. That it can be interpreted with a high degree of accuracy in a given culture has often been demonstrated, but variations among cultural groups can be great. For example, direct eye contact has very different meanings in Japan and the United States, and among Caucasian Americans and native Americans. People in small groups often use eye contact to seek feedback, when they want to be spoken to, and when they want to participate more actively.[8] In a group, the meaning of eye contact is determined by the context and type of climate. In a competitive situation eye contact probably means "let's fight," whereas in a cooperative climate it signals friendship and cohesiveness.[9] A great deal of response can be given to another with facial expressions and head gestures. Looking at a speaker indicates interest, and facial cues can be expanded to signal agreement, puzzlement, disagreement, support, disgust, and so on. A group of people who respond openly and extensively with such facial signals can communicate much more efficiently than those who are less expressive facially.

Posture and Movement—Posture, general bodily orientation, and movements can reveal much of how we feel toward a speaker of the moment or the group as a whole. Signs of tension show in the degree of rigidity of various parts of the body and continuous motion such as twisting hands or a swinging foot. Frequent changes in posture are indicators of primary or secondary tension which may need to be dealt with. Mehrabian and Friar found that a positive attitude toward another was conveyed by a slight lean of the torso, moving closer, and facing toward the other.[10] Persons with congruent orientations may imitate each other's positions or movements. For example, one person in a group may lean forward, followed by others doing the same. People with different points of view often reflect this divergence with different body positions.

Seating Arrangements—Where you sit in a discussion group may have a lot to do with your status or relationships with other members. Early in the history of group research it was found that when seated in a circle discussants show a strong tendency to speak more often to those across from them than to those adjacent to them.[11] However, if a highly directive leader presides, discussants

8. James McCroskey, Carl Larson, and Mark Knapp, *An Introduction to Interpersonal Communication* (Englewood Cliffs, N.J.: Prentice-Hall, Inc., 1971), pp. 110-114.

9. R.V. Exline, "Explorations in the Process of Person Perception: Visual Interaction in Relation to Competition, Sex, and the Need for Affiliation," *Journal of Personality* 31 (1963), pp. 1-20.

10. Albert Mehrabian and J. Friar, "Encoding of Attitude by a Seated Communicator via Posture and Positional Cues," *Journal of Consulting and Clinical Psychology* 33 (1969), pp. 330-336.

11. Bernard Steinzor, "The Spatial Factor in Face-to-Face Discussion Groups," *Journal of Abnormal and Social Psychology* 45 (1950), pp. 552-555.

then show a tendency to speak more to people seated beside them.[12] Persons who sit at the end of a rectangular table are more likely to emerge as leaders than those who sit along the sides, and those at the corners tend to be least active in a discussion.[13] Many members of continuing groups will show signs of tension when the designated leader sits at one side rather than at the end of a rectangular table; the end is a nonverbal sign of leadership. When I did this intentionally in two different committees that I chaired, there was much sign of tension. Then I moved to the end of the table, and all returned to normal in both groups. When one member of a group chooses to sit outside the circle of chairs, this is a good indication that the person does not feel involved or accepted in the group.

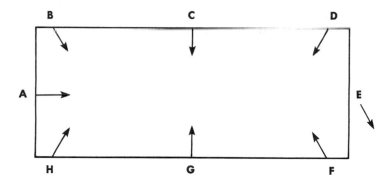

A & E are most likely to emerge as leaders.
B, D, F & H are likely to be less frequent speakers than are A, C, E & G.

E is showing low
   interest, primary
   tension, or feeling of
   rejection

Figure 3.2. Seating arrangements indicate status relationships and feelings.

Vocal Cues—Vocal cues such as tone, rate of speaking, pitch changes, articulation of sounds, and force convey much information about a speaker and his affective state. Listeners tend to agree on the characteristics they ascribe to

---

12. George Hearn, "Leadership and the Spatial Factor in Small Groups," *Journal of Abnormal and Social Psychology* 54 (1957), pp. 269-272.
13. A. Paul Hare and R.F. Bales, "Seating Position and Small Group Interaction," *Sociometry* 26 (1963), pp. 164-168.

speakers based on vocal cues, as shown by extensive research since the 1930s.[14] Included are such characteristics as aptitudes and interests, personality traits, adjustment, ethnic group, education, anxiety, and other emotional states.[15] The tone of voice has been recognized as an excellent indicator of a person's self-concept and mood. How we react to statements such as "I agree" or "Okay" depends much more on the pitch patterns and tone of voice than on the words themselves. Anxiety about communicating has been related to nonfluencies such as introjections ("uh"), repetitions, hesitations, sentence corrections, and even stuttering. To discover how much you infer from vocal cues, tape record a discussion. Everyone in the group should listen just to the voices, trying to ignore the words, and then write a description of the mood, feelings, or attitudes of each other person in the group. A comparison of the results often shows strikingly high agreement.

Physical Environment—We are all aware that the physical setting in which a discussion occurs can make a real difference in the communication among group members. Mintz concluded that an ugly room produced such effects as monotony, fatigue, headaches, irritability, and hostility, whereas a beautiful room produced feelings of comfort, pleasure, energy, importance, enjoyment, and a desire to continue the activity.[16] When free to choose, people in a group will sit closer together in a large room than in a small room (see Figure 3.3). Few people

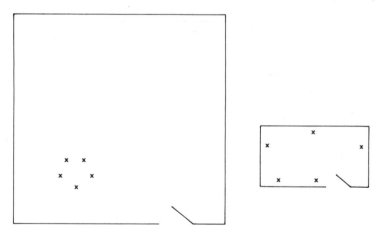

Figure 3.3. Room size influences seating.

14. D. Addington, "The Relationship of Selected Vocal Characteristics to Personality Perception," *Speech Monographs* 35 (1968), p. 492, and Ernest Kramer, "Judgment of Personal Characteristics and Emotions from Nonverbal Properties of Speech," *Psychological Bulletin* 60 (1963), pp. 408-420.

15. Joel R. Davitz and Lois Davitz, "Nonverbal Vocal Communication of Feelings," *Journal of Communication* 11 (1961), pp. 81-86.

16. N.L. Mintz, "Effects of Esthetic Surroundings: II. Prolonged and Repeated Experience in a 'Beautiful' and an 'Ugly' Room," *Journal of Psychology* 41 (1956), pp. 459-466.

will use profanity in a church, and voices will tend to be muted. In a student union snack bar voices get loud, there is much use of slang, and a great deal of vocal and physical animation while talking. Many members of student project groups have reported less primary tension, more informality, increased self-disclosure, and a greater feeling of cohesiveness when they moved from a class-room to a member's apartment or living room. Obviously we ignore the meeting room, its decor and the seating arrangements for a discussion group at our peril!

THE COMPLETED COMMUNICATION CIRCUIT

The idea of a completed communication transaction has already been touched upon. For a complete and validated interpersonal transaction to occur there must be a response to any initial message and an acknowledgement of that response so that both parties to the interchange know that they have communicated as desired. Thus if member A says, "What happened in the student center that everyone is talking about?" (Initiation), B might say, "A big fight broke out between members of two fraternities" (Response), to which A would possibly nod or say "Oh, I see" (Acknowledgement). In the case of a small group, each speaker addressing the group as a whole needs a response of some perceivable sort from each other member (maybe only a nod or a frown), and needs, in turn, to acknowledge that response. He may find that he has to correct or revise the original message because the response indicates he was not understood as in-tended. Or the response may be the lack of response—in which case he has two choices: to drop it or to restate in a more forceful or different way. Nothing is more dampening to cohesiveness, interest, and enthusiasm than a lack of perceiv-able response—"feedback"—denying the speaker's very existence by indicating "you matter not at all; you are not worth responding to." To be passive during group interaction is to be a very negative force. Passivity displays an attitude of rejection of others, and of noninvolvement in the group.

Notice if there is a difference in the amount of response to each other by members of groups in which you participate. With which do you find yourself most comfortable—those who react openly and clearly, or those who give little response? I suggest that you monitor your own response behavior, and change it if you find that you are a discussant who fails to respond actively to speakers; in short, don't break the communication circuit. Many student journals have had statements like this: "Even though Jean didn't say much, I was able to tell where she stood. You could tell from her face and movements that she was involved. Ed was another story. It was hard to tell how he felt, and I never could trust him."

ATTITUDES OF CONSTRUCTIVE DISCUSSANTS

Responsibility to the Group

A whole set of constructive attitudes can be summarized in the phrase *a sense of responsibility for the success of the group.* The constructive discussant feels a personal responsibility to see that the group achieves its goals, and will do what he or she reasonably can to help. Likewise, such a person will encourage others to manifest the same types of responsible behaviors. Such a person cannot "let George do it"; this participant is George.

In Chapter 2 we explored the negative impact of self-centered as opposed to group-oriented behaviors. The kind of group commitment which leads to consensus decisions has been related to the pronouns used by group members. Research has shown a significantly higher ratio of self-reference pronouns (I, me, my, mine, myself) to other or group referent pronouns (you, your, yours, we, us, our) in groups that failed to reach consensus than in groups that did. A discussant's use of pronouns will indicate the degree to which she is responsible to the group.

A responsible member can be depended upon to do an assignment which she has accepted and on which the group depends. If she agrees to bring certain information to the next meeting, it will be there. If she agrees to arrange a meeting place, she will do so without fail. If such a member cannot attend a meeting at which her participation is vital (and in a very small group it always is), she will let the group know of this in advance and as soon as possible.

This responsibility to the group continues after the discussion. The ideal discussant supports the group decisions. He speaks of "we" rather than "I" and "they." He accepts a full share of the blame for any group failure, and no more than his share of credit for group success. He carries out any task which he accepted as a representative of the group, never accepting any responsibility which he cannot or will not discharge. This discussant respects the confidence and trust of other group members, not revealing what they have stated in confidence during a discussion.

Objectivity in Acceptance of Ideas

An ideal discussant displays an attitude of scientific objectivity toward the subject of discussion. He realizes that all knowledge is subject to the frailties of the human observers from whom it came. He is aware that we do not know everything about anything, and so maintains a mood of open-minded inquiry, seeking further information from other group members. Such a participant is willing to change interpretations, beliefs, or values in the light of new information. He not only listens patiently to a new or different point of view; he does so eagerly.

She realizes that it is vital to understand the information, ideas, and feelings of all other members, and can accept these as their statements without having to agree, feel the same, or change the other member who thinks or feels differently. For example, this sort of discussant, even if feeling strongly that all abortion is wrong, can nevertheless listen fully to the views and feelings of another who strongly urges a free abortion law.

While the good discussant is open-minded, she is not a spineless weather vane, shifting to conform to each new idea or point of view. On the contrary, she can make up her mind and support an idea, but only so far as it is supported by evidence and reasoning.

But if a discussant's view of communication is that it is a process of changing or persuading others to accept her views, clash is inevitable and cooperation is possible only if someone *gives in* (notice the language of combat and conflict). If discussants begin with the assumption that the purpose of communicating in a discussion group is to achieve understanding of each other's points of view, beliefs, and information, then *voluntary change* and *cooperation* are possible. Only the person who has freely and voluntarily changed her mind will be a strong supporter of a new point of view.

Jack R. Gibb did extensive study on how defensiveness is engendered in discussion groups and the effects of this feeling on the communication among members. Defensive behavior results from perceiving a threat or anticipating a threat from other group members.

The person who behaves defensively, even though giving some attention to the common task, devotes considerable energy to the defense of self. Besides talking about the topic, he thinks about how he appears to others, how he may be seen more favorably, how he may win, dominate, impress, or escape punishment, and/or how he may avoid or mitigate a perceived or an anticipated attack.[17] Such behaviors evoke similar defensiveness in other members, producing a spiral effect which is very damaging to group cohesiveness and productivity. Defensive listening blocks productive understanding and produces all kinds of verbal and nonverbal cues which likewise put the original speaker on the defensive. Gibb found that as people became more defensive, their understanding of each other became less and less accurate.

What produces such unobjective responses? Gibb spent eight years analyzing tape recordings of discussions from many settings in seeking an answer to that question. What he found is very instructive to the importance of objectivity in acceptance of ideas and of other discussants. He listed six categories of personal attitudes and concomitant behaviors which characterized defensive and suppor-

17. Jack R. Gibb, "Defensive Communication," in Robert S. Cathcart and L.A. Samovar, eds., *Small Group Communication: A Reader* (Dubuque: Wm. C. Brown Company Publishers, 1970), p. 300.

tive climates; the defensive category is first in each of the six pairs of terms: (1) evaluation vs. description; (2) control vs. problem orientation; (3) strategy vs. spontaneity; (4) neutrality vs. empathy; (5) superiority vs. equality; (6) certainty vs. provisionalism. Briefly we will explore each of these pairs of terms so you can examine your actions and attitudes toward others in a discussion group, and in turn help them be aware of their defensive behaviors which block productive communication based on objectivity.

"Evaluation" means that something in the words, voice, or actions of the sender seems *to the listener* to be judging him. "Descriptive" speaking behavior arouses a minimum of defensiveness; descriptions are expressions of feelings, events, beliefs, and so on, which do not in any way suggest that the listener change his behavior or attitude. They are limited to descriptions of the *speaker's* perceptions, beliefs, feelings, and values. It can be very difficult to even ask, "When did that happen?" so that it does not appear evaluative, unless the speaker sincerely feels only a desire to understand, not to judge.

Some examples of evaluative and descriptive expressions of opinion and feelings are compared below. Notice that in one case the speaker describes how she feels, whereas in the other way of speaking the feeling is only implied instead of being described, and the other person may be evaluated or blamed.

Descriptive	Evaluative
"I really like that idea."	"That's a wonderful idea."
I'm angry at you, Joe, for blaming me for not getting out notices of the meeting. I mailed them over a week ago."	"Joe, you're awfully dumb to say that, for you just don't know what you're talking about."

Closely related to evaluation is the "control" orientation, which comes from a desire on the part of the speaker to dominate or change the listener. Most of us do not take kindly to orders from persons we perceive as our equals in authority. If attempts to control are expressed openly as the desires of the speaker rather than as orders, the likelihood of defensive responses is much less. Usually the would-be controller has a belief that the way to get work done in a group is for one person to take charge and to tell all the others what to do. Such a person may say something like "Now here's our problem, and what we're going to do about it. Sandy, you get. . . ." The problem-oriented discussant would say something like "We have a problem, as I see it, of raising enough money to buy a new church bus. How might we go about doing that?" The discussant with a "problem" orientation has no predetermined attitude, method, or solution. Rather, she is seeking to find the best alternative by cooperative thinking.

"Strategy" refers to attempts to manipulate another through a less than open statement of purpose. Feigned emotions, withholding information, or playing games are all seen as strategic ploys as opposed to completely open, guileless, and honest speaking. On the other hand, freedom from any deception, withholding, or game-playing produces acceptance, objectivity, and cooperation.

An attitude of "neutrality" is the very opposite of the sense of responsibility for the group and its members discussed in the beginning of this chapter; it arouses defensiveness. Who can trust someone who does not care what happens to the group or other members? On the other hand, an open manner which conveys empathy and a belief that others have productive motives tends to produce nondefensive listening.

Any behavior by which one discussant indicates feelings of superiority to another is likely to put that other on the defensive and so reduce objectivity and listening accuracy. The superiority shown may be based on education, power, wealth, status, intellectual ability, physical attributes, or anything—the resulting feelings of inadequacy on the part of a listener will reduce his or her openness and objectivity toward information and ideals. Competition is set up between a "top dog" and a "bottom dog." As Gibb says, ". . . differences in talent, ability, worth, appearance, status, and power . . . exist, but the low defense communicator seems to attach little importance to these distinctions."[18]

"Certainty" refers to the attitude of being right, dogmatism. Those who seem to have *the* answers and regard themselves as teachers rather than as coworkers put others on guard. Gibb found that people perceived as dogmatic were seen as needing to win an argument rather than solve a problem, as needing to be right while the other's view must be wrong, or as seeing their ideas as immutable truth. Dogmatists do not accept disagreement graciously. The converse is the person who is willing to test his attitudes and ideas objectively, who holds provisional attitudes and beliefs, who investigates rather than affirms. Persons preferred as future fellow discussants were found to express their opinions much more provisionally than people rejected as future fellow discussants.[19]   Perhaps no one really wants to be put down and on the defensive by fellow members. Not everyone's ideas are equally worthy, but everyone's ideas merit attention. Everyone deserves to have his questions answered without sarcasm or suspicion and to have his suggestions accorded respectful consideration.

Objective evaluation of all ideas is part of the supportive climate which reduces defensiveness and face-saving behaviors. "Evaluation" refers as much to too ready an agreeing or accepting as it does to negative judgments. We need to guard against the halo effect in which we support what another does or says because of some general acceptance of his person or the position he occupies. A

18. *Ibid.*, p. 306.

19. John K. Brilhart, "An Exploratory Study of Relationships Between the Evaluating Process and Associated Behaviors of Participants in Six Study-Groups," (Ph.D. dissertation, Pennsylvania State University, 1962), pp. 180-185.

very fluent person is not necessarily correct, nor is his summary necessarily adequate. A person who produced one superior idea may produce a dud the next time. Advertisers use the halo effect extensively; we are not objective or engendering of a supportive climate if we fall into the assumption on which such advertising rests—that because a person is outstanding in one area makes his judgments in another area of great merit. A man may be a great quarterback, but that does not make his judgment of aftershave lotion better than yours, nor is the recommendation of a presidential candidate by Robert Redford or Glen Campbell to be taken at face value just because both are outstanding entertainers. It has been suggested that we view all "experts" and great men as if they were in underwear—at least that might help us maintain the objectivity that neither accepts nor rejects information and ideas on the basis of the person who presents them. Objectivity in discussion means we neither indicate that others should accept our ideas because of who we are nor that we accept or reject the idea of another because of whom he may be. Goodwill, friendship, trust, and respect for a person *as a person* must not cloud our thinking or limit our search for the best possible ideas, information, or criteria. The author often has students sign a card which says, "I understand that I do not have to believe a single thing I hear the instructor say nor a single thing I read in connection with this course." Amazingly, many students are shocked at this and some instructors almost panicked at the idea of suggesting this to students! But as cooperative group members, we need the sense of equality and objectivity this card is intended to foster.

A particular danger of status differences is that high-status persons tend to ignore or reject ideas from persons of lower status. Low-status persons tend to accept or reject uncritically the ideas of high-status persons. In the one case, the low-status person accepts an authority figure uncritically; in the other, he acts defensively. To help assure that all discussants will be given an equitable hearing, it is helpful to have all addressed in a similar manner, for instance, by first names, titles, or "Mr.," "Mrs.," "Miss," and "Ms."

In summary, to be effective discussants we need to develop attitudes and procedures that make for trust and cooperation, which focus on information, issues, and ideas rather than on the persons who utter them. We need to have a real concern for both the well-being of each other as members of a group and the quality of our joint efforts.

Desire to Communicate

Think of your speaking during discussion in comparison to a scale ranging from "trying hard, wanting to be heard and understood" to "not really trying nor caring to be heard or understood." Where do you fall on such a scale? If you fall near the "not caring" end, ask yourself why you act this way. Just maybe you don't care, but if so you do not belong in the group.

It may be that you are reticent, unduly apprehensive about how others will judge you if you speak. The "shy" person who experiences an exceptionally high level of apprehension about speaking up usually has a low self-concept. Have you often failed to say something during a discussion, thinking you might look foolish to others, and then later wished you had said it? Or have you rejected one of your ideas without even stating it, and later heard someone else suggest that very idea and seen the group adopt it? Before you can be an effective discussant you will have to correct any serious misgivings about yourself.

A number of steps which you can take may prove helpful. If you have doubts about your knowledge, prepare thoroughly. A technique in wide use today to reduce communication apprehension is called "systematic desensitization." Your instructor will be able to arrange for you to participate in such a training program if it is in use at your school. You will first complete a scale to measure your degree of apprehension about speaking up. Then you will undergo training in maintaining a state of relaxation while envisioning yourself in threatening situations as a speaker. A feedback session such as is described later in this book may be quite helpful. If you can, participate in a group training laboratory (T-group) or encounter group as a way of gaining a more positive self-concept. Most colleges and universities provide a staff of counselling psychologists who can also provide assistance.

COMMUNICATION SKILLS OF AN IDEAL DISCUSSANT

While the attitudes discussed in the previous section are prerequisites to being an effective discussant, there are many specific skills you can learn which will also make you a more effective discussant. These concern *what* you contribute, *when* you contribute, and *how* you contribute.

Communicate Effectively

Be Open

The effective discussant reacts so others can be constantly aware of his or her state of mind. There is nothing so depressing as a group of people sitting like zombies while another is speaking. Response and reaction are essential to cooperative thinking and good interpersonal relations. When you agree, show it with a nod or verbal assent. When you disagree, show it. When you have a question, ask it. When you have a feeling of warmth for others, communicate it with a word, smile, or gesture. Nothing is quite so inconsiderate of another as ignoring; lack of response, at least from the other person's point of view, is ignoring. Disclosing what you feel, what you want, and who you see yourself to be is a great way to build trust and cohesiveness in a continuing small group.

Speak Effectively

Speak to the group. To keep the channels for participation open to all, address your remarks to the entire group. You may begin a response to an individual, but extend your eye contact to include all members. Speaking to a chairperson especially restricts spontaneity and effectiveness of group thinking. What you say should be of interest to everyone, and everyone should be made to feel equally free to respond.

Organize your remarks. A useful comment does not come at random, nor is it randomly expressed. A general pattern to follow is this: relate the contribution to what has already been said by another; state the idea; develop and support it; connect the contribution to the topic or phase of the problem being discussed. You will notice that this format provides an answer to the three basic questions to be asked when evaluating any extended contribution: What is the point? How do you know? How does it matter at this time? For example:

> Helen, you said many magazine articles have been cut out. I also found that every encyclopedia had articles removed from it. The librarian told me it costs about $1,000.00 per year to replace damaged encyclopedias. So we can see that a serious part of the problem is the loss of widely used reference materials.

State one point at a time. This is not an inviolable rule, but generally speaking, you should not contribute more than one idea in a single speech. A several-point speech is definitely out. A group can discuss only one idea at a time; confusion is likely to result if you try to make several points at once. A comment in which you attempt to give all the data on an issue or present a series of points is likely to be too involved to be grasped and responded to.

Speak concisely. If listeners appear bored or restive, you have spoken at too great length. Try to state your ideas as simply and briefly as possible. Some participants restate every point several times, or take two hundred words to say what could be stated in twenty. This reduces the opportunity for others to participate, and often results in the long speech being tuned out by others. If you notice that when others restate your ideas they do so much more briefly than you spoke, you may want to work for a more concise style.

Use appropriate language. Vague, general words often lead to misunderstanding. Language that is not a part of the vocabulary of the group members will help no one. The purpose is not to display your erudition, but to contribute to group understanding. Concrete instances or examples, an analogy relating a new idea to a familiar one, or vivid description are just as important in discussion as in public speaking.

Presenting information and ideas in a helpful style and showing off one's knowledge are very different. A person who is most concerned with making a good impression may talk very rapidly and use a lot ot technical words not familiar to other members of the group. By using words to confuse and obscure, he may gain the self-centered objective of impressing others with his knowledge and prevent them from asking embarrassing questions. The expert who is a skilled speaker introduces technical concepts slowly, defines them carefully with language familiar to the listeners, and invites questions.

Don't Monopolize

You should, of course, enter the discussion whenever you have anything new, relevant, and useful to offer. But watch to see that you are not monopolizing time or discouraging others from participating. Remember that the larger the group, the greater the probability that a few members will overparticipate.

Help Maintain Order and Organization

The ideal discussant shares in the responsibility for procedural leadership, if only by following the pattern and procedures agreed on by the group. If a change in procedure or topic appears needed, make this known. Then act in concert with the majority, whether or not they accept your proposed change. In addition, relate all comments to the previous remarks and the issue under consideration. When the group gets off track or loses sight of its goals, point this out. After a fantasy chain has tapered off you can bring the group back to the issue previously being discussed. For example, you might say, "We were trying to plan the menu for our picnic, but now we are talking about dating. Are we ready to get back to the menu?"

Listen to Understand

Effective listening is an active process, requiring as much effort as speaking. Unless we listen closely, we will not have all the information needed to make sound decisions. Often several discussants in turn say almost the same thing, as if they had never heard what the first person said. This wastes time. Of course during the early stages of the emergence of a new group, while roles are in flux, not much listening may be in evidence as members vie for status and roles. But if this continues at length something needs to be done.

It is especially important to listen to understand the other person's meaning before reacting. The sidetracking and irrelevancy which result from half listening are costly of time and goodwill. A good test of your listening is to restate, in your own words, the meaning of the previous speaker. The author's discussion classes often do this as an exercise to develop effective listening. Each discussant is required to restate the prior speaker's ideas to the person's satisfaction. If the restatement is not accepted as accurate, then the new speaker loses the floor. In many groups, more than fifty percent of the restatements are rejected as being inaccurate or incomplete. If misunderstanding is so common even when great effort to understand is being made, how common must it be in ordinary discussions?

One effect of listening to understand is a slowing down of the discussion. One cannot listen well while thinking up what to say next. If you are not used to listening so carefully that you could restate what another has said to her satisfaction, at first you may find you have nothing to say for a moment after another has finished. But keep at it; soon you will find yourself making spontaneous responses in place of strategically preplanned remarks. Your comments will be more relevant to what preceded, and cooperation will be enhanced in your groups.

Only when you are sure you understand another person's point of view should you evaluate his comment. Then critical listening is in order. Was his comment pertinent? Is there a basis in evidence and experience for what he said? Is his statement logically valid? Does he present a biased picture of events? Good listening is a process of understanding what the speaker meant from his point of view, and then evaluating the significance and dependability of his comments.

Maintain a Balanced Perspective

Perspective is needed on the expenditure of time. Some impatient discussants expect a group to move to a conclusion as rapidly as an individual. These people show no tolerance for the time-consuming process of talking out an idea until it is understood by all the members. They want immediate solutions rather than mutually acceptable ones, not realizing that hasty decisions may have to be made all over again because differences in belief were suppressed. People are not computers. Only people can solve new and important problems. And only people can interpret the breakdowns in understanding involved in social upheaval. Time spent in achieving understanding and mutually acceptable solutions is an investment in future efficiency. On the other hand, time wasted on irrelevancies, on interpersonal conflicts, on rambling speeches, or on misunderstandings due to poor listening is time lost forever.

Perspective is needed on group norms: what are they, what are they producing? Profanity is permitted in some discussion groups, in others it is taboo. Some groups are very formal, while others are relaxed and casual. The effective discussant detects the norms of his group and adapts to them. Later, if it is handicapping the group or some of its members, he can bring the norm to the attention of the group, point out what he feels is wrong with it, and suggest an alternative. But only a person lacking in perspective on group process would make an immediate frontal assault on norms and values long accepted by other members.

Perspective is needed on the power to produce conformity. Many studies have demonstrated that a group can exert great pressure on its members to conform in judgment, belief, and action. Summarizing these studies, Hare concluded that a group member is likely to change his opinion *"when the object to be judged is ambiguous,* if he must make his *opinion public,* if the *majority holding a con-*

trary opinion is large, and if the *group is especially friendly or close knit.* "[20] All of these conditions are likely to be found in a continuing discussion group.

There is much you can do to reduce conformity of opinions. First, if members are made aware of the pressure to conform they can resist it more successfully. Support from one other person, especially a designated discussion leader, is often sufficient to help a person maintain a point of view until the idea has been tested on its own merits. It is wise to establish a group norm of considering all minority points of view before reaching a decision. Certainly we need the kind of perspective that comes from remembering that every new idea in the world was at its inception in a minority of one.

Finally, we need perspective when one of our pet ideas has been rejected. The ideal discussant realizes that even though evidence and inferences are rejected, the person presenting them is not rejected. He or she should continue to do everything possible to help the group reach the best possible solution, and then support the final group decision.

IMPROVING VERBALIZATION DURING DISCUSSIONS

Thus far in this chapter attention has been focused on the attitudes and behaviors of constructive members of discussion groups. The total process of interpersonal communication in the small group has been described in some detail, but no specific analysis has been made of the language and verbal communication among members. In this section we turn to assumptions and language behaviors which lead to bypassing, confusion, unnecessary conflict, and stoppages of the process of members thinking cooperatively.

Miscommunication Through Language

Bypassing

Two people bypass each other when they have different meanings for the same word or phrase. Each hears the same words, but the images each creates are so different as to represent a serious misunderstanding. They are "talking past each other." For example, the writer once listened to a group discussing religious beliefs argue for about half an hour (wasted time!) about whether or not man had free will. The group formed sides, led by an atheist and an avowed Methodist. After listening to a tape recording of the discussion and getting to specific cases they realized that they were actually in agreement! Each side had been using the term "free will" to refer to a very different phenomenon. They were able to see that all believed man had free will (Type 1, some ability to make

---

20. A. Paul Hare, *Handbook of Small Group Research* (New York: The Free Press of Glencoe, 1962), pp. 30-31.

conscious choices among alternatives), but did not have a free will (Type 2, much of what happens in life is beyond our control and is determined by the converging of forces within and without). In a very simple case of bypassing a young nurse reported this: "I left a pan of water, soap, washcloth, and towel with a new patient, telling him it was time for his bed bath. When I returned in half an hour I found him scrubbing his bed with the cloth, but personally unwashed. He was not supposed to get out of bed!" In another instance a man whose car battery was too low to turn over the engine told a helpful motorist who had stopped that because he had an automatic transmission she would have to push him about thirty-five miles per hour. You guessed it—she backed up and rammed into his rear bumper at thirty-five miles per hour, doing $300 damage![21] I have watched members of many groups go on talking blithely as if they understood each other when any careful observer could tell that members had very different meanings for some key term. This usually results in conflict at a later date, especially if the misunderstanding is over some course of action to be taken by the group. Tempers flare, people go on the defensive, and time is wasted—and sometimes serious damage is done—as a result of bypassing.

This type of verbal misunderstanding comes from several assumptions about language. First, the container myth, is that *words have meaning.* If a word has meaning in itself and I give you the right word, you are bound to get the meaning. But there is no intrinsic connection between any word and any thing, experience, or relationship. Words are symbols for experiences, representing whatever we have in mind when we use the words. *Meaning resides in the users of the words,* never in the words. We make a grievous error when we argue what a word means instead of trying to uncover what the user of the word means. Words have only arbitrary connections to events. Although in a given language each word tends to be used in a limited way with a range of meanings, these uses are conventional, assigned by the users. We can only play the word game, as any game, when we agree on the usage at a given time (just as in poker we must agree on the value of each chip color for the game). We must determine from the context, what we know about the background of the user of the words, and his nonverbal cues what he probably means. Even then our meanings may be far apart, and will always differ slightly in the fullest sense of the term "meaning." For example, although we may both refer to animals-that-wag-tails-when-happy with the word *dog* (we might in our culture also refer to used cars, unattractive girls, clamps, etc.), each of us is likely to have considerably different feelings related to this term and to conjure up very different pictures. Persons attempting to communicate must discover whether or not their meanings for terms are sufficiently similar to refer to the same thing before they can know what has been communicated between them.

21. William V. Haney, *Communication and Organizational Behavior,* 3rd ed. (Home-wood, Ill.: Richard D. Irwin, 1973), p. 246.

The second assumption is that *words have monousage* (single usage). Although patently ridiculous, we often *act* as if it were valid. Only in the realm of highly technical jargon is this assumption likely to be correct; for example, sodium chloride has virtually one usage among chemists. But "salt" does not. The same word, in different contexts, may be used to refer to many things of the same type, and many types of things. Even *word* has fourteen definitions in a collegiate dictionary. In short, words have many usages, even in the denotative area. As the general semanticians also point out, words are used at many orders of abstraction. For instance, the word "unit" can refer to a single soldier, a platoon, a company, a command, or even a whole army. "Love" not only can be used to refer to many types of feeling and behavior, but to different orders of behavior of the same type, as in "the love of love" or even "the love of the love of love"—possibly talking about having a positive feeling toward people who love the act of loving! We may realize in a moment of reflection that words do not have monousage, but during the heat of conflict among group members, this understanding may be forgotten, with bypassing the wasteful result.

What can a discussant do to prevent or correct instances of bypassing?

1. *Be person-centered rather than word-centered.* As you listen, look beyond the words for the speaker's probable meaning; when you speak, consider what the listeners might mean when they use a word you are about to use. "What would it mean if I were in his or her position?" "Is my interpretation consistent with other things that I know about the speaker's professional background, previous statements, experience, and so forth?" Always listen to hear the speaker out, avoiding judgments of meaning or value until you are pretty certain of what the speaker means.
2. *Question and paraphrase.* When there seems to be any possibility of bypassing, ask for clarification. Try putting what you understood into your own words, and ask if that is what the speaker meant. When you have spoken an important message, encourage paraphrasing and questioning by the listeners; sometimes you may even insist on it.
3. *Consider the context.* Note what preceded and what follows. How does your present interpretation fit with other things you have heard the person say?

Ambiguity and Vagueness

In discussion, many of the statements are necessarily abstract, and much misunderstanding can occur. The vagueness resulting from abstractness can be reduced. Ambiguity results from language which could have either of two meanings in the context in which it is used.

As one moves away from terms referring to specific, individual, and unique items, the degree of abstractness and ambiguity increases. A high-level abstraction is a term or phrase that could reasonably be interpreted in many ways by a person familiar with the term. Consider the following set of terms, each of which is higher in level of abstraction (and more vague) than the ones that precede it:

the jar of "Squishy" peanut butter on my cupboard shelf
"Squishy" peanut butter
spreads
food
commodities
merchandise

When the first term is used between people both familiar with "Squishy," the picture in the speaker's head is likely to be very similar to the picture in the head of the listener, and the listener could pick out the object if asked to do so. But when we talk of "spreads," "merchandise," "politicians," or "democracy," the pictures in the heads of speakers and listeners will often differ significantly—and the feelings even more so! Only terms which name unique objects are likely to be free of vagueness. For example, one discussant said: "Lecturing is a poor method of teaching." Another responded: "Oh, no it isn't." An argument ensued until a third discussant asked for some examples (lower order abstractions). The speakers were then able to agree on specific instances of effective and ineffective lecturing, especially when some quantitative research data were introduced. The vagueness reduced, the group reached agreement on a less abstract statement: "Lecturing, if well organized, filled with concrete instances, and done by a skilled speaker, can be an effective means of presenting factual information and theoretical concepts. It is usually less effective than discussion for changing attitudes or developing thinking skills."

Leathers studied the impact of abstract statements on a series of laboratory discussions. He found that the abstract statements consistently had a disruptive effect on subsequent discussion, and that the degree of disruption increased as the statements became more highly abstract. His groups contained "plant" discussants who were trained to say things like "Don't you think this is a matter of historical dialectism?" After such a statement, most of the naive discussants became confused and tense, and some just withdrew from further participation.[22]

Ambiguity results from phrases which could readily have either of two types of meaning to the listeners. For example, "I just can't say enough that is good about his effort for the company." What does the speaker mean? That the employee being discussed made such extensive contributions that it is impossible to describe them all, or that he did so little that the speaker cannot give the kind

---

22. Dale G. Leathers, "Process Disruption and Measurement in Small Group Communication," *Quarterly Journal of Speech* 55 (1969), pp. 288-298.

of recommendation the listeners want for a possible candidate for a new position? In such a case, even vocal cues may not clear up the ambiguity.

Ambiguity can also result from a "mixed" message, one in which the words seem to imply one meaning but the vocal cues indicate something different. For example a speaker might say "That seems like a great idea" in a flat pitch with little emphasis, thus implying with her voice that she does not really care about the idea. Or a speaker might say "Take as long as you like to think this through" while glancing at his watch. Such ambiguous actions are highly disruptive to a discussion.

What to do? Spotting vague or ambiguous statements and asking the speaker to clarify can do much to prevent misunderstanding. Ask for specific examples. Paraphrase in less abstract terms and ask for confirmation. Use concrete examples to illustrate your own abstract statements. Use approximate synonyms. Instead of beginning a discussion with a vague or ambiguous question, you can often prevent confusion by introducing a specific case problem including details of what happened.

STOPPERS

Certain ways of talking serve as *stoppers* to the discussion process. They tend to get emotional reactions, reducing the thinking component of discussion. Stigma words, clichés, and the mood of dismissal are especially likely to stop consideration of an issue.

STIGMA WORDS AND NAME-CALLING

A *stigma* word is one used by the speaker or perceived by the listener to indicate a negative evaluation of the referent. Even though the speaker may not intend to stigmatize, the important thing to the listener is that he hears a stigmatizing term. Sensitivity to current usage and to the meanings and feelings of listeners is very important. For example, a white speaker with no prejudicial intention may say "colored," and a Black listener may respond defensively—to the listener "colored" indicates that the speaker is a racist. One discussant might say "Nebraska has a socialistic form of electric power generation and distribution," meaning that all such facilities are owned by the public and managed by a board elected by the registered voters. Some Nebraskans would react to such a statement in a very defensive way, stopping forward progress of the group to wrangle about "socialism." Or perhaps one discussant expresses his judgment or suggests a solution, and another replies: "Why that's nothing but _____ !" "You're proposing _____ !" "That's _____ !" In the blanks may go any word or phrase used to label something strongly disliked or feared, and for which the respondent has a highly unpleasant connotation: *communism, facism, federal control, racism, childishness, chauvinism,* or others words used in derogation. The speaker has now been identified with something ugly or fearful. He may stop cold, deny and argue, or call the speaker some name. The group will likely get caught in a sidetrack of whether the subject of discussion should be called by the stigmatic term. The goal is forgotten, harmony is lost, feelings are hurt, and members lose face. Even if the group gets reoriented, residual antagonism is likely to hamper cooperation: "Nobody gets away with that!"

The use of sexist terms has become a major problem for many groups. Terms which were once used interchangeably to refer to all people and to males specifically are now being rejected as biased against women. For instance, the word "man" has been used in the past when the person referred to could be either male or female (patrolman, chairman, businessman). Some words have a special ending to indicate a woman, but no such ending to indicate a man: usherette, aviatrix, Jewess, and poetess are examples. Much preferred are the root forms which do not imply the sex of the person referred to: usher, aviator, Jew, and poet. Many people resent any word which implies an inappropriate sex criterion for filling any role or performing any task, and this resentment will often disrupt a discussion. Most certainly if you view women as inherently inferior to men, beings who should be "kept in their place, the home," you are in for some serious relearning. Consciously eliminating all sexually stereotyping terms from your speaking vocabulary may be necessary if you are to avoid being disruptive in many discussions.

The worst form of stigmatizing is out-and-out name-calling. Adrenalin rises and physiologically we prepare to fight when called by such names as "pig," "male chauvinist," or "nigger." Such behavior is sure to turn attention from the issues before a group, reduce trust, and evoke defensive reactions.

What can you do to prevent, reduce, and alleviate stigmatizing? First, recognize that people have feelings about everything, and these feelings are not to be rejected. Then, be aware that your feelings and evaluations are just that—YOUR feelings or the other person's—and not characteristics of some objective reality outside yourself. Some labelling and stigmatizing are likely to occur when people express how they feel about things. We can reduce it in ourselves, using phrases to remind others and ourselves that our judgments are our judgments: "I don't like . . ." or "It seems to *me* that . . .," for example. When someone expresses a stigma or red-flag term, another participant or designated leader can directly reduce the danger of direct and wasteful conflict or defensiveness by inviting contrasting feelings and points of view, first restating the stigmatic statement in unloaded terms. For example: "Joe has called the ACTION program phony and fascistic. That's one point of view. What are some others?" "Okay, Helen's belief is that public power is socialistic. Are there other ways of looking at it?" Rephrasing might go like this (to "Cops are brutal pigs"): "Joe feels that police officers are insensitive and brutal in their dealing with the public. Has this been the experience of others?" Thus by replacing the stigma terms with more denotative ones and having obtained other evaluations and feelings, one can then ask for a description of the idea or proposal based on more complete information. Talk can now be directed to the facts of the situation and the goals of the group.

If no one is ready or willing to express a point of view contrary to that of the stigmatizer, the designated leader can sometimes help remove the block to objectivity by playing the devil's advocate. He or she expresses a point of view contrary to that of the stigmatizer, indicating that it is one that ought to be considered in order to objectively weigh the proposal from all points of view and on its own merits. For instance, he might say: "Joan has called the loan fund socialistic. Let's consider another judgment of it which I've heard expressed by. . . . They say it helps students develop independence."

All of this points to the importance of trying to develop group norms against the use of stigma terms, and an objective examination of all evidence and points of view. A periodic examination of the values and norms implicit in the language we choose and the ways we express our feelings and beliefs can be quite constructive in a group plagued by language barriers to communication.

DOUBLESPEAK

Doublespeak refers to the use of language to confuse or deceive by speaking in confusing and affectively neutral circumlocutions. The user of doublespeak, when asked a direct question, will try to give the impression of having answered while actually evading the question. The listener is confused by the lengthy and vague utterance, but gets the general impression that he was answered in sophisticated language beyond his ken. Rather than appear "dumb" by insisting on a clear answer, he lets the diversion pass. A vivid example of doublespeak was given by Ron Ziegler, press secretary to President Nixon, when he was asked if the Watergate tapes were intact. His reply:

> I would feel that most of the conversations that took place in those areas of the White House that did have the recording system would in almost their entirety be in existence but the special prosecutor, the court, and I think, the American people are sufficiently familiar with the recording system to know where the recording devices existed and to know the situation in terms of the recording process but I feel, although the process has not been undertaken yet in the preparation of material to abide by the court decision, really, what the answer to the question is.

Bureaucrats, diplomats, and military spokesmen seem especially prone to use doublespeak. Consider such examples as calling a shovel a "combat emplacement evacuator," a parachute "an aerodynamic personnel accelerator," or illegal wiretapping "intelligence gathering."[23] When someone answers your question with

23. H. Kahane, *Logic and Contemporary Rhetoric: The Use of Logic in Everyday Life* (Belmont, Cal.: Wadsworth Publishing Co., Inc., 1976), p. 102.

doublespeak, insist on an answer you are sure you understand or the discussion will all too often go awry.

Clichés

Another frequent stopper of objective thinking and realistic consideration of ideas is the *cliché* or proverb. It is easy to say, "A stitch in time saves nine," or "A penny saved is a penny earned, you know." These sayings seem so obvious that no one bothers to look further at the merits of a proposal clobbered by the cliché. The wheels of group thinking grind to a halt on the cliché.

How can you undo the effects of a cliché? First, keep in mind that no two situations or problems are identical. Second, be on guard for easy answers, proverbs, or clichés with their stopping effects. When you spot one, you can point it out as such and suggest an examination of the details of the new proposal, especially to discover if it is different from any other. For example, you might say, "That seems too pat. Are there any differences between this proposal and . . .?" Sometimes you can counter a cliché with another proverb, or cliché; every cliché seems to have an antithesis. For instance, if someone says, "Don't put off till tomorrow," you might counter with, "True in some cases, but also remember that 'haste makes waste.' Now why don't we look further into this proposal?"

Dismissal

Perhaps the deadliest pitfall to group communication is the *mood of dismissal,* or *allness.* It is the mood which seems to say, "This isn't worth considering," "It won't work," or "My mind is made up. Don't confuse me with the facts." Common to all forms of dismissal is the wish—perhaps unconscious—to stop communication about an idea. As Lee described it, this is the mood in which a man indicates "he wishes to go no farther, to talk no more about something which is to him impossible, unthinkable, wrong, unnecessary, or just plain out of the question. He has spoken and there is little use in trying to make him see otherwise."[24] He may declare, "We've done it another way and we just aren't going to try something new and dangerous, I refuse to listen to such nonsense." "How naive can you be?," or "Let's not waste time with that one." Such comments indicate what Phillips calls the game of "It Can't be Done," in which a speaker may even give a tightly reasoned argument to show the apparent impossibility of solving a problem ("the best minds have failed to solve it") or of implementing a proposal.[25] This verbal-emotional game can be constructive, but

24. Lee, *How to Talk with People.* (New York: Harper & Row, Publishers, 1952), p.46.
25. Gerald M. Philips, *Communication and the Small Group,* 2nd ed. (Indianapolis: The Bobbs-Merrill Company, 1973), p. 145.

only if all contradictory ideas and alternatives that can be thought of are first examined.

Dismissal comments display unmitigated arrogance on the part of the speaker. He assumes he knows all there is to know or all that needs to be known, in effect forgetting that the world of reality is complex, constantly changing, and known to him only in part. Such a dogmatic person has a closed belief system. He does not or cannot entertain new or different beliefs that are contradictory to ones he already holds. Often dogmatic persons conclude the very opposite of what others conclude from the same evidence. For example, Dwight Eisenhower was almost universally regarded as highly patriotic and loyal. To reactionaries, this was strong evidence that he was a Communist dupe. Most of us like to think that we are open-minded, but careful analysis of many statements from discussions indicates that many discussants' minds are more closed than open. Your mind is closed to the degree that you (1) consistently and absolutely reject ideas which you disbelieve; (2) you cannot distinguish among beliefs different from your own but see them as the same; and (3) you can see no similarity between your own beliefs and disbeliefs.[26]

What can be done to offset the mood of dismissal? First you might try asking for other points of view, much as you would in responding to a stigma. In a continuing group it would be well to tackle the problem head-on by discussing the attitude itself with the group. An effective way to do this is to discuss specific cases of people acting with a mood of dismissal. Few people will persist in making allness statements if they are aware that other group members perceive them to be closed-minded. Taking the short form of the Dogmatism Test and discussing the results may have a positive effect on the members of a group inclined to dismissal and dogmatic statements.[27] It may help to keep reminding the group that mutual respect must be given if group cooperation is to be possible.

ASKING QUESTIONS TO IMPROVE COMMUNICATION

It has often been said that, "To know how to ask the right questions is more important than knowing the answers." Every propositional statement is an answer to some question, whether that question is stated aloud or not. The entire process of dialectic—a search for truth through dialogue—is a search for answers to questions. Effective discussions are always that, a search for answers

---

26. Dale G. Leathers, "Belief-Disbelief Systems: The Communicative Vacuum of the Radical Right," in C.J. Stewart, D.J. Ochs, and G.P. Mohrman, eds., *Explorations in Rhetorical Criticism* (University Park, Pa.: The Pennsylvania State University Press, 1973), pp. 127-131.

27. V.C. Troldahl and F.A. Powell, "A Short Form Dogmatism Scale for Use in Field Studies," *Social Forces* 44 (1965), pp. 211-214.

to questions. A number of criteria-questions need to be applied to the general questions to which a small group addresses itself:

Is this question of interest to the members? Do they need an answer to it?

Is the question within the area of freedom of the group?

Is the question within the competence of the group to answer?

Is the question sufficiently specific, clear, and delimited to be dealt with thoroughly in the time available?

If the answer to any of these questions is "no" the discussion will in all probability be chaotic and vacuous, the interaction listless and apathetic, and the end result satisfactory to no one.

Very often the content of a discussion can be greatly improved by simply asking the question, "What question are we now discussing?" An open statement of the question or issue and its implications will reveal what is wrong when a group seems to be going awry. After examining the frequency with which themes or topics are switched in many discussions, it often appears as if no one knows what the issue is much of the time. Many discussions could be characterized as answers looking for questions. Both *what* we ask and *how* we ask it are vital to the communication among members of a small group. For that reason, this section is addressed to the types of questions we talk about and how we phrase them.

First, all questions can be classified as either *answerable* or *unanswerable*. As Weinburg pointed out, just because we can put a question mark after a string of words does not mean we have asked a meaningful or answerable question. If "answers" are given to an unanswerable question and we are unable to choose among them on any objective basis, there is no way to tell which is the correct or best answer.[28] To illustrate, consider the following: "What is the population of China today?" "What was the population of Omaha according to the 1976 census?" "How fast can a greyhound run?" and "Why did God punish the Martins by burning their house?" Most people would agree that a factual answer, based on specific methods of census taking, could provide an objective answer to the first question even though such an answer may not now be available. Thus it is *potentially* answerable, but not answerable at the moment without extensive nonverbal activity. The second is readily answerable; records will give a specific uncontrovertible answer to what the report says. The third question is ambiguous because it contains variable terms—it can only be answered when specific conditions are stated naming the dog, and such conditions as time and place. Thus it could be made meaningful by asking, "How fast did Diamond Jack run in the third race at the Atokad Greyhound Race Track on July 3, 1973?" The

---

28. Harry L. Weinberg, *Levels of Knowing and Existence* (New York: Harper & Row, Publishers, 1959), pp. 213-216.

fourth question is meaningless, because it refers to nonobjective concepts, unobservables. That question assumes some personal force called God, and that this God took direct causative action. To answer it, what would we observe? Under what conditions? How? Such a "question" cannot be answered by any known means, so there is nothing to be gained by discussing it except confusion and conflict. You can help a group by pointing this out, and suggesting that the question either be dropped as meaningless or else be rephrased in a meaningful way which provides for some sort of observational answer (e.g., "What beliefs do each of us have about why the Martins' house may have burned?"—our beliefs can at least be stated and observed *as our beliefs*).

Second, all questions can be classified as *limited* or *open-ended*. Limited questions ask for a specific, brief answer, such as information, or if another person agrees or disagrees with some proposition. Such questions do not encourage elaboration or different points of view. Implied in a limited question is that there are only one, two, or a very few possible responses. Once a short answer has been given, there is no room for further response. For example: "How old are you?" "Do you think age is related to wisdom?" "Did you like that movie?" "When must we submit our report?" or "Which side do you think is right, the students or the administration?" Especially be wary of questions which suggest a one- or two-valued orientation. Although there are useful two-valued ways of classifying things, in most cases such thinking leads us to overlook matters of degree. Few things are either all good or bad, all black or white. If something were pure black, no light would reflect from it. But even lampblack reflects some light. Digitalis is poisonous in some quantities, but a powerful medicine in others. To ask, "Is this painting beautiful?" is to imply that it is either all beautiful or all ugly. As a rule phrase questions in terms of degree, not as either-or.

Open-ended questions imply a wide variety of possible answers, encouraging elaboration and numerous points of view. They imply more than a one-word or brief answer, with room for many responses. For example: "How beautiful do you think she is?" "What did you like about the movie?" "What are the relative merits of both the students' and the administration's points of view?" "Can anyone tell me more about that?"

Many types of answerable questions have been listed by writers on the subject, but most of them can be reduced to questions concerned with orientation, information, interpretation and value, policy, and procedure.

Questions of Orientation

Questions of orientation seek answers which will orient the group and help determine its goals. Early in a discussion it is important that the interdependent purposes, the area of freedom, and the type of end results which the discussion is to achieve be established. Questions seeking such information and decisions are most helpful if asked explicitly during this time, and may be needed whenever the group seems to have lost its orientation toward a clear goal. Some questions of orientation may need to be of the limited type, such as when asking about the group's area of freedom. Consider the following examples:

"What are the purposes of this meeting?"

"How many nominees are we to report for each position to be filled?"

"Should we be trying to reach an agreement on what is the best policy regarding capital punishment, or just understanding the arguments for various proposed policies?"

"Where are we now? We were discussing the extent of the problem, but now we seem to be talking about a possible solution to it."

Questions of Information

Questions of information are those which ask for specific statements of fact. They may refer to observations of something which has occurred, to what somebody said earlier, or for clarification of some statement. The answers should be limited to such reports without interpretations or inferences being confused with the fact; confusion often arises when a question of fact is responded to with a guess, hunch, theory, or pet belief. A fact as such is not discussable; it can merely be reported and possibly verified by further observation. Examples of meaningful questions of information or fact (those which can be answered from observations based on specific steps or operations) illustrate this type:

"What factors did the fire chief say contributed to the burning of the Martins' house?" (To verify, ask him or ask someone who heard him.)

"How did you do on the English CLEP exam?"

"What did you say, Sally, was the number of abortions in University Hospital last year?"

"By 'police' did you mean all law enforcement officers or only uniformed patrolmen?"

"What does anybody know about the extent of crimes of violence in our city?"

The answers to such questions may be true or false, depending on whether or not the answer conforms to what happened. The accuracy is discussable, but a fact itself is not subject to discussion—only to observation. It is important to determine whether what appears to be a question of information is really such, or if it is ambiguous or meaningless (does not refer to any observable event).

Questions of Interpretation

Questions of interpretation or judgment are those concerned with the meaning of a fact or group of facts. Such a question asks not just what happened, but what are the implications of events. Since they ask for opinions or judgments, there is much room for discussion of questions of interpretation. Many groups have as their goal the answering of such questions. For example, a grand jury collects information, then decides whether or not to file charges against a suspect. A so-called "fact-finding" committee of a legislature first ascertains what has happened, then interprets the meanings of these facts and may even recommend policy actions. The facts about heroin usage in a particular city will undoubtedly be judged as indicating a serious (or not so serious) problem. Examples of this type of question, such as the following, can be found in any discussion:

	Limited	Open-Ended
Unanswerable (nonsense)		
Answerable (sense)	Orientation Information Interpretation & value Policy Rhetorical or "leading"	Orientation Information Interpretation & value Policy

Figure 3.4. Types of questions.

"Has auto theft increased in seriousness in our city since 1975?"

"How have the attitudes of college students changed since 1970?"

"What conditions appear to have contributed to the decline in the number of family-owned farms?"

"How effective is capital punishment in reducing the murder rate?"

"What are the relative merits of these proposals for improving the delivery of mail?"

To answer any such question requires information, but the answer will be an interpretation of that information.

Questions of interpretation are vital in both learning and problem-solving discussions. To analyze a problem means to interpret the extent and seriousness of it; and to get at its roots means to judge how events are related. Thus questions of "What caused this?" are invariably questions of interpretation. It is vital to keep in mind that answers are not absolute and totally objective, as can be the answers to questions of fact. There is room for disagreement among reasonable persons. The goal of a group is to arrive at the best *group* judgment possible.

Questions of value are special types of questions of interpretation in which discussants are asked to assess the merit or worth of something. A comparison is always involved or implied in answering a question of value. This may be a comparison to specific criteria (standards of judgment) or to a similar type of object or idea. For example:

"Is using coal to reduce our dependency on oil or reducing air pollution more important to our way of life?"

"Which political party has done more to improve the living conditions for the poor?"

"Should individuals have the right to use dangerous stimulants?"

"How moral is capital punishment?"

When individual and personal valuations are called for, it is important to remember that there is no need for agreement. There is no sense arguing about answers to such questions as: "Is this a good painting?" "Do you like this poem?" or "Is pork or chicken better?" A learning group has no need to agree on matters of value, but merely to understand what the questions imply and the basis for different answers to them. On the other hand, a group trying to arrive at a solution to a problem, when facing a choice among possible courses of action, must agree on the values or criteria in order to arrive at a specific recommendation or plan of action. For such a problem-solving group, arriving at agreement on values may well be essential if they are ever to agree on a decision.

Questions of Policy

Questions of policy ask, "What should be done to . . .?" The key word is *should*. Such a question asks for a solution to a problem or a general plan of action. For example: "How many credits of science should be required for liberal arts graduates?" "What should we do to reduce littering in our town?" Obviously, an answer to such questions that will be acceptable to all members of a group can be found after answers to questions of interpretation and value have been agreed upon. When communication breaks down in a group trying to agree upon a solution, it is usually wise to raise questions of value, asking what criteria are actually being applied. It may also be necessary to collect more facts and interpret them. The patterns for problem-solving discussion provide for discussion of fact, interpretation, value, and policy in that order. But sometimes the discussion is too sketchy at some stage in the process of problem solving to provide a basis for agreement on a policy statement. In this event the group may need to backtrack to answer questions of fact, interpretation, or value previously overlooked.

Questions About Procedure

Such questions are not so frequent in a group discussion as are those concerning information, opinion, and policy, but they are vital to a group. They must be answered if group members are to work together in a cooperative way. Asking a question of procedure will often help to organize group work or to clarify a vague proposal. The following examples show what these questions are like:

"How should we proceed to evaluate this list of ideas?"

"How would such a plan be put into effect?"

"What topics will we take up first?"

"Who will write up our report for us?"

"What questions should we discuss in order to understand this problem fully?"

When no procedure has been agreed upon or announced to a discussion group, or if you do not understand what to do next or who is to do what, that is a good indication that a question of procedure will facilitate cooperative group work.

Questions with Rhetorical Intent

Rhetorical questions are not questions at all in the sense that they seek answers; rather, they are affirmations couched in the language of questions, often called "leading" questions. For example: "Wouldn't it be a good idea to brainstorm this question?" "Why don't we recommend that the school buy a bus to transport debate teams?" or "Don't you think prostitution should be legalized?" When a discussant hears a rhetorical question he can often clarify or prevent confusion by restating it as a declarative sentence, such as: "You seem to think we should brainstorm this issue. I agree." "You are recommending that the school buy a bus for the debate team." "You seem to favor legalizing prostitution."

A large number of additional types of questions could be listed here, such as questions of choice, questions asking for agreement or disagreement, and so on, but all of these can be included in one of the above types. The important thing is to understand the questions being discussed, to ask those needed at each stage of discussion, to understand the implications of each type of question, and to respond relevantly.

REPORTING THE RESULTS OF A DISCUSSION

Efficient communication within a continuing group depends upon records and reports of meetings. Although learning groups rarely keep records of their meetings since the outcomes are individual learnings, problem-solving groups always should. Even a single-meeting *ad hoc* group usually benefits from a written report of the meeting, as a reminder to all members of what was discussed and decided, and to assure that all agree with the understanding of the secretary or reporter. Most committees of larger groups are required to keep records of their meetings, and they usually must submit reports not only to all members of the committee, but also to the parent organization (and sometimes to other interested groups). For example, at the university where the author works, the committees of the Faculty Senate must write reports of each meeting, and the reports are distributed to all members of the Senate and sometimes to selected administrators.

The purpose of such reports is to preserve a record of the essential *content* of the discussion, not of the process. The format and type of detail included in meeting reports may take various forms, depending upon the nature of the group, its objectives, and the type of report it must submit to others. Sometimes an advisory committee will submit a written resolution to a parent body. This resolution may also include arguments for the resolution, often called "whereas" clauses. For example, consider the following resolution:

> Whereas, the Academic Affairs Committee of the Senate has determined that students transferring from the University of Nebraska at Lincoln to the University of Nebraska at Omaha bring transcripts and academic averages based on grades which include plus and minus indicators and UNO students receive only straight letter grades of A, B, C, D, or F; and
> Whereas, this practice can make the academic average of a UNL student significantly higher than the academic average of a UNO student doing comparable work, thus placing UNO students at a disadvantage in the competition for scholarly recognition; and
> Whereas, the majority of institutions of higher education in the United States award only straight letter grades of A through F;
> Therefore, Be it Resolved: that the Chancellor be requested to seek a common system of grading symbols and quality points throughout the entire University of Nebraska System, preferably based on straight letter grades of A through F and quality points of 4 through 0.

The reports of some committees and judicial groups must, as directed by the constitution of the organization, be kept in the form of minutes with a record of all items on the agenda, including reports, actions by consent, motions, and votes. Such a report does not necessarily indicate that the committee employed all possible parliamentary rules, but only that it kept complete records of all actions and voted where necessary to confirm decisions. Here is an example of committee minutes which you could use as a guide:

Minutes of April 12, 1977 Meeting of Committee A

Committee A held a special meet at 1:30 P.M. on Thursday, April 14, 1977 in room 14 of the Jones Library.

    Attendance: Walter Bradley, Marlynn Jones, George Smith, Barbara Trekheld, and Michael Williams.

    Absent were Jantha Calamus and Peter Shiuoka.

1. The minutes of the April 4 meeting were approved as distributed.

2. Two nominations for membership in the graduate faculty were considered. A subcommittee of Bradley and Trekheld reported that their investigation indicated that Dr. Robert Jordon met all criteria for Membership. Williams moved that Professor Jordan be recommended to Dean Bryant for Membership in the Graduate Faculty. The vote was unanimously in favor.

The nomination of Professor Andrea Long was discussed; it was concluded that she met all criteria, and that the nomination had been processed properly. Jones moved that Professor Long be recommended for appointment to the Graduate Faculty. The motion was passed unanimously.

3. Encouragement of grant activity. Discussion next centered on the question of how to encourage more faculty members to submit proposals for funding grants. Several ideas were discussed. Bradley moved that we recommend to President Yardley that:

    a. A policy be established to grant reduced teaching loads to all professorial faculty who submit two or more grant proposals in a semester; and

    b. That ten percent of all grant overhead be returned to the department which obtained the grant for use in any appropriate way.

This motion was approved unanimously.

4. It was agreed that our next meeting will be in Carter Hall 241 on Friday, May 6, at 1:30 P.M. All members were asked to send agenda items to Professor Jones by April 24.

5. The meeting was adjourned at 3:45 P.M.

Submitted by,
Marlynn Jones, Chair

More typically the report of a problem-solving group takes the form of a brief summary of attendance, time and place of the meeting, the purpose of the meeting, the problem(s) discussed, the findings, the ideas considered, any criteria used to weigh ideas, the final solution accepted by the group, and who is responsible for what action. The following report is given as a model which you may use as a guide for format, or modify to suit the needs of particular groups and meetings.

Report of February Meeting of the Field Trial Committee
Pine Ridge Beagle Club

Time and Place of Meeting: 7:30 P.M. at home of Henry Lewis, February 4, 1974.

Attendance:	Joe Hamilton, Marshall Frazier, Henry Lewis, George Brown, and Jack Brilhart. Absent was Mark Jones.
Purpose:	The committee met to select dates for the 1974 licensed trial, and to prepare a slate of judges to recommend at the next membership meeting.
Findings:	The predicted entry, based on past records and AKC registration trends, will be 10-15 15″ males, 15-20 15″ females, 20-25 13″ males, and 25-30 13″ females.
	A letter from AKC indicated we could hold our trial on September 5-8, September 30-October 3, or November 5-6. Because of costs, it was felt we should have two judges cover all classes.
Criteria for Judges:	1. They should have attended an AKC seminar, and give performance priority over style. 2. They should have a reputation for tact. 3. They should live within 400 miles in order to hold down transportation costs.
Possible Judges:	Twelve names were proposed by the committee: Jack Jones, Evlyn Smith, Tim Coasley, Mike O'Neil, Harry Lampdon, Pete Bradovich, Ed Ponza, Mack Lambert, Walt Smith, Betty Candler, Jim Johnson, and Bugs Gower.
Decisions:	We decided to recommend a 3-day trial, September 30-October 2, with both 15″ classes the first day, followed by 13″ males and 13″ females. Earlier might be too hot, and later runs into the Hawkeye trial dates. For judges we nominated: Pete Bradovich, Betty Candler, Jack Jones, and Harry Lampdon.
Action:	Chairman Hamilton will write to AKC requesting approval for the dates selected. Secretary Lewis will call the four judges to determine if they are available.

Reported by,
Henry Lewis, Secretary

Such records as the above will help members recall from meeting to meeting just what facts were presented, what assignments were accepted for research, what progress was made toward finding a commonly accepted solution, and so on. Without such a written report, each meeting of a group tends to "begin from scratch." Much time is wasted, and often members forget what was decided, leading to needless argument and even open conflict. Further, such a report can give a sense of accomplishment to the group and help to foster cohesiveness among members.

It is wise for each member to keep some record of the meeting as it progresses, but the writing of the report (or "minutes") is usually the assigned duty of the chair or an appointed recorder (or "secretary"). Regardless, even as the content of the discussion is the responsibility and the property of all members, so is the report. It is usually unwise to report *who* suggested what solution or idea, or who presented what information. Sometimes this could be threatening to the members, and so may stifle creativity if they fear the responses of some superior administrator in an organization (e.g., the Chancellor in the case of a university committee, or the instructor in the case of a class committee). So record all information, all ideas, all accepted criteria, all decisions, and all responsibilities for action—but only in the latter case report the name unless legal minutes are required.

Effective communication among members of small groups depends on many factors, but none so important as an understanding that communication is a process of interpersonal transactions by which we send and perceive signals both verbal and nonverbal. Constructive discussants strive for completed transactions establishing as high a degree of mutual understanding as possible. Productive members never forget that language is symbolic and that meanings are in people. They listen to understand empathically, and keep their remarks as relevant, concise, and concrete as possible. They avoid evoking defensiveness in each other, and seek objectivity toward self, evidence, ideas, and other participants. A sensitivity to the problems inherent in language is part of their equipment, helping them to avoid fact-inference confusions, bypassing, ambiguity and vagueness, stigmatizing, and stoppers of all types. They become skilled at determining the questions or issues being discussed, the implications of those questions, and appropriate answers. Finally, they keep accurate records and write reports to facilitate recall and action.

Bibliography

Bormann, Ernest, *Discussion and Group Methods: Theory and Practice,* 2nd ed., New York: Harper & Row, Publishers, 1975.

Cathcart, Robert S., and Samovar, Larry A., eds., *Small Group Communication: A Reader,* 2nd ed., Dubuque: Wm. C. Brown Company Publishers, 1974.

Fast, Julian, *Body Language,* New York: M. Evans and Company, 1970.

Gulley, Halbert E., and Leathers, Dale G., *Communication and Group Process: Techniques for Improving the Quality of Small-Group Communication,* 3rd ed., New York: Holt, Rinehart and Winston, Inc., 1977; especially Parts 1 and 3.

Haney, William, *Communication and Organizational Behavior,* 3rd ed., Homewood, Ill.: Richard D. Irwin, Inc., 1973.

Hayakawa, S.I., *Language in Thought and Action,* New York: Harcourt, Brace and Company, 1949.

Johnson, Wendell, *People in Quandaries,* New York: Harper & Row, Publishers, 1946.

Knapp, Mark L., *Nonverbal Communication in Human Interaction,* New York: Holt, Rinehart and Winston, Inc., 1972.

Lee, Irving J., *How to Talk with People,* New York: Harper & Row, Publishers, 1952.

Phillips, Gerald M., *Communication and the Small Group,* 2nd ed., Indianapolis: The Bobbs-Merrill Co., Inc., 1973.

Rosenfeld, Lawrence B., *Human Interaction in the Small Group Setting,* Columbus, Ohio: Charles E. Merrill Publishing Company, 1973.

Taylor, Anita, *et al., Communicating,* Englewood Cliffs, N.J.: Prentice-Hall, Inc., 1977; especially Chapters 4, 5, 7, and 11.

Weinberg, Harry L., *Levels of Knowing and Existence,* New York: Harper & Row, Publishers, 1959.

Key Concepts

Bypassing—misunderstanding resulting from two persons not realizing they have different referents/meanings for the same words.

Complete communication circuit—open interchange system in which both persons send and receive signals, so that a signal from one is responded to by the other, and the response is acknowledged.

Concrete words—low-level abstractions, referring to a specific object, experience, relationship, etc.

Defensive listening—interpretation and response of other's statement characterized by evaluation, control, strategy, neutrality, superiority, or certainty in the listener.

Dismissal—communicative acts manifesting allness, dogmatism, closed-mindedness, and rigidity of belief.

Doublespeak—lengthy and abstruse statements designed to avoid a clear answer or to confuse.

Empathic listening—interpretation and response to other's statements characterized by active attempts to understand other's point of view and feelings, without evaluating.

Feedback—perception of one's own behavior or response of another, which perception modifies further communicative output.

High-level abstraction—word or phrase commonly used to refer to a broad category of objects, relationships, concepts, etc.

Interpersonal communication—transactional process in which one person's verbal and nonverbal behavior evokes meaning in another.

Minutes—written sequential report of every item included in the agenda actually followed in a group meeting, with complete record of all motions and votes.

Nonverbal communication—process of perceiving, interpreting, and responding to signals other than words themselves.

Question—verbal request for a response, interrogational statement.

> **Answerable**—one for which an answer can be provided from some sort of observation or interpretation of observations.
> **Limited**—implies only one, two, or few possible answers.
> **Open-ended**—implies a broad range of possible answers.
> **Of orientation**—seeks answer that will help define context or external structure and goals.
> **Of information**—seeks specific statements of fact.
> **Of interpretation**—seeks judgments or opinions about the meaning of a body of related facts.
> **Of value**—special type of question of interpretation seeking assessment or judgment of goodness, merit, or worth.
> **Of policy**—asks for solutions or general plan of action.

Of procedure—seeks guidelines, modes of operation, or cooperation.

Resolution—a formal recommendation or proposal, often including a rationale in the form of "whereas" clauses.

Stopper—any of several types of responses which interrupt the flow of a discussion, including stigma terms, name-calling, racist or sexist language, clichés, and tangential humor.

Symbol—anything used to represent something else with which it has no necessary or inherent relationship; all words are symbols.

Exercises

1. See how well you understand the kinds of statements and behaviors which foster defensiveness and openness-trust in a group, and how these relate to a cooperative vs. competitive climate by matching the following:

   _____ evaluation   A. cooperative relationships
   _____ empathy   B. competitive relationships
   _____ control
   _____ certainty
   _____ spontaneity
   _____ description
   _____ neutrality
   _____ strategies
   _____ provisionalism
   _____ problem solving

2. Study carefully the diagram of communication process presented in Figure 3.1, page 60. What elements and processes seem to you to be omitted or inadequately represented? How would you improve, simplify, or elaborate this model? Your instructor may make this an individual or group assignment.

3. During a fishbowl discussion (one group in center engaged in discussion, encircled by nonparticipating observers), any observer may call "freeze" at any time, at which point each discussant should remain motionless without changing even so much as eye direction. Then the observer asks each other observer to comment on what each discussant's posture, position in the group, eye direction, and nonverbal behavior seems to indicate about his or her feelings toward the group. After this, both observers and participants may discuss the implications of these observer comments and the basis for them.

4. During a "feedback" session, each member of a small project group should practice stating his or her feelings toward the group as a whole and other members of it, its procedures, objectives, and other aspects of the discussion. These should be stated in a direct, "owning" fashion. To "own" your feelings, state them this way, never as accusations:
   "I am angry that. . . ."
   "When Sue said . . . I felt very. . . ."
   "I feel very frustrated that. . . ."

5. Any member of a learning or project group may, during a special session when the group adopts this rule, call "freeze feelings" at any point he or

she wants to do so, and each participant then must state exactly what he or she was *feeling* and thinking about at the instant of the call.

6. In a practice session, group discussants should first refrain from giving any bodily or vocal responses to comments of others (i.e., no head nods, leaning forward, hand gestures while another talks, "un-huh" comments, facial expressions, etc.) for about ten minutes. Then, during the next ten minutes, everyone should react nonverbally (both physically and vocally) as fully and completely as possible. Members should then describe how they felt in each situation, why, and what this shows about group communication.

7. The same discussion group should meet in three very different settings over a short time span (1 or 2 days), with different seating, room size, lighting, etc. Then report your observations of the effects of the environment in a short paper or as a journal entry, summarize findings in each small group of your class, and have a member of each group report the group's findings to the entire class. This may also be done for different seating arrangements and distances among discussants in the regular classroom.

8. Practice the rule that "each discussant must rephrase in his own words his understanding of the previous speaker's meanings (ideas *and* feelings) to that speaker's *complete* satisfaction (as indicated verbally or by a head nod) before he may have the floor and add anything to the discussion." If the rephrasing is not accepted, the original speaker may then clarify, the rephraser may try again, or someone else may try. One member of the group should not participate, but keep an accurate count of the number of times rephrasings are accepted and rejected. Be sure to count each attempt to rephrase. Discuss the implications of listening, how to improve communication, and how you felt during this project.

9. After one or a series of several meetings, members of each project group should evaluate the apparent sense of responsibility each member of the group has shown for the success of the group on a scale of ten (very responsible) to one (no responsibility for the group). Also, record the basis for each such assessment. Then tabulate the results and discuss them within the group.

10. During fishbowl discussions, the observers should rate each participant on each of the polar scales of defensive vs. supportive communication, by making an X in the appropriate space:

evaluative	___:___:___:___:___:___:___	descriptive
controlling	___:___:___:___:___:___:___	problem-solving
strategic	___:___:___:___:___:___:___	spontaneous
neutral	___:___:___:___:___:___:___	empathic
superior	___:___:___:___:___:___:___	equal
certain	___:___:___:___:___:___:___	provisional
	1 2 3 4 5 6 7	

Now give numbers to each scale, from 1 to 7, and sum the six scales for a score of "cooperativeness." These ratings should be given to the participants. Each person may then want to listen to a recording of the discussion and prepare a plan for making any changes she feels appropriate in the way she speaks during discussions.

11. Analyze a tape-recorded discussion of your group, tallying and briefly describing all instances of:
    bypassing
    ambiguity or vagueness
    stigmatizing or name-calling
    clichés
    dismissal
    sexism or racism
    Note in each instance the effect on group communication, if the problem was corrected, and if not, what might have been done to correct it.

12. As you listen to a tape-recorded discussion, make up a sheet listing each of the *types* of questions, thus getting a frequency count of each type. Also record each actual question and the appropriateness of the response to it. Compare your results with those of other members of your group who listen to the same recorded discussion.

13. With others, listen to a tape-recorded discussion. Each time the group seems to be discussing a new question or issue, stop the recorder, write out what you judge the question under discussion to be, and the logical-psychological implications of it. Compare results with others listening to the same discussion.

14. Each member of a small group should write up a formal report of the discussion. Distribute these to all group members. Evaluate them in a discussion, seeking to determine guidelines for an adequate report.

15. Write up a complete recommendation based on an advisory discussion, with a formal resolution to be presented to a parent body of which you are (or pretend to be) a committee. You may want to include "Whereas" clauses setting forth the arguments for the policy, and then begin the policy proposition with the phrase "Be it resolved, that. . . ."

16. Carry on a conversation with two or three other persons in which you can only make statements in the form of questions. Leading or rhetorical questions are okay. Discuss what you learn from doing this.

17. Videotape record three discussions during the term. Make an analysis of the nonverbal communication in these discussions:
    a. What cues were used in response to each other?
    b. Did the nonverbals seem to facilitate or detract from goal achievement by the group?
    c. What did you infer about feelings and relationships among the members from the nonverbal cues?
    d. How might nonverbal cues have been used more effectively?

4
Preparing
to Discuss

"A discussion is a group of people, none of whom is individually capable of doing anything, deciding collectively that nothing can be done." The wag who coined this definition must have listened to many of the verbal interchanges which pass for problem-solving discussion. Perhaps it is because we discuss at the drop of a hat in daily contacts that so many people look upon discussion as something which no one (except possibly a leader) would prepare for. But for most discussions, as in so many human ventures, to fail to prepare is to prepare to fail.

Effective discussion, like effective public speaking, grows out of dependable knowledge and clear thinking, which can come only from preparation. Of course there are productive discussions for which nobody seems to have made specific preparations. But appearances here, as in many situations, are deceiving. Participating in such discussions are people who by nature of their work, life, and study are well prepared: a group of speech communication teachers discussing how to help students overcome reticence, graduate students in public administration talking about reforms needed in the city charter, or a group of dog fanciers talking about how to train their animals.

Even the experts can do a better job if they prepare specifically. In the modern organization most problems are far too complex for any one person to have enough information to solve them (e.g., engine design, guidance systems, market decisions, pollution control, registration procedures). Consequently, discussion by task, research, and action groups is the basic process by which major decisions are made in organizations. The skills of organization, including discussion, are the key to twentieth century society and industrial success. Western Europe used American economic aid so much more productively after World War II than have most developing nations largely because the knowledge of how to set up and operate complex organizations was there even if the factories and tools were not. Third world nations, if they are to advance their standards of living, need to know how to develop and maintain complex organizations, how to gather objective information, and how to engage in effective small group discussion even more than they need actual financial help.

All of which further indicates that effective group discussion is never a pool of ignorance. Every dependable conclusion, solution, interpretation, or belief rests on dependable evidence and valid reasoning from the evidence. Half-informed participants can reach only half-informed decisions. The valuable participant has plumbed his subject deeply. Think for a moment of a group of college students trying to intelligently discuss such topics as capital punishment or the control of atomic arms without having studied the topic. Would you place credence in the findings of such a group?

How highly group members value the prepared, informed participant was shown in research on emergent leadership in leaderless discussion groups. Geier found that being perceived as uninformed was the greatest single reason why members of leaderless discussion groups were quickly eliminated from any bid for major influence in the group.[1] You simply can't bluff for long in a group that is at all informed and critical of information and ideas. Group members are well advised to make serious individual efforts to be well informed.

Groups are frequently plagued by playboys who keep telling irrelevant jokes or pulling the group off the topic. Such nuisances are almost always poorly informed. One promotor of study-discussion programs advocated this policy: "If anyone has not read the materials, he is not permitted to speak unless to ask a question." Needless to say, this policy produced prepared participants and satisfying discussions. Many study-discussion leaders report that when the participants have not prepared, the ensuing discussion is listless, disorganized, shallow, and frustrating. Many students in my small group communication courses have reported in case studies of their project groups that little progress was made until finally everyone did the research needed. Then a lot was accomplished in a short time with the needed information now available.

Not only do discussants need information if their groups are to be effective, but it must be relevant, accurate, valid, and as complete as possible. This means that tests of the quality of information must be applied both while preparing for and participating in discussions. The evidence on which decisions are reached may include such nonverbal materials as maps, photos, and objects (e.g., sample products, weapons, tools), and such verbal materials as statements of fact,

1. John G. Geier, "A Trait Approach to the Study of Leadership in Small Groups," in Robert S. Cathcart and Larry A. Samovar, eds., *Small Group Communication: A Reader* (Dubuque: Wm. C. Brown Company Publishers, 1970), p. 414.

opinion, and advice or policy. How reliable and valid the information may be is crucial in deciding whether or not to use it—an out-of-date map, a "salted" ore sample, a biased set of statistics, an uninformed opinion, an untested bit of advice, or an outdated concept (e.g., "women belong in the home") can lead to very poor group decisions indeed!

The contrast between being uninformed and informed was discovered by a group of students at a large university. They began attacking the university food service, with a host of complaints about what was wrong and what should be done to improve it. Fortunately, they soon realized that they knew very little about the facts of the subject except for what they had seen and heard as students and customers. Thus, they decided to conduct a careful investigation. The labor was divided among the group members, some studying menu planning, others studying food preparation, others looking into costs, and others investigating food service at other schools. Information was gathered from home economists, dieticians, food service employees, journals, and books. At the next meeting this group of informed students pooled their knowledge, and came to the conclusion that they had the finest food service of any university in their section of the country, that meals were reasonably priced, that menus were better planned than most family diets, and that many of the complaints were due to ignorance or to misuse of the food service by students. The problem soon changed to, "How can we get the students at our university to appreciate the excellence of our food service, and to take better advantage of it?" They also made a few recommendations for minor improvements in the food service, all based on the facts of the case. These suggestions were well received by the man in charge of the service, who expressed his appreciation and put several of them into effect.

Since preparation is so important, the question now becomes, "What can we do to prepare ourselves to discuss effectively?" No answer will suffice for all occasions, but a plan for preparing to engage in group problem solving, a plan for preparing to engage in group learning discussion, and suggestions for preparing one's self to engage in other types of discussion will be presented next. The last section of this chapter is devoted to the special preparations which should be made by a designated leader, including notices, preparation of facilities, and group planning sessions. As a result of studying this chapter you should:

1. Desire that discussants be prepared, or else delay decision making until they are adequately informed.
2. Be able to locate information efficiently in all sources available to you.
3. Be able to construct a bibliography of resources in any major library.
4. Understand a series of steps to take in a definite time order in gathering information efficiently.

5. Be able to distinguish between statements of fact and statements of inference with a high degree of accuracy (80 percent at least).
6. Know what to do to prepare for meetings as a leader—chairperson, moderator, or supervisor.

PREPARING FOR PROBLEM-SOLVING DISCUSSIONS

Each member of a problem-solving or decision-making group should prepare whenever possible. The steps in preparing are outlined below in the order in which they should be taken. This procedure may be modified somewhat if you are well versed in the problem area. But none of these steps can be omitted without a loss in effectiveness.

1. *Review and organize your own stock of information and ideas on the subject.* Undoubtedly you already have some information and experience on the subject, or you would not be discussing it. Taking a systematic inventory of this knowledge can save you much time in preparation, and will enable you to recall what you need when you need to. To begin reading at this point would be wasteful and inefficient.

> a. Place the problem or subject in perspective. To what is it related? What will it affect, or by what is it affected? For example, in trying to plan a scholarship program for a corporation, one should consider the corporation's financial condition, long-range plans, obligations to the community, public relations, types of employees, and the like.
> b. Make an inventory of what you know about the subject. An approach that may help you recall is to list courses taken, jobs held, reports, firsthand experiences, articles read, books, ideas, and so forth. Additional headings will suggest themselves as you proceed. These headings can be put on sheets of scratch paper. Then jot down in brief form everything that comes to mind. Let your mind be "freewheeling," without being concerned with the degree of importance, relevance, or even validity.
> c. Organize your information into a problem-solving outline. This can be in a rough pencil draft. Look over your notes for main issues, topics, or questions about the problem, being guided by a model outline suggested in Chapter 5.
> d. Look for deficiencies. Your outline of information will reveal what you do *not* know, where specific information is needed, and which ideas or opinions are unsupported.

2. *Gather needed information.* You are now ready to plan research to correct some of the deficiencies in your knowledge and thinking. We will review briefly the means for getting this information and recording it, for this topic has probably been covered previously in your speech and English classes.

Information and ideas slip from memory or twist themselves in recall unless we make *accurate* and *complete* notes. Carrying books, magazines, and recordings to a discussion would at best be clumsy, and you might get so lost in the mess that you distract your group.

The best system of note-taking is to record each bit of information or idea on a separate 3 by 5 note card. Put a topic heading on the card, followed by the specific subject. Then list exact details of the source, just as you would for a bibliography. Finally, record the information, idea, or quotation. The following example shows how to do this:

PREPARING TO DISCUSS   Get General Understanding First

   Harnack, R. Victor and Fest, Thorrel B., Group Discussion: Theory and Technique New York: Appleton-Century-Crofts, 1964, pp. 118-119.
   "Unless the member is already rather thoroughly acquainted with the nature of the problem to be solved, he ought to spend some time investigating the nature of the overall problem before he begins looking for the specific evidence that is his assignment. . . . Looking at the whole problem will help the individual in three ways. First, he will be better able to fit his specific assignment into the total picture. Second, he will be prepared to understand and evaluate the contributions made by others with different assignments. Third, he may discover some evidence or ideas that may have escaped the notice of those investigating the other aspects of the problem."

Figure 4.1.

The note cards provide both accuracy and flexibility. One can arrange them in various groups as he synthesizes and interprets the evidence he has collected. They can be consulted with ease during discussion without having to leaf through a disorganized notebook. Full reference data permit others to evaluate the credibility of the evidence. It is virtually useless to say something appeared in *The New York Times* or *Newsweek* or "a book by some psychologist."

Your information may come from many sources:

   a.   *Personal observation.* When feasible, gather information firsthand. For example, before discussing how to reduce traffic jams on a campus, you will want to look at the traffic flow from the perspective of your problem and the questions you have generated. A group of students desiring to improve conditions in a self-service campus coffee shop spent some time observing what was happening there at various times throughout the day. They recorded the number of people who did and did not bus their waste materials, the kinds of litter on the floor and tables, the placement and condition of waste containers, and the kinds of signs encouraging users to keep the room clean.

   b.   *Interviews.* Where you can see only a small part or where you are not sufficiently knowledgeable to observe meaningfully, inquire of people who are trained observers or who have firsthand contact with your problem. The students referred to above interviewed users of the coffee shop to determine how they felt about its condition and their reasons for busing or not busing their cups, plates, and leftover food. They also questioned the manager about why plastic plates and utensils were used, costs, waste containers, use of employees, efforts made to keep the coffee shop clean, and so on.

If only a few people need to be consulted, members of a group may want to conduct an in-depth interview with several open-ended questions designed to obtain responses bearing on the problem or topic. Open-ended questions will often elicit unexpected information which the interviewer would not have obtained in response to limited questions. If several group members will be interviewing a larger number of persons, each interviewer should have the same set of questions to ask, with forms on which to record the answers. If the questions have been properly planned the results can be tabulated and easily interpreted. For example, study the questions asked and the summary of answers reported in a newspaper carrying one of the national polls (such as those conducted by Gallup or Harris). One group of discussion students did a project to discover differences between first dates of approximately thirty years ago and today. They selected a sample of interviewees from two age groups, then asked all these persons the same set of questions:

1. Do you remember your first date? Yes _____ No _____
2. How old were you at the time of your first date? _____
3. How did you first become acquainted with the person you dated?
4. Was this a solo or double date?
5. If you remember, what did you do on this date?
6. Did you get a kiss on this date? Yes _____ No _____

    c.   *Reading.* On many topics, the biggest pool of information will be found in books, journals, newspapers, and other printed pages. You may need to read widely and thoroughly.

First, you will need to compile a *bibliography* of possible written sources. A bibliography is a list of published works bearing on a specific issue or topic. Ideally, you would locate and evaluate all the relevant recent printed information before making any final description of a problem or reaching any decisions about a solution. Most certainly you should not limit your reading to only one or a few sources. To do so is to risk getting biased information and opinions, with no way to cross check the truth of what you read, or to compare various positions on the subject. To be as efficient and thorough as possible, first prepare a list of key terms bearing on the topic to guide your search for bibliographic items. The group can do this most effectively, perhaps by using the technique of brainstorming described on page 140. Of course other key terms will be discovered as you proceed with library research. For example, in preparing to discuss "What type of lottery, if any, should our state run?" the key words might include: lottery, sweepstakes, gambling, victimless crime, wagering, revenue, taxes, and betting.

A good library manual, available at virtually every college or university library, is a great help in building a bibliography and locating materials. You may find help in bibliographies of bibliographies, which list special published bibliographies by topic, such as: *A World Bibliography of Bibliographies and of Bibliographic Catalogues . . ., Bibliographical Index,* and *Bulletin of Bibliography and Magazine Notes.* Bibliographies will be found at the end of many books, doctoral dissertations (see *Dissertation Abstracts* to locate these), and research articles. The subject section of the card catalog of the library may reveal books not previously located. You can locate materials in magazines, journals, and newspapers with such special indexes as: *The Reader's Guide to Periodical Literature, Applied Science and Technology Index, The Education Index,* and *The New York Times Index.* Do not overlook publications by federal and state governments. Most libraries have special sections of such material. Most helpful in locating relevant information in these publications is the *Monthly Catalog of U.S. Government Publications,* followed by the *Monthly Checklist of State Publications.*

Often much labor can be saved in a group by dividing up a bibliography, so that a few key materials are read by all discussants but most writings are examined by one or two members. However, there is a very real danger in dividing up a bibliography by topics, one member per topic. Each person then becomes a specialist, with no one to check on his or her findings, interpretations, and conclusions. There is likely to be little disagreement about the probable truth of statements—whatever the group "expert" says on this topic is likely to be accepted with very little questioning, whether or not it is accurate. If one or more members does not do a competent job of investigating and interpreting, the group may suffer greatly from incorrect or inadequate information. Interaction among the members and cohesiveness will both likely suffer.

Read wisely. Instead of reading an entire book look in the index and table of contents for clues to what is pertinent. Skim rapidly until you find something of value to your group's special purpose. Read the summary of an article to see if the entire article warrants your time.

d. *Other sources.* One of the best ways to get ideas and information is to talk to your acquaintances about the problem you are investigating. Listen for new ideas, expressions of feeling, and specific information which you can later check for validity. Useful information and ideas may crop up anywhere or anytime, perhaps when least expected. You may find something in a television program, from a lecture, or from a radio show. Keep your ears open and a supply of note cards handy.

3. *Evaluate your information and ideas.* In the light of all you have learned in individual research of the problem, it is now time to evaluate your information and ideas. Many of your ideas may collapse before new evidence. Some of your information may be spurious, in direct conflict with other information, or from highly suspect sources. Some will be virtually irrelevant to the problem facing

the group. Now is the time to cull the misleading, false, suspect, unsubstantiated, or irrelevant so you do not misinform, confuse, or delay your group.

It is especially important, both in gathering data and evaluating it during discussion, to distinguish between statements of fact and statements of inference, opinion, advice, preference, or definition.

The major difference between statements of fact and all other types of statements is that factual statements are *true* or *false* in a special sense of these terms. *A statement of fact* is a declarative sentence that refers to an *observation* of some event in the world. The event is described, and the statement includes or implies a method of observing by which the statement could be tested for truth or accuracy. It is a *true* statement of fact if accurate to the observed events, and can only refer to a *past* event actually observed. Facts either exist or do not exist; they are not discussable as such. The truth or validity of such a statement may or may not be directly verifiable. If the statement refers to a presently ongoing situation accessible to the group, it can be verified. If not, only the presence of the statement can be verified (that is, if the statement refers to something that is not continuing or is not accessible to the group). For example, we could not verify that George III occupied the throne of England in 1773—only that records indicate he was king. However, if several independent sources report the same information as fact, you can be more confident than if it comes from only one unverified source. You might not be able to directly verify the population of Australia, but only what the census report at a given date revealed. As benchmarks to help you recognize them, statements of fact:

are limited to description;

can be made only *after* observation;

are limited in the number that can be made;

if primary, can be made only by a direct observer;

are as close to certain as humans can get.

On the other hand, statements of opinion and inference:

go *beyond* what was directly observed;

can be made at any time without regard to observation;

are unlimited in the number that can be made about anything;

can be made by anyone, observer or not;

entail some degree of probability, of inferential risk, or uncertainty.

Statements of advice, taste, or preference do not refer to direct observation, but report a personal liking, choice, value, or taste of someone.

A few examples may help to clarify these differences:

Statements of Fact:

The population of Omaha recorded in the 1970 census was 363,421.

On June 3, 1976, Jack Egrat owned two cats.

Three men with guns held up the Bank of Ralston on May 20, 1970, and escaped with $5,200.

Statements of Opinion and Inference:

Omaha is growing rapidly.

Jack Egart likes cats.

The heart of a good university is its (library, faculty, standards).

We should legalize gambling to reduce the state tax.

You will get to New York from Cleveland by following I-80 (not if you have a wreck!).

Occasionally a student, when first introduced to the differences between statements of fact and of opinion, tends to act as if statements of opinion are unwise or unnecessary in a discussion. Hardly so! As was said before, facts as such are not even discussable, but provide the basis for our discussions of what to do, what values to accept, etc. A group must not only deal with the world as it has been observed, but also determine priorities of value, ethics, goals, and procedures acceptable to all. Inferences must be made as to what will probably happen *if* we adopt each possible course of action. The facts regarding combustion pollution as they affect the environment and the use of resources must be examined, but what to do depends on values, opinions, and judgments acceptable to all if a rational law is to be adopted.

Unexamined opinions are poor guides to belief or action. Statements of inference and opinion cannot be tested for truth or falsity by direct observation as can statements of fact, but they can be examined. First consider the *source* of the opinion. Is this person a recognized expert in the field? How do other experts in the field regard the person who expressed the opinion? If they hold differing opinions, how might these be explained? Does the source have anything personal to gain from implications of the opinion (a vested interest)? How correct have her predictions and opinions been in the past? Has the source been consistent in this opinion? If not, is there an acceptable explanation for the change?

Second, consider the *implications* of the opinion. To what further inferences or conclusions does it logically lead, and are these acceptable to the group? For example, some writer may argue that outlawing private ownership of handguns would protect us from accidents and murderers. What are the implications of this opinion? That dangerous devices should not be allowed in the hands of citizens at large? That only unessential dangerous tools that could be used as murder weapons should be restricted? That eventually all potential weapons of murder should be removed from citizens? That less innocent people would be killed if handguns were taken from the public? Another writer may argue that anyone should be allowed to own a handgun after demonstrating competence in handling it safely and correctly and if the person has no felony record. What are the implications of that opinion? That only convicted felons will use handguns to kill other people? That most accidents would be prevented if people knew how to handle guns safely? That handguns are useful to many people? Still another may argue that legislation controlling handgun ownership is not needed, but that stringent and certain punishment should be meted out to anyone using a handgun in the commission of a crime; that this would solve the "real problem" without creating new problems. What are the assumptions of this position? That the threat of certain punishment is an effective deterrent? That killings by handguns are acts of only criminal "types"? Probably you can detect many implications of each of the above opinions. The point is this—when a group decision depends on opinions, it is most important to *test* these opinions, especially for what they assume and imply. To do so is the essence of discussion. Not to do so is to assure very poor group decisions and policies.

A careful review of all the factual statements and opinions you have collected will help you to weed out the irrelevant and undependable. Apply the following additional tests to your information:

Are these data related to the question to be discussed?

Is the statement from a direct observer, or a secondary source?

Was the source capable of accurate observations?

Is the method of computing statistics explained, and is it appropriate? Was the sampling procedure likely to give an accurate picture?[2]

4. *Reorganize your information and ideas.* Form a tentative analysis outline, using the major headings for a problem-solving pattern (see Chapter 5). It is very important to ask, "What are all the questions which must be answered to arrive at a full understanding of the problem and determine our group's goals?" Arrange your cards into piles (clarifying and limiting the problem, describing and analyzing the problem, criteria, possible solutions, and evaluating the solutions). Then the material helping you to clarify and analyze the problem can be further arranged according to details or symptoms of the problem, contributing factors, and the like. This arrangement will simplify the writing of your outline. Such an analysis of the problem situation will greatly improve the quality of group decisions; preparing it will "get your head together" about what needs to be considered and discussed by the group.

Your outline may contain some possible solutions; doubtless it should. You may have some evidence and reasoning which shows how similar solutions were

---

2. For a simple explanation of dangers in statistical data, see Darrell C. Huff, *How to Lie with Statistics* (New York: W.W. Norton & Company, Inc., 1954).

tried on similar problems. You may even have some suggestions on how to put a plan into effect, how to check to see if it works, and how to make adjustments. However, such thinking and planning is tentative. The worst sort of preparation is to go to a group discussion prepared to advocate a particular solution against all comers. Just as bad is to feel that one's personal definition and understanding of the problem is the complete problem. If researching and outlining make a participant closed-minded, it is better to remain ignorant. At least an ignorant person will not deadlock the group, and perhaps will listen and learn from others. Remember that the experts in almost any field, the people at the very frontier of knowledge, are the least dogmatic and sure of themselves. From these people the discussant who has read widely, thought long, and made a detailed outline should take heed. At the best he or she will now be prepared to contribute some reliable information, some ideas for testing in the forge of the group's collective knowledge and thinking, and perhaps most important, to listen with more understanding, to ask knowing questions, and thus to shape an image of and a solution to the problem. No one person could devise all of this alone.

PREPARING FOR ENLIGHTENMENT DISCUSSION

Much of what has been said about preparing for a problem-solving discussion applies also to preparing one's self for participation in a learning discussion. Usually a discussant needs to take stock of personal knowledge and experience, and to investigate the subject carefully. Outlining information may be omitted in some cases, or if done, the form of the outline would now be according to one of the patterns suggested for organizing group learning discussions.

Preparation for enlightenment discussion will vary depending on the nature of the subject and the group purposes. Usually there is a program of necessary reading. All members of the group discussing a subject need some common background. One should first attempt to get an overview of the subject, perhaps by reading a general article or by skimming an entire set of readings, an entire chapter, book, or whatever is to be discussed. Then the discussant should either be guided by a study outline prepared for the group, or else should prepare questions to answer through reading. For example, before reading an article by the late Secretary of State John Foster Dulles, one might ask such questions as, "What did Dulles think our relationship with Latin America should be?" "What evidence did he give to support his belief?" "What did he predict would happen if we did not follow his policy?"[3]

When preparing to discuss a controversial topic, your reading should encompass as many contrasting interpretations or points of view as possible. To

3. If you think this procedure is like the famous SQ3R method of studying, you are right!

learn, we must consider that which *does not conform* with our present beliefs; we must perceive, accept, and adapt to new knowledge. *This is most difficult to do.* We tend to listen to people who believe as we do, and to read what we want to read. We tend to be undercritical of these sources, and to be overcritical of evidence or opinions contrary to what we know and believe. It has been proven that we tend to forget new evidence or beliefs that are different from our own.[4] While reading, the study-discussant should make notes of the following:

Significant issues for the group to discuss;

Controversial points of view or policies that the group should examine;

Passages which are unclear, and any questions she wants to raise;

How a proposition of a writer relates to his personal life and experience;

Any other related information or experience that comes to mind.

Thus armed, you will now be a most valuable member of the discussion group. You will be able to understand the comments and questions raised by others. You will be prepared to help guide the discussion into the most important issues. You will see that the questions of concern are discussed. And you will recognize the limitations of your own points of view and those of others.

When the discussion is designed to explore works of art, study the art carefully, shifting the focus as you do. With a painting, you might shift attention from outline, to color, to spaces, to planes, to texture, and so forth. With a poem, you would first try to interpret it, then note how it is constructed, and finally form some tentative opinion of its worth or meaningfulness. Make notes of your questions and the stanzas which puzzle you; record your reactions. By all means, *read the poem aloud.*

In summary, focus on the materials—readings, visuals, or whatever—which will be discussed. Look at the subject of your forthcoming discussion from as many angles and points of view as possible, deferring final judgment. And most important, put *yourself* into the preparation—what do you see, understand, feel, or believe in response? Put down the most important of your observations and musings in brief notes as a possible springboard for remarks during the discussion. Then go to the group meeting in a mood of inquiry, ready to discover, not to persuade.

THE LEADER'S SPECIAL PREPARATIONS

Regardless of the type of discussion, when there is time for advance planning and preparation, a designated discussion leader (called chairperson, moderator,

---

4. Sir Frederic Bartlett, *Thinking: An Experimental and Social Study* (New York: Basic Books, Inc., Publishers, 1958).

etc.) has a special responsibility to help the participants by coordinating group preparation. This may include planning an agenda, seeing that each discussant is notified or reminded of the meeting, planning an outline for guiding the discussion of each problem, making resource materials available, and making clear what is expected of each participant.

When possible, each participant should receive a notice of the meeting far enough in advance so he can sufficiently prepare himself. The nature and timing of this notice will depend on the details of the discussion and the basis for the group's existence. A chairperson of a newly appointed committee might call the members to find a suitable time for them to meet, then send a notice to each member somewhat like that shown in Figure 4.2.

This notice gives the members the exact time and place of the meeting, expected participants, purpose of the meeting, preparation, and some basic information about the task.

July 23, 1977

From: Charles Snow, Search Committee Chairperson
To: Walter Brown, Helen Davis, Mike Rubenstein, and Betty Yalnoske
Subject: Meeting to Select a Lab Assistant

We will meet in room 24-B of the University Library at 9:30 A.M. on Friday, July 29.

The purpose of the meeting is to evaluate the credentials of the ten applicants for the position of lab assistant, and to decide whom we want to recommend for the position.

A complete file of the applicants' credentials is in Mrs. Brown's office. Please study these carefully and tentatively rank them before coming to the meeting. If you know anyone who might be acquainted with any of the applicants you might contact such persons for additional information.

Figure 4.2. Notice of meeting.

Sometimes a designated leader will need to plan an agenda of problems to be dealt with by a group. He or she might ask the discussants what problems the group should deal with, then arrange an agenda which will be sent to all members in time for them to prepare. For example, when the author was scheduled to participate in a panel which was to explore ways to train adult leaders, he was invited by the chairperson to submit questions for the discussion. The chairperson synthesized all the suggested questions into a five-question outline. This outline, along with the time and place of the public meeting and some suggestions for preparation, was sent to all panelists. The result was the panelists were well prepared for and satisfied with the discussion.

Sometimes a designated leader may find it feasible to call a preliminary meeting of the group in order to plan an agenda or perhaps to plan how the group will get the information it needs. At such a meeting the group would clarify the problem facing them, decide what information they need and how to get it, and divide up the work of research. It is always important to convene a panel or other public discussion group before they face the audience. Even if it is just before the discussion is presented, the members can be introduced to each other, the pattern of questions to be discussed can be made clear, and procedures can be explained. Such a meeting should not include a rehearsal; this will make you sound stale to the audience.

The designated leader of a study-discussion group has the special responsibility of working out a plan or pattern for guiding the discussion. He or she will need both a set of questions about the basic issues and follow-up questions to help bring out details; such a leader will need excerpts of readings, points of view, and feelings. Such preparation is covered in detail in the next three chapters.

Sometimes the leader of a learning-discussion group is given a manual or outline. In using it, the leader is wise to study the materials for the discussion first, making notes about major questions and issues. Only then should he or she turn to the leader's guide, comparing the suggested questions with personally prepared ones. As a general rule, it is best to use your own questions even though these may be primarily adaptations of questions suggested in a manual. Finally, arrange the questions into a sequence that is likely to be acceptable to the group.

PHYSICAL ARRANGEMENTS

An otherwise effective discussion can almost be ruined by poor physical arrangements. Someone, usually the designated leader, must see that facilities have been prepared.

The optimum for private discussion is a circular seating arrangement with members seated close together. In most discussions, each member should also have a writing surface. If the group meets in a classroom with flexible seating, have the participants push chairs into a circle (or a semicircle where everyone can see the chalkboard). In a room with fixed seating, a few portable chairs can be brought in or some participants can sit sideways in their chairs in order to form a rough circle. If you have a long rectangular table, get the people at the middle of each side to push their chairs out from the table, thus allowing for some eye contact between all members. If possible, do not seat anyone at the very corners of a square or rectangular table. A few small tables can be arranged to approximate a circle. See Figure 4.4.

Figure 4.3. All ready for the committee to gather.

If group members are not well acquainted, each should be given a tag or "tent" on which to write or print the name. Satisfactory name tags can be made from 3 by 5 file cards, with the name printed with crayon or felt-tip pen, and held in place with a straight pin. A plain 5 by 8 file card makes a good name tent when folded lengthwise. It is printed on both sides and set in front of the discussant so all members of the group can readily read the name.

If smoking is permitted, each discussant should have easy access to an ashtray. Of course it should be determined that no one is bothered by smoke before anyone lights up. Sometimes printed materials, note pads, pencils, or other supplies may be placed at each seat. If any special visual materials are to be used, be sure they are prepared and in good working order: enough handouts to go around, charts arranged in the order in which they are to be displayed, film projector threaded and focused, slides in correct order, or audiotape ready to play.

Adequate lighting, comfortable temperature, and ventilation should be arranged as for any meeting. The room should be quiet and free from intruders. The writer has seen several meetings thrown off track by someone wandering into a library room, children playing in an adjoining room, or workmen passing through. Extravagance is not important, but comfort, convenience, and freedom from distraction are essential. Special arrangements for public discussions are explained in Chapter 8.

The theme of this chapter has been that effective discussion comes from people who have prepared themselves to discuss. By getting as broad a perspective as possible on the group topic, discussants are at once informed, yet humble

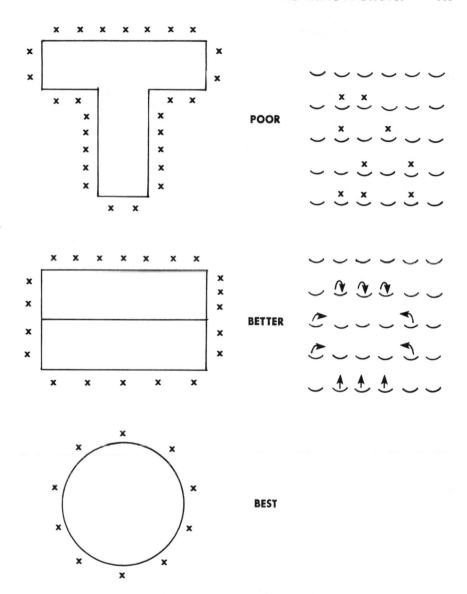

POOR

BETTER

BEST

Figure 4.4. Seating arrangements for discussion groups.

in the knowledge that they are only partially informed. It has been pointed out that good group thinking can only come from good individual thinking. Leaders have a special responsibility to help discussants prepare. Finally, a group must have physical arrangements which will facilitate a productive interchange. No book can tell you exactly how to prepare for a specific discussion, but you can take certain steps which, modified to suit the situation, can greatly increase the probability of a successful and satisfying discussion.

Bibliography

Bormann, Earnest G., *Discussion and Group Methods: Theory and Practice,* 2nd ed., New York: Harper & Row, Publishers, 1975; Chapters 4-6.

Ehninger, Douglas, and Brockriede, Wayne, *Decision by Debate,* New York: Dodd, Mead & Company, 1963; Part III.

Gulley, Halbert E., and Leathers, Dale G., *Communication and Group Process: Techniques for Improving the Quality of Small-Group Communication,* 3rd ed., New York: Holt, Rinehart and Winston, Inc., 1977; Chapter 5.

Huff, Darrell C., *How to Lie with Statistics,* New York: W.W. Norton & Company, Inc., 1954.

Key Concepts

Assumption—a belief that is taken for granted, and used in reasoning *as if* it were a statement of fact without checking for evidence of its truthfulness.

Bibliography—a list of readings or print sources, including books, journals and magazines, research papers, pamphlets, newspapers, etc., bearing on a given topic, problem, or issue.

Fact, statement of—a description of a specific event that was observed by some person, often including in the statement when, how, and by whom the observation was made; may be either true or false.

Implication—a statement which is a logical derivative, extension, or conclusion of a belief or opinion.

Inference, statement of—any statement which includes more than a description of some event, involving some degree of uncertainty and probability; cannot be checked for truth or falsity by observation.

Notice of meeting—a memorandum, card, or letter sent in advance of a meeting to all members of a group to inform them of the time, place, purpose, and preparations needed for discussion.

Exercises

1. Your instructor may want to have you take one of the available fact-inference tests, such as that produced by William V. Haney.

2. Your instructor will give you an essay to analyze for statements of fact, inference and opinion, and taste or value. Label each statement as to type. If a statement of fact, indicate whether or not it could be verified, and how such verification could be made.

3. Write a notice for a committee meeting, one for a learning discussion, and one for a panel discussion.

4. Plan how to arrange your meeting room for a problem-solving discussion by the entire class and for three or four simultaneous problem-solving discussions by subgroups of the class. Put your plans in the form of diagrams.

5. You may be assigned to get acquainted with the bibliographic tools mentioned in this chapter (and perhaps some others) by locating assigned materials.

6. In class, select a topic or problem of interest to all. Then:
   a. Prepare a bibliography of references on the topic, keeping a record of all the bibliographic sources you used;
   b. Prepare yourself to discuss the subject, including a detailed outline and the note cards from all the sources you consulted. These may be submitted to your instructor following the discussion. Be sure your outline contains all the questions you can think of that must be answered by the group to fully understand the problem, arrive at common goals and values, and reach a decision.

7. Observe a discussion (perhaps in fishbowl fashion in your classroom) for the amount of information, the quality of the information, the consistency of the statements of opinion expressed, and the implications of the values expressed.

8. Take several statements of opinion and value, and for each write out any (1) assumptions on which it rests; and (2) any implications of the statement. Compare the assumptions you detected and the implications you drew from each statement with the lists of these prepared by several classmates in a small group discussion. What conclusions can your group make as guidelines for testing statements of opinion and value?

   Your instructor may choose to take the statements from a recording of your actual discussions at an earlier date, from the list below, or some other source.

   "No new buildings should be connected to gas mains."

   "Country-western music is better than rock."

   "Natural wood makes better paneling than does fiberboard."

   "X-rated films should not be shown on television."

   "Physical assaults and killings are more obscene than any sex practices of consenting adults."

   "Religion is essential to a wholesome life."

   "Any person who is conscious should have the right to die when he or she chooses."

5
Procedures for Effective Decision Making and Problem Solving

The old joke that "a camel is a horse designed by a committee" reflects our concern for the quality of group decision making and problem solving. That groups can devise superior solutions to the types of problems for which there is no single "correct" answer has been demonstrated repeatedly, both in carefully designed research studies and from observation of real-life groups. But groups can and do often make poor decisions and plans of action, depending to a great degree on the procedures they follow. If you ask most educated people how to solve a problem, they will say something like "get the facts, weigh the alternatives, and make a decision." That's not too bad a procedure, but extensive observation of both individual and group problem solving reveals all sorts of procedures, mostly haphazard and unsystematic, more intuitive than analytical. Problem solving by groups, if it is to be maximally effective, requires systematic procedures to coordinate the thinking of several people, just as playing winning football requires systematic coordination of the actions of all players during each play and an overall game plan.

In the all too typical problem-solving discussion, someone outlines a problem, then immediately someone else suggests what to do to solve it, followed by a brief period of discussion evaluating this idea. Then another idea is suggested, discussed and dropped. Maybe at this point the group goes back to talking about the problem. A third idea for solving the problem is proposed, and possibly forgotten along with the first two. Finally, time begins to run out and a decision is made quickly, usually the last idea discussed, even though the proposals made earlier might have solved the problem more effectively. All too often the group adjourns without making plans for actually getting anything done.

This chapter will give principles and procedures for making prob-

118

lem-solving discussions efficient and effective. As a result of your reading, study, and practice in connection with this chapter, you should:

1. Appreciate the value of a careful analysis of a problem, and be able to ask the questions that will bring out a thorough understanding of a problem.
2. Understand the differences among decision making by consensus, majority, averaging, chance, attrition, expert, and leader, and be able to list advantages and disadvantages of each method.
3. Prefer to make major decisions by consensus in a group of peers, or whenever you are in a position of leadership.
4. Be able to distinguish between problem questions and solution questions.
5. Be able to adapt three different problem-solving procedures to appropriate kinds of problems, including writing detailed outlines of questions for organizing discussions of problems.
6. Be able to conduct a brainstorming session.
7. Know how to write or state criteria as standards for evaluating possible solutions.
8. Insist that any problem-solving group work out a plan to implement and follow up on a solution before ending its deliberations on the problem.

Many of us are so used to discussing anything, anywhere, anytime that planning and following a pattern or outline when discussing may seem unnecessary or even a bit ridiculous. We resist such constraints. After all, we've discussed problems, made decisions, and taken action as members of groups without much thought about the pattern of our thinking together. Yet the most common complaint by participants in adult groups I have observed was that leaders failed to keep the group on track and the discussion organized. Such complaints have also been reported by investigators of real-life, problem-solving groups.

Have you noticed how easy it is to overlook some important fact when you tackle a problem alone? Do you find your thoughts often coming in a random, jumbled, helter-skelter fashion? Have you regretted decisions made before all the needed evidence was considered or possible alternatives explored? If individual thinking is often haphazard, consider what can happen when a group of people try to think together toward a common aim. Each person may have a different way of approaching the subject or problem. If each follows his own lead, there will not be a group discussion, but individuals talking to themselves. Perhaps you have noticed how often conversation is shallow and vacuous, shifting aimlessly from topic to topic, with no one getting his feelings and meanings clearly expressed about anything. Berg used a technique of content analysis to locate the themes in discussions by task-oriented groups. He reported that these groups averaged changing themes or topics every 58 seconds. "Though the same themes frequently reappeared several times, groups were often unable to complete discussion of these topics." Although his procedure for theme analysis contributed somewhat to the finding that the themes were discussed very briefly, the conclusion that these problem-solving discussions were badly organized is inescapable.[1]

Two examples of discussion by adult study-discussion groups further illustrate the need for a systematic procedure to outline and organize discussions. In the first group, ten persons were responding to a set of readings on "Status and Role" in societies. In one swoop they went from an exploration of conflicting roles of a contemporary African leader to one discussant's troubles with a trucking union. Next they jumped to unions in general, then to contemporary literary magazines—all in the span of five minutes. They never did get back to the readings.

Quite different was a discussion in which eighteen adults were analyzing two of E.E. Cummings' poems. Talk was excited and spontaneous, but the remarks were clearly interrelated. One speaker mentioned the picture he thought the poet wanted to create with a particular line of the poem. A second added a further interpretation. The third speaker explained why she disagreed somewhat, followed by nods and verbal agreement. A fourth speaker gave his views on the next stanza. The designated discussion leader asked if there was anything in the poem to support this interpretation. The prior speaker began to explain, then stopped, and began again with, "Now I see what you mean." On and on went the group in a gradual unfolding of the poem. Finally, one speaker attempted a synthesis of many varying points expressed. As the discussion closed, the members spoke of how much they enjoyed it and how much better they now understood and appreciated the poem.

These two brief examples illustrate several differences between disorganized talk and organized group thinking. In the first instance, the talk was scattered among many topics and going nowhere; in the second, the talk was easy to follow, fruitful of understanding, with each comment a natural outgrowth of what had preceded it. In the first case, the discussion sounded like an undisciplined train of free association; in the second, the statements resembled the workings of a trained, controlled mind. This chapter is designed to help you achieve discussions like the second. First, we will compare the concepts of "decision making" and "problem solving"; second, we will compare several ways in which decisions are made in small groups; third, we will examine the characteristics of effective group problem solving; and last, we will look at some specific patterns or procedures for organizing group problem-solving discussions.

DECISION MAKING vs. PROBLEM SOLVING

"Problem solving" refers to a procedure by which an individual or group moves through time from a state of dissatisfaction with something to a plan for

---

1. David M. Berg, "A Descriptive Analysis of the Distribution and Duration of Themes Discussed by Task-oriented Small Groups," *Speech Monographs* 34 (1967) pp. 172-175.

arriving at a satisfactory condition. A series of stages or steps is always involved in problem solving, and entails many decisions. Problem solving is explained in depth in the rest of this chapter.

Although some writers have used the term "decision making" as if it were a synonym for problem solving, there is a major and vital difference between these concepts. "Decision making" refers to *choosing* among two or more possible alternatives. Thus you make a decision when selecting which of three available psychology courses to register for, whether to take the bus or drive to work on a snowy morning, which of several pairs of slacks to wear, or which of several pins in a display case to purchase. In the process of problem solving many decisions must be made, such as what factual data to accept as true, which is the most probable precipitating cause of an unsatisfactory situation, the order in which to arrange several criteria, when and where to hold a discussion of the problem, and even when to take up a specific issue. Some decisions must be made of weighty matters, such as which of several possible solutions to a problem to adopt. Some are of a trivial nature, such as when to take a refreshment break. Often group members are not even aware that a decision has been made; at other times the group may spend a long time deciding how to make a decision. No one way of making decisions will be used at all times by a group, as different circumstances and issues call for different ways of deciding. On complex or vital matters a group can usually make far better decisions than can any individual member.[2] In our society such important matters as guilt or innocence of persons accused of a felony, size of tax levies, and permissable uses of media are generally made by groups.

MAKING DECISIONS IN SMALL GROUPS

How do you prefer that decisions be made in small groups of which you are a member? If you are reading this book for a course in discussion or small group communication, your instructor may ask you to divide into groups of three to five persons and do the exercises on pages 151 to 154 as a way to explore and experience the different ways in which decisions are made in small groups. There are at least seven different ways in which groups make their decisions: by consensus, by majority vote, by popularity or averaging, by attrition, by chance, by an "expert" member, or by the leader.

Decision by Consensus

A consensus decision is one which all members agree is the best they can *all* accept or agree to; it is not necessarily the most preferred decision of all mem-

2. Marvin E. Shaw, *Group Dynamics: The Psychology of Small Group Behavior,* 2nd ed. (New York: McGraw-Hill Book Company, 1976), pp. 60-65.

bers. Deciding by consensus produces superior results in quality, in member satisfaction with the decision, and in acceptance of the result. But reaching consensus usually takes more time than any other method of deciding, especially if unanimity is achieved, and sometimes consensus is not possible. Unanimity is a state of perfect consensus in which every member of a group believes that the decision reached is the best that could be made, not just the best that the group could agree upon. Often this is not possible. All members of a group understand a consensus decision and the reasons for it, and all will usually support it even though it is not the decision one or a few persons would have preferred. The process of arriving at a consensus gives all members a chance to express how they feel about it, and an equitable chance to influence the final outcome.

Consensus depends on careful listening so that all important information and points of view are understood similarly by all discussants. A consensual decision is often a synergistic outcome in which the group produces something superior to a summation of individual ideas and thinking. In arriving at a consensus, conflicts and differences of opinion must be viewed as a means for clarification and testing of alternatives, not as interpersonal competition for power. Guidelines for making decisions by consensus were outlined by Hall:

1. Don't argue stubbornly for your own position. Present your position as clearly and logically as possible, being sure you listen to all reactions and consider them carefully.
2. When a stalemate seems to have occurred, avoid looking at it as a situation in which someone must win and someone else lose. Rather, see if you can find a next best alternative that is acceptable to everyone. This may take conscious effort.
3. When an agreement is reached too easily and quickly, be on guard. Don't change your position simply to avoid conflict and reach agreement quickly. Through discussion, be certain that everyone accepts the solution for similar or complementary reasons.
4. Don't use such techniques as majority vote, averaging, coin tossing, or swapping off.
5. Seek out differences of opinion; they are to be expected and can be most helpful in testing ideas. Get every member involved in the decision-making process. If you have a wide range of information and ideas the group has a better chance of finding a truly excellent solution.[3]

To understand this process of making decisions in a group by consensus you must participate in it. To gain such experience, a class can be divided into groups of 4-7 members each for exercise 2 at the end of this chapter.

3. Adapted from Jay Hall, "Decisions, Decisions, Decisions," *Psychology Today* 5 (November, 1971), pp. 51-54, 86-87.

Decision by Majority Vote

Majority vote is the basis for deciding in most large, democratic groups. As soon as 51 percent of the members voting support one alternative, the decision has been reached. Voting in a small group can be done by voice ("aye"), a show of hands, or even by ballot (slips of paper). This method of deciding is much easier and faster than consensus as a rule, but all too frequently the members in the minority ("losers") are not satisfied that their ideas have been fully understood and considered or that the best possible decision the group could make has been achieved. Not only does the quality of the decision frequently suffer, but also the cohesiveness and commitment to the decision. In some committees the constitution of the parent organization requires that votes be taken and recorded on major issues. If so, the group can discuss until a consensus decision has emerged, then vote to confirm it "legally." Exercise 3 will give you a guided experience in making a decision by majority vote and analyzing some of the impact of deciding by majority.

Decision by Expert

When a group contains one member with much greater knowledge than other members, the group may let this person decide an issue and then inform the group of the decision. In some cases this may indeed provide a technically excellent decision. But letting the expert decide for a group has drawbacks: only the expert may understand the reasons for the decision, beliefs and values of other members may be violated, important information held by other members may not be available to the expert, and other members may not work well to carry out the decision. In short, if the expert has a truly superior solution, taking time to make it a consensus of the group may be well worthwhile. To explore this method of decision making, you can do exercise 4, page 153.

Decision by Leader

Sometimes a designated or emergent leader makes a decision and announces it for the group. This may be done after some discussion of the facts, ideas, and issues involved; in other cases, an authoritarian leader will think the problem through alone and simply state his decision without discussion. The result may or may not be a good one in light of the facts of the problem situation, but other outcomes will often be resentment from other group members, lowered cohesiveness, halfhearted support for the decision, and a loss of effective influence on later decisions. Indeed, the members may not only "drag their heels," but even work to make the solution fail, as classic studies in management have shown.[4] Even while I write this I am caught up in a small group that is working to have a designated leader removed from his position for making a series of decisions for the group unilaterally; we refuse to accept an autocrat as our leader.

Decisions by persons in places of authority is quite common in some organizations, and of course may be desirable in some matters such as calling plays during a football game or a military fire fight. However, in groups of peers there is usually time for major decisions to be made by the group. In a class your instructor may wish to set up small groups (decision by leader), appoint leaders for these groups, and have the leader announce the decision for each group as explained in exercise 5.

Other Methods

Decisions can also be made in small groups by random choice among alternatives (coin toss, drawing, etc.), averaging a set of member ranks or ratings, allowing a subcommittee to decide, or other nonconsensus means. All of these can be practiced at times, but have little to favor them except convenience and saving of time. None makes optimum use of information or the reasoning of all members. You can check out the average ranks in exercise 2, if you do that exercise, and compare them to the consensus decisions. In groups where I have done this, the consensus decisions are superior to the averages about 80 percent of the time. Another way to compare decision by averaging with consensus is to have one person bring a glass jar with a large number of beans in it. Each group member examines the jar carefully and records a best guess of the number of beans. These are collected on slips of paper and tabulated in secret by the person having the correct count. Then the group discusses the number until a consensus is arrived at. These numbers can be compared for accuracy.

In summary, there are many ways in which decisions are made in small groups. When there is no standard of "correctness," the quality of a decision can be estimated from these guidelines: (1) To what degree was the information and thinking of *all* members used? (2) How satisfied are members with the decision, and how committed to working for it? (3) What effect has the decision-making procedure had on the atmosphere in the group, especially cohesiveness? Group decisions take longer to make than do individual ones, but extensive research shows they are superior for a number of reasons. Although arriving at a majority takes longer than averaging, and arriving at a consensus takes longer than a simple majority, the results are usually worth the extra time. First, complementary knowledge of members is pooled. Second, members perform better on

---

4. Many such studies have been reported; perhaps the most famous is Lester Coch and John R.P. French, Jr., "Overcoming Resistance to Change," *Human Relations* 1 (1948), pp. 512-532.

many tasks when working in the presence of others. Third, conscientious and knowledgeable people tend to put out greater effort in decision making than do less well-informed members, assuring that the best possible outcome is achieved. Fourth, mistakes and errors in individual thinking are likely to be detected and corrected by other members of a group if honest conflict is encouraged. Fifth, discussants often stimulate each other to recall information and think up creative alternatives which could not have been done when working alone, or by making a quick decision by majority vote or averaging. When possible, consensus is the best way to make decisions on solutions in small groups.

Thinking in the context of a group is still a process which occurs within the nervous system of each individual, not in the group in some suprapersonal way. But when each member understands and utilizes all that he can of the other member's statements in advancing the group—whether or not one chooses to call this occurrence group thinking—we can say that *promotively interdependent thinking* has occurred. Most of the statements and nonverbal reactions of group members are dovetailed; each is related to, based upon, and to some degree assimilated with what has preceded. The discussion is directed toward the discovery of common ends and of mutually acceptable means to the goals. Minds are attuned like players in a "jam" session, with each discussant contributing to the total effect, catching his cues from what his fellows are doing, and being guided throughout by a central theme or "melody" which serves to organize and give power.

Such group thinking does not result merely from following rules of logic or some preplanned outline. Procedure need not be projected and controlled by one member (leader). Nor is such thinking by group members necessarily the result of studying discussion techniques. But some shared logic or mode of thinking is essential to it. Training in discussion techniques, procedural methods, and an understanding of the modes of critical thinking will contribute much to intellectual teamwork if other necessary conditions exist.

ORGANIZING PROBLEM-SOLVING DISCUSSIONS

We have already considered some of the preconditions necessary for promotively interdependent thinking: well-informed members, a structure of roles, accepted norms. Next, we will consider some procedural patterns for group problem solving (as opposed to decision making). Some pattern appropriate to the problem is invariably evident in the talk of groups which display a high degree of cooperative interdependence in their thinking. Organizing the discussion of several persons concerned with a problem so that it is efficient and effective is not something we can do "naturally" or instinctively. It is highly complex, *learned* behavior. It takes extensive training to develop an expert diagnostician of diseases, or to learn to apply the scientific method in individual problem solving. Even so it takes considerable training to learn to organize problem-solving discussions.

Research Findings

The first studies surveyed describe how groups discussed problems, but did not consider how effectively they did so. Other studies considered the effectiveness of different ways in which problem-solving discussions can be organized. Out of these studies emerge some prescriptions for how to organize group problem solving for maximum effectiveness.

Studies to explain how groups solve problems have been made for a long time, beginning with the work of Bales and Strodtbeck using the "Interaction Process Analysis" system to classify behaviors of discussion groups (a very general set of categories for group interaction study). They interpreted their findings into three phases of group problem solving: (1) orientation; (2) evaluation; and (3) control. In the *orientation* phase, the frequency of asking for and giving information, orientation, repetition, and confirmation was at a peak. In the *evaluation* phase, there was some decrease in orienting types of remarks, with a significant increase in the evaluative types: seeking and giving opinions, evaluations, analyses, and feelings. In the final phase, *control,* there was a further decline in orienting-informing types of statements, and an increase in seeking and giving suggestions, direction, and courses of possible action, along with more expressing of agreement and disagreement.[5] However, even in the third phase the percentage of control-type remarks was far less than the percentage of orienting and evaluating ones, and the percentage of evaluating-type remarks declined only slightly from phase two. For the most part, the groups were without assigned or emergent leaders, had no history or future, lacked any plan for conducting their discussions, and had no training in group problem solving. The final outcomes of these discussions may or may not have been particularly effective or the process efficient—these factors were not evaluated in the research. The IPA scoring system is much too general to reveal details of the problem-solving process. All the Bales-Strodtbeck research really tells us is that naive groups tended to shift in frequency of types of behaviors through time, not what would be a productive pattern to follow. By way of comparison, if we study various cultures, we would find most people being very unscientific, unsystematic, and less than optimally productive. The general procedure of scientific investigation or engineering design is highly prescriptive and "unnatural," but it has yielded fantastic results in technological and social control when applied. It is *not* based on a description of how naive thinkers or groups work. Scientific

5. Robert F. Bales and Fred L. Strodtbeck, "Phases in Group Problem-Solving," *Journal of Abnormal and Social Psychology* 46 (1951), pp. 485-495.

method is highly prescriptive, guiding *optimal* human problem-solving behavior as we know it today, not the typical. So although some writers have urged use of Bales' early work as a guide to organizing problem-solving discussions, I urge just the opposite. Bales described the behavior of untrained collections of people who were being paid to discuss and "solve" problems with which they were not personally involved.

Schiedel and Crowell in 1964 questioned whether the pattern a problem-solving group follows is ". . . a linear progression from a problem through the various reflective-thinking steps to a conclusion." Using a five-dimension category system, they analyzed parts of ten discussions. Participants were students midway in a course on "the principles of group discussion," and each group had a designated chairperson. The task was to evaluate *The Seattle Times* as a metropolitan newspaper, so did not involve the full problem-solving process. Only one section of each discussion was analyzed, focusing on either the development of one criterion or its application. Schiedel and Crowell found a circular anchoring or spiral process to be characteristic of each segment of discussion analyzed, and from this finding they say they would ". . . replace the typical linear development illustration seen in many textbooks with a *spiraling model for group problem solving.*" They do acknowledge that the groups could be seen as moving toward a solution in a linear fashion overall, with a spiraling process during each phase of the meeting.[6] Crowell published a discussion textbook in which she set forth a linear reflective thinking model for group problem solving.[7] So what does their study mean as we investigate ways to organize group discussion? This: the process of group discussion, even though the pattern overall may be generally outlineable and linear, involves considerable spiraling in which members spend about one-fourth of their comments in confirming statements already made and another fourth clarifying and elaborating ideas, picking up more facts, referring back to those previously mentioned, and re-diagnosing the problem. One member advances an idea which is then elaborated and tested with clarification, substantiation, and verbalized acceptance or rejection by the group. Thus any outline for guiding the problem-solving process in a group discussion must not be followed too rigidly as a step-by-step procedure to be adhered to without any overlapping or doubling back to earlier questions or information about the situation. Forward movement toward a solution is sometimes accompanied by backward steps to anchor ideas in prior discussion and lateral moves to consolidate the thinking of all members. Fantasy themes and comments to deal with secondary tensions may intrude on the logical order of

6. Thomas M. Schiedel and Laura Crowell, "Idea Development in Small Groups," *Quarterly Journal of Speech* 50 (1964), pp. 140-145.

7. Laura Crowell, *Discussion: Method of Democracy* (Chicago: Scott, Foresman and Company, 1963).

an outline, but only for relatively brief periods of time. The overall discussion can be planned as a definite sequence of steps or phases in a procedure.

Fisher, unlike his predecessors, attempted ". . . to discover the nature of the interaction process across time leading to group consensus on decision-making tasks." He tape recorded ten very different groups in nonclassroom contexts, then subjected transcripts of the recordings to a special category system which omitted all socializing and procedural comments. Each comment was scored on three dimensions: (1) asserted or seeking; (2) the content as interpretation, substantiation, clarification, modification, summary, or agreement; and (3) as favorable, unfavorable, or ambiguous toward a proposal. Also recorded was the origination of each proposal and any subsequent introductions of it after the group had stopped talking about it for a time. He found that all ten groups displayed four phases in the movement toward consensus, with the phases blending into one another in a continuous and gradual change of interaction patterns, not necessarily typical of all groups but probably fitting most. Task behavior in phase one, "orientation," was characterized by much ambiguity and tentativeness in expressing ideas and opinions, by clarification and agreement. Phase two, the "conflict" phase, was characterized by disputation, with definite expressions of opinions, and both favorable and unfavorable comments—with much less tentativeness and ambiguity than in phase one, and a considerable amount of persuasion and argument being attempted by coalitions of members. Phase three, the "emergence" phase, showed a drop in conflict, argument, and reinforcement of unfavorable opinions. The level of conflict gradually dropped off, but ambiguity again rose as a means of gradually shifting attitudes toward proposals without loss of face—dissent, ambiguity, assent. Coalitions now tended to disappear. By the fourth phase, "reinforcement," a decision had been reached and it was now being fully understood and confirmed by members of the group. Much interpretation and favorable substantiating occurred, with almost no dissent. Thus Fisher has presented us with a descriptive picture of the *task* dimension of decision-making group interaction which shows group members express positions tentatively at first, then test them through conflict, gradually reduce the number of alternatives as a decision begins to emerge, and finally confirm the emergent decision. Unfortunately his category system focuses only on *proposals,* and has no room for information *apart from* some proposal, thus possibly indicating more conflict and less fact-orientated behavior than is present in many groups.[8]

What practical guidance can we get from these three major studies of group thinking? Even though different category systems for classifying interaction

8. B. Aubrey Fisher, "Decision Emergence: Phases in Group Decision-Making," *Speech Monographs* 37 (1970), pp. 53-66.

were used, some important findings about decision-making discussion emerged. First, during the early part of group problem solving discussants focus on orienting themselves to the problem and to each other's values and attitudes toward the problem, and tend to be very tentative in expressing any proposals. Then as proposals emerge, so do coalitions and conflict. By a process of elimination the group gradually reduces the number of alternatives until a consensus decision begins to emerge, which is then clarified, restated, and confirmed by all. While the overall process is somewhat linear (and strikingly similar in reports by Strodtbeck and Bales and by Fisher), the forward movement is also characterized by cycling on each issue or proposal as it is explored, tested, and a consensus for or against it is reached.

Such studies can give us guidance in developing and using pattern outlines for guiding group thinking, but they do not obviate the need for such outlines or procedures. Consider an analogy of group thinking to traveling. Before starting on a journey, we first develop some idea of the destination even though we may have never been there before. We map out in advance the sequence of routes we will follow, the major cities and landmarks that should be noticed as we proceed from point of origin to goal. We watch for these as we proceed, sometimes making unplanned detours or stops, and correcting our course after every deviation from the planned route. So, too, must be the conduct of those who wish to be effective in the art of discussion. They must have a planned route to follow from problem analysis to arrival at a solution, with ways to check their progress along the route of discussion.

A limited amount of research has been done on the merits of various "patterns" or procedures for conducting problem-solving discussions. Maier and Maier found that a "developmental pattern," while taking more patience and skill on the part of the designated leader, produced a better quality of decision than did a simpler problem-solution ("free") pattern.[9] The "developmental pattern" breaks the problem into a series of distinct issues and steps. It forces the group to map out the problem thoroughly and systematically. In a "free" discussion the group tries to find a solution without following any systematic outline to guide the analysis of the problem. In a similar study, Maier and Solem found that a leader technique for delaying the group decision produced solutions to a "change of work procedure" problem superior to those solutions produced when "free" discussion was permitted.[10] Pyron and Sharp found that problem-solving discussants whose performance was ranked high by both fellow discussants and

9. N.R.F. Maier and R.A. Maier, "An Experimental Test of the Effects of 'Developmental' vs. 'Free' Discussions on the Quality of Group Decisions," *Journal of Applied Psychology* 41 (1957), pp. 320-323.

10. N.R.F. Maier and A.R. Solem, "The Contribution of a Discussion Leader to the Quality of Group Thinking: The Effective Use of Minority Opinions," *Human Relations* 5 (1952), pp. 277-288.

observers did significantly better on a test of reflective thinking ability than did discussants ranked low on performance.[11] Ability to engage in patterned problem solving seems to be an important part of the skills of anyone who would be an effective discussant, and discussants can learn to follow procedures which lead to better quality solutions than they would arrive at otherwise. In short, certain prescriptive procedures can make the orientation, conflict, and emergence phases of decision making more productive. As Stech and Ratliffe wrote, "Seldom, if ever, do task or interpersonal aspects of group work just 'happen' if maximum group effectiveness is desired. Members must intentionally function in ways that cause them to happen effectively."[12]

The effects of three different prescriptive patterns for problem-solving discussion were compared experimentally by Brilhart and Jochem. A creative problem-solving pattern produced more possible solutions, and more solutions judged to be good ideas by independent judges. Participants preferred the complex creative problem-solving outline to a simpler pattern of "problem-possible solutions-final solution." Significantly more subjects also preferred a creative problem-solving pattern in which possible solutions preceded criteria to one in which discussion of criteria preceded possible solutions. Several subjects indicated that they felt discussing criteria first reduced their freedom to express novel ideas.[13]

In a subsequent unpublished study, Brilhart compared the creative problem-solving sequence and a simpler reflective thinking sequence in which each idea was evaluated when first mentioned. Discussants in this later study made decisions on problems which affected them personally: how to distribute grade points among themselves, and the date of the final examination in their speech course. Again, significantly more subjects preferred the detailed creative problem-solving pattern after using both.

Parnes and his associates have found that brainstorming techniques, in which no judging or criticism of any type is permitted while ideas are being proposed and listed, produced many more new and good ideas than did ordinary problem-solving procedures. Parnes also recommended establishing detailed criteria only after possible ideas have been listed by the group.[14]

11. H.C. Pyron and H. Sharp, "A Quantitative Study of Reflective Thinking and Performance in Problem-Solving Discussion," *Journal of Communication* 13 (1963), pp. 46-53.

12. Ernest Stech and Sharon A. Ratliffe, *Working in Groups* (Skokie, Ill.: National Textbook Company, 1976), p. 199.

13. John K. Brilhart and Lurene M. Jochem, "Effects of Different Patterns on Outcomes of Problem-Solving Discussion," *Journal of Applied Psychology* 48 (1964), pp. 175-179.

14. Sidney J. Parnes and Harold F. Harding, eds., *A Source Book for Creative Thinking* (New York: Charles Scribner's Sons, 1962), pp. 19-30, 185-191, 283-290.

Sidney J. Parnes, "Effects of Extended Effort in Creative Problem-Solving," *Journal of Educational Psychology* 52 (1961), pp. 117-122.

Sidney J. Parnes and Arnold Meadow, "Effects of 'Brainstorming' Instructions on Creative Problem-Solving by Trained and Untrained Subjects," *Journal of Educational Psychology* 50 (1959), pp. 171-176.

Larson used untrained student groups to discuss industrial relations problems for which a "best" solution (opinion of experts) was known. This was one of five possible solutions given to each group. Four different analysis formats were compared, with eight different groups using each: "no pattern," in which the group was given the problem to solve but no systematic analytic outline to follow; "single question form," which like Maier's developmental pattern gets the group to analyze the problem systematically; "ideal solution form," which focuses attention on the desires and values of all people affected by a decision; and the "reflective thinking form." Any of the three prescriptive patterns for guiding group problem solving produced more correct solutions than did no prescriptive pattern. The "single question" and "ideal solution" forms produced significantly more correct solutions than did the "reflective thinking" format. However, the groups did not have to generate ideas but only to choose among alternatives, and they had only twenty minutes in which to discuss each problem. How far these results can be extrapolated to the kinds of problems on which discussion groups must spend hours and for which there is no convenient list of five solutions is questionable, but at least the merits of some prescriptive pattern for organizing group thinking were demonstrated.[15]

While personally participating in and leading innumerable problem-solving discussion by all sorts of groups, I have found it often difficult for a new or untrained group to follow a systematic problem-solving outline. Doubtless, you also have noticed this. But I have also found that most one-meeting groups will stick pretty close to an outline if it is suggested to them, and that when a continuing group has settled the role structure it can and will follow a prescriptive model of problem solving, *if* the members understand the pattern and accept it as a logical way to achieve their goal. Even when the group has members who keep pulling off on tangents or rushing to find a quick and easy decision, having an outline based on a systematic problem-solving pattern can help get them to look again before jumping to a less than satisfactory solution.

From these research findings and other experience with discussions, we can establish some basic principles which apply regardless of the specific pattern outline being followed by the group.

General Principles

Focus on the Problem Before Solutions

What would you think if you drove into a garage with a car that was running poorly and the mechanic almost immediately said, "What you need to fix this buggy is a new carburetor and a set of spark plugs." If your reaction is like mine,

---

15. Carl E. Larson, "Forms of Analysis and Small Group Problem-Solving," *Speech Monographs* 36 (1969), pp. 452-455.

you would get out of there as fast as your ailing auto would let you. A competent mechanic, after he asked questions about how the car was acting and observed how it ran, would put it on an electronic engine analyzer. After gathering information by these means he would make a tentative diagnosis, which he would check by direct examination of the suspected parts. Only then would he say something like, "The problem is that two of your valves are burned, and the carburetor is so badly worn that it won't stay adjusted properly."

Our two hypothetical mechanics illustrate one of the most common failings in group (and individual) problem solving: solution centeredness. Irving Lee, after observing many problem-solving conferences and discussions, found that in most of the groups he studied there was "a deeply held assumption that because the problem was announced it was understood. People seemed too often to consider a complaint equivalent to a description, a charge the same as a specification."[16] Maier, after many years of studying problem-solving discussions in business and industry, stated that "participants as well as discussion leaders focus on the objective of arriving at a solution and fail to give due consideration to an exploration of the problem."[17] Groups tend to act like a surgeon who scheduled an operation when a patient complained of a pain in his abdomen, like a judge who handed down a decision as soon as he had read the indictment, or like the hunter who shot at a noise in the bushes and killed his son. Solution-centeredness has harmful effects:

1. *Partisanship is encouraged.* Participants spend a lot of time arguing the merits of their pet proposals. Often this is due to their having different ideas about the group objective, factual information not having been shared, and a failure to discuss what may have caused the unsatisfactory situation. Only when members first agree on the nature of the problem are they likely to be able to agree on what to do about it; otherwise the group may become hopelessly split or generate interpersonal tensions which hurt future group work.

2. *Ineffectual solutions tend to be adopted.* There is a tendency to spend much time debating the first and most obvious solutions, which are usually taken bodily from other situations and are not based on the facts of the present case. New, innovative ideas are not considered. When a careful analysis of the combination of forces and conditions producing the problem ("causes") has not been made, often only symptoms are treated with the basic problem getting worse instead of being solved. To illustrate,

16. Irving J. Lee, *How to Talk with People* (New York: Harper & Row, Publishers, 1952), p. 62.

17. Norman R.F. Maier, *Problem-Solving Discussions and Conferences* (New York: McGraw-Hill Book Company, 1963), p. 123.

think of what happens if you put better gasoline in a car badly out of tune, or a doctor gives aspirin to pull down the fever of someone with pneumonia without treating the cause of the fever.

3. *Time is wasted.* Solution-at-once methods often result in a sort of pin-wheel pattern. The problem is mentioned; someone proposes a solution which is argued at length; someone points out that an important aspect of the problem has been neglected; someone then goes back to the problem to see if this is so. This problem-solution cycle may be repeated indefinitely, wasting time on solutions which do not fit the facts of the case. At first, focus on what has gone wrong rather than what shall be done about it.

BEGIN WITH A PROBLEM QUESTION RATHER THAN A SOLUTION OR CHOICE QUESTION

How the problem is initially presented to a group and phrased as a question is vital to what follows. Begin with a *problem* question rather than a *solution* question; these are contrasted in Figure 5.1. Consider the following

SOLUTION QUESTIONS	PROBLEM QUESTIONS
One type of action is suggested. Focus is on *what to do.* *Different images* of what is wrong; information not pooled. *Partisan conflicts* likely to split group.	*Many alternative courses* implied, none suggested. Focus is on *what's wrong* and why. *Shared image* of problem, based on pooled information. *Consensus possible,* even probable.

Figure 5.1. Differences between *Problem Questions* and *Solution Questions.*

situation: a student leader asks his group, "How can we get rid of a club president who is not doing his job, without further disrupting the club?" Such a statement of the problem appears insoluble, like how to eat a cake and have it too. The apparent dilemma is the result of incorporating a solution (get rid of the president) into the statement of the problem. The better procedure is to separate the solution from the problem, then focus on understanding the details of the problem. Once this has been done, appropriate solutions will usually emerge. Our student leader might ask, "How might we get good leadership for our club?" Then the group can dig into what is expected of the president, how the incumbent is acting, what members are complaining about, what is wrong, and why. Answers to these questions about the problem may lead to tentative solutions: "Send him to a leadership training workshop," "Have the sponsor instruct him in his duties," "Ask him to resign," "Temporarily assign part of his duties to the executive committee members," and the like.

See if you can distinguish between the following questions which include solutions (solution questions) and those which focus on what is wrong (problem):

How can I transfer a man who is popular in the work group but slows down the work of others?

What can be done to alleviate complaints about inadequate parking space at our college?

How will we reduce shoplifting in our store?

How will we get more students to shape up by taking physical education?

What action shall we take in the case of Joe Blevins who is accused of cheating on Professor Lamdeau's exam?

MAP THE PROBLEM SITUATION

To help develop problem mindedness, think of the problem as a large uncharted map with only vague boundaries. The first task facing the problem-solving group is to make the map as complete as possible (in other words, to fully diagnose the situation). The leader of the group should urge the members to tell all they know about the situation: facts, complaints, conditions, circumstances, factors, details, happenings, relationships, disturbances, effects. In short, what have you observed? What have others observed? What have you heard?

Figure 5.2 illustrates this process of gathering and sharing information to "map out" a problem so that all members have virtually the same understanding of it. The large outer circle represents the entire problem in a context. Each of the four members of the group (A, B, C, D) has some information about the problem, a unique personal map represented by one of the four inner circles. Some of the information is shared by two members (light shading), some by three members (dark shading), and some by all four (dark center area), when the discussion gets underway. As the discussants share their information in a systematic analysis of the problem, they come to have at least very similar images or maps of the problem; no longer do they have four problems, but a shared problem. This map of the situation facing them is far better than any one or two members could have constructed (indicated by circle in right half of Figure 5.2).

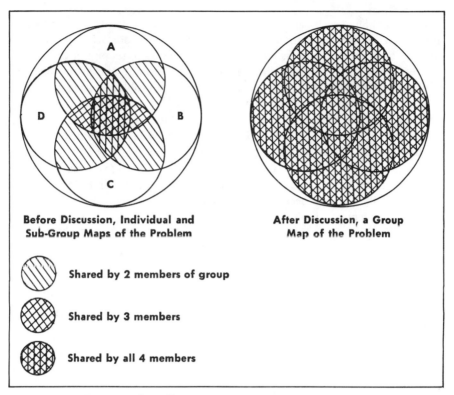

Before Discussion, Individual and Sub-Group Maps of the Problem

After Discussion, a Group Map of the Problem

Shared by 2 members of group

Shared by 3 members

Shared by all 4 members

Figure 5.2. "Maps" of a problem before and after discussion.

At best the "map" of the problem will be incomplete, with full detail in some parts, but gaps or faint outlines in others. Members will disagree on some details. Some observations may be spotty and fleeting. Sometimes the members will admit they do not know enough about the problem to deal with it intelligently. The author remembers a group of students concerned with recommending solutions to a severe shortage of parking space at a large university. The discussants soon decided they did not have enough information to make wise recommendations. They tried to list the types of information they would need before proceeding to talk about solutions. Soon investigating teams were out interviewing, getting maps, collecting records, and reading. The subsequent discussions led to a clear description of the many problems involved, and ultimately to a set of recommendations with which the entire group was pleased. These recommendations were presented to proper authorities, and most of them put into effect within three years. When a group gets into a discussion of what must be done to get needed information, the spirit of teamwork is something to behold! And the solutions usually work.

Every problem can be analyzed into three basic components: a present situation, a goal (desired situation), and some obstacle or obstacles to the goal. Problem solving is the process by which we find a way to remove or get around the obstacles. A goal to which there are no obstacles is not a problem. Members of a group who have different goals cannot engage in problem solving until they first agree on the goal to be achieved. So a cooperative group must first agree on what the discussants hope to achieve, then understand where they are at present in relation to that goal, and what obstacles lie between them and the goal. A solution question leads to looking at a means before the obstacles have been fully mapped out. Effective solutions are those which overcome real obstacles *which the group has power to do something about.* Sometimes it becomes necessary to modify the goal because of unsurmountable obstacles. Figure 5.3 illustrates this concept of a problem.

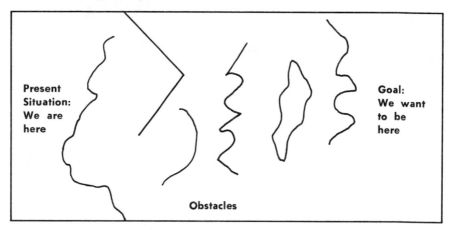

Figure 5.3. The elements of a problem.

A similar concept of a problem was developed by Kepner and Tregoe:

A problem is a deviation between what *should* be happening and what *actually* is happening that is important enough to make someone think the deviation ought to be corrected.[18]

This concept of a problem was diagrammed by Kepner and Tregoe as shown in Figure 5.4. The "problem" is the difference between what *should* be going on (desired state of affairs) and what is *actually* going on (present undesired state of affairs). The goal is to get the course of events to lead back to the desired state, "what should be going on." A group using this model of a problem must deter-

18. Charles H. Kepner and Benjamin B. Tregoe, *The Rational Manager* (New York: McGraw-Hill Book Company, 1965), p. 20.

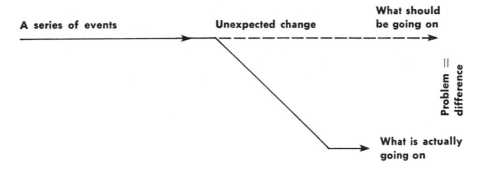

Figure 5.4. Kepner-Tregoe model of a problem.

mine the details of the difference: what is wrong. Then they must decide what produced or caused the unexpected change in order to create an appropriate solution. The Kepner and Tregoe model of a problem may help you to map out such problems as a change in the frequency of accidents, a machine that is not running properly, or even a change in the relationships among members of a family. Regardless of the model, a group does not understand a problem adequately to come up with an effective solution until all members agree on what is the desired situation, what is the actual situation, and the causes or obstacles producing the difference. Such "mapping" should be as precise and detailed as possible. You might be guided by such examples as the investigation of a murder by a team of trained detectives, the investigation of a plane crash by the Federal Aviation Administration, or the investigation by medical researchers of a series of deaths from some unknown disease. As Kepner and Tregoe pointed out, one of the greatest dangers is that a group will too quickly accept an apparent cause without adequate gathering of facts, analysis, and interpretation of them— "jumping to a conclusion about cause." Instead of being very critical in comparison of possible causative forces, discussants may collect arguments in support of a pet theory, resist other possible explanations of the problem, and pridefully fight to protect their theories of why things are not satisfactory. It is very important to "closely examine each hypothesis, looking for loopholes, for inconsistencies, for exceptions, for partial explanations," even with regard to one's own brainchildren.[19]

Perhaps the greatest obstacle to problem-centered thinking is the leader or member who comes to the group with the problem all solved in his mind. The presenter of a problem to a group must therefore set aside his solution and focus on the goal he wants to achieve if true discussion is to occur. Even in a consultative discussion where one member brings a problem to the group for advice, the

19. *Ibid.*, pp. 117-118.

discussion will frequently bring that person to see the problem very differently. Being willing to explore any and all solutions without having a favorite is an essential attitude for problem-solving discussion. Clarifying relationships between goals, obstacles, and the present state of affairs must be done if the solution is to be maximally effective. Remember, also, to focus on what *can* be done, what obstacles *can* be overcome.

Be Sure the Group Agrees on Criteria

Many times there is a lack of "reality testing" before a decision is made final. Other times, a group cannot agree on which of two or more possible solutions to adopt. If the problem has been fully explored, the most likely source of difficulty is a lack of clear-cut standards, criteria, or objectives. In many discussions there is a need for two considerations of criteria: first, when formulating the specific objectives of the group; second, when stating specific standards to be used in judging among solutions. Until agreement (explicit or intuitive) is reached on criteria, agreement on a solution is unlikely.

Many criteria are expressions of values shared by members of a group. Rubenstein gave an example of a problem which brought out very different values from different persons, and thus disagreement over the appropriate course of action (solution). Imagine that a man is in a small boat with his mother, wife, and child. The boat capsizes. The man is the only person in the boat who can swim. He can save only one of the other three persons. Which one should he save? Rubenstein found that all the Arabs he asked would save the mother, explaining that a man can always get another wife and children but not another mother. Of 100 American college freshmen asked this same question, 60 said they would save the wife and 40 the child. These Americans laughed at the idea of saving the mother. Why these great differences in choices? The criteria, based on different values, are different for most Arabs and most Americans. Hence, said Rubenstein,

> This is the problem of problems, the subjective element of problem solving and decision making. Man's value system, his priorities, guide his behavior as manifested in problem solving and decision making. Two people using the same rational tools of problem solving may arrive at different solutions because they operate from different frames of values, and therefore, their behavior is different.[20]

So a consensus of values relevant to the problem must be arrived at before a group can arrive at a consensus decision. It may take much time for a group to search out common values and beliefs. This is an important function of fantasy

---

20. Moshe F. Rubenstein, *Patterns of Problem Solving* (Englewood Cliffs, N.J.: Prentice-Hall, Inc., 1975), pp. 1-2.

chains, the establishment of common frames of values. When a group cannot seem to agree on a solution, look for differences in values, bring these up for discussion, and see if it is possible to agree. It may *not* be. The Kidney Machine case presented at the end of Chapter 2 is an excellent exercise for exploring and experiencing the role of values as criteria in discussions where decisions must be made.

From the beginning of the discussion, the group needs to be clearly aware of the limitations placed upon it. This is sometimes called the group's area of freedom. The group which tries to make decisions affecting matters over which it has no authority will be both confused and frustrated. For example, the area of freedom for a group of university students includes recommending changes in teaching methods, but students have no authority to make or enforce policy governing such changes. A committee may be given power to recommend plans for the building, but not to make the final decision and contract for the building. Any policy decision or plan of action must be judged by whether or not it fits into the group's area of freedom. Thus, if a committee is authorized to spend up to $500.00, it must evaluate all possible ideas by that absolute criterion.

It is important to rank criteria, giving priority to those which must be met. Ideas proposed can be rated "yes" or "no" on whether they meet all the absolute criteria, and from "excellent" to "poor" on how well they measure up to the less important criteria.

Single words, such as *efficient*, are not criteria, but categories of criteria. Such words are so vague that they are meaningless when applied to possible solutions. They can be used to find specific criteria. Criteria should be worded as questions or absolute statements. For example, the following criteria might be applied to plans for a club's annual banquet:

Absolute— Must not cost over $400.00 for entertainment.
            Must be enjoyable to both members and their families.

Questions— How convenient is the location for members?
            How comfortable is the room?

The importance of valid facts as criteria is suggested by Maier. Any solution not based on unchallenged facts or interpretations of facts available to the group should be rejected, and any solution based only on challenged information or interpretations should not be given further consideration.[21]

Defer Judgment When Seeking Solutions

Instead of evaluating each possible solution when it is first proposed, it is more efficient to defer judgment until a complete list of possible solutions has

---

21. Norman R.F. Maier, *Problem Solving and Creativity* (Belmont, Cal.: Brooks Publishing Company, 1970), pp. 453-455.

been produced. Much of the research already quoted indicates that the process of *idea gathering* should be separated from *idea evaluation*. Judgment stifles unusual and novel ideas. It is a good idea to list the proposed solutions on a chart or chalkboard. Encouragement should be given to combine, modify, or build upon previous suggestions.

For some types of problems, there are few options open to a group. If so, some discussion of each idea when it is proposed may be appropriate, but no final decision should be made until all alternatives that group members can think of have been recorded. At other times a very thorough exploration of the problem and causes will lead to a sudden insight into a solution. In such a case, the group should still try to think of other ideas with which the first one can be compared—"What *else* might we do?" If nothing is discovered, that solution should still be evaluated very thoroughly, and in the process it may undergo considerable revision and improvement.

Employ Brainstorming

Occasionally a problem-solving group may want to engage in a full-fledged brainstorming discussion. Brainstorming depends on the deferment of judgment; many auxiliary skills and techniques can be used to advantage. Brainstorming can be applied to any problem if there is a wide range of possible solutions, none of which can in advance be said to be just right. The process of brainstorming can be applied to any phase of the discussion: finding information (What information do we need? How might we get this information?), finding criteria (What criteria might we use to test ideas?), finding ideas (What might we do?), or implementation (How might we put our decision into effect?). In addition to what has been said about creative problem solving, the following rules of brainstorming should be presented to the group:

1. *All criticism is ruled out while brainstorming.*
2. *The wilder the ideas, the better.* Even offbeat, impractical suggestions may suggest practical ideas to other members.
3. *Quantity is wanted.* The more ideas, the more likelihood of good ones.
4. *Combination and improvement are wanted.* If you see a way to improve on a previous idea, snap your fingers to get attention so it can be recorded at once.

It is often advantageous to have in the discussion group both people with experience and people quite new to the specific problem (for a fresh point of view). A full-time recorder is needed to write down ideas as fast as they are suggested. Sometimes this can be done with a tape recorder, but a visual record that all can see is best. Be sure the recorder gets all ideas in accurate form.

The flow of possible solutions can sometimes be increased by asking idea-spurring questions. One can ask: "How can we adapt (modify, rearrange, reverse, combine, minimize, maximize) *any general solution?*" A concrete suggestion can

Figure 5.5. Brainstorming produces lots of ideas.

be used to open up creative thinking in a whole area. For example, someone might suggest: "Place a guard at each door." The leader could then ask, "What else might be done to increase security?" When the group seems to have run out of ideas, try reviewing the list rapidly; then ask for a definite number of additional suggestions to see if you can get more ideas. Usually you will get many more, including some very good ones.

A few warnings about applying brainstorming should be mentioned. A thorough job of creating new ideas, based on a full understanding of the problem, takes time. If time is short, use a more conventional and simple pattern. Be sure to stop all criticism, whether stated or implied by voice or manner. Everyone must feel completely free to express any idea that occurs to him as a possible solution. There are a few people who seem to be unable to separate ideation from evaluation. If a few attempts fail to stop a person from criticizing ideas, ask him to follow the rules, stay quiet, or leave the group. The problem must be clear, carefully analyzed, and closely limited and defined. Broad, sweeping problems must be broken down into subproblems. Vague generalities cannot be put into action, so be sure to clarify and elaborate all courses of action before adopting them.

Use Constructive Argument to Avoid "Groupthink"

As mentioned earlier, Irving Janis has used the term "groupthink" to refer to conformity to the belief of a head person or a majority in a group. "Groupthink" sometimes occurs when members begin to think they are infallible, or that the ideas of high status members should not be challenged. Leaders who promote their own solutions invite groupthink, but this phenomenon can occur in any group. Examples of the results of groupthink outcomes are the invasion of the Bay of Pigs, the decision to escalate the United States involvement in South Vietnam, and the Watergate espionage. Contributing to groupthink are pressures for consensus at the price of repressing doubts and contradictory evidence, cohesiveness based on less than open communication, a lack of critical scrutiny of all pros and cons, a failure to look for more alternatives, a failure to examine moral or ethical considerations, stereotyping of opposing groups, pressure from high status members, ignoring of facts and interpretations which do not support a majority view, failure to consult with available experts, and an illusion of unanimity based on suppression of doubts.[22]

Appropriate norms or rules for arguing can do much to produce constructive argument. Any problem-solving group needs norms such as those which follow. If your group is suffering from "groupthink" it might be a good idea to make a copy of these rules for everybody to discuss at one meeting.

1. Arguments should not lead to some persons being perceived as "winners" and other members as "losers;" everyone wins when a more creative, adequate solution is achieved.

2. Each member of the group should participate openly, expressing feelings, ideas, and positions. Even intuitions and hunches should be expressed and evaluated.

3. Members should insist on exploring the assumptions and implications of every idea; it is especially important that the person who first suggests a solution ask for such critical evaluation of the idea.

4. Every response to one's ideas should be valued and taken seriously. Every idea deserves an interested hearing.

5. Members should be critical of *all* ideas, but not of the members who express the ideas. Disagreement should not be person-centered but idea-centered. No one should try to put another on the defensive if the best possible thinking is to be done. Uptight discussants do not think clearly.

6. Members should frequently state what they think are the positions, feelings, and values of others with whose ideas they disagree. This will avoid much bypassing, and needless secondary tension.

7. All ideas should be evaluated on their own merits, not on the basis of who suggests them. In so far as possible, status power should be equalized so all members have the same chance to participate and be listened to, regardless of position or power in the external structure of the group or even role in the group.

22. Irving L. Janis, "Groupthink," *Psychology Today* 5 (Nov., 1971), pp. 43-46, 74-76.

8. The importance of teamwork in striving for consensus decisions which all can support should be stressed, perhaps often.
9. Controversy should be introduced when there is enough time to discuss the point at issue thoroughly, not just before the meeting must adjourn.
10. Trickery, bargaining, manipulation, and deception should be assiduously avoided, and pointed out and rebuked if detected.[23]

Plan How to Implement and Follow Up

Many times a group will arrive to no avail at a policy decision, a solution to a problem, a resolution, or some advice. No plans are made for putting a policy into effect or to see how recommendations are received. Every problem-solving discussion should terminate in some plan for action; no such group should consider its work finished until agreement is reached on who is to do exactly what, by what time, and how. If a committee is to make recommendations to a parent body, the committee should decide who will make the report, when she will make it, and in what form. If this report is to be made at a membership meeting, the committee members may then decide to prepare seconding or supporting speeches, may decide how to prepare the general membership to accept their recommendations, and so forth. A neighborhood group that has decided to turn a vacant lot into a playground would have to plan how to get legal clearances, who to get to do the work, where to get the materials (or at least from whom), and how to check on the use children get from the playground. No good chairperson or leader of a problem-solving group would fail to see that the group worked out details of how to put their decisions into effect.

Phillips has suggested the use of PERT ("Program Evaluation and Review Technique") as an adjunct to the discussion process for working out the details of a complex solution.[24] It can be very useful for implementing a complex plan of action such as is involved in constructing a building, conducting a promotional campaign, scheduling the making of a movie, or producing a play, etc. PERT involves identifying all events that must take place in sequences, estimating the time and resources needed for each, determining the allocation of personnel and material, and deciding whether a target date can likely be achieved. Although not needed for most plans of action, it is an excellent means for working out a plan based on statistical estimates rather than personal whim or guesswork. You may want to study it in one of the many excellent manuals on the process, but it must be practiced, not merely read about. Regardless of

---

23. Partly adapted from David W. Johnson and Frank P. Johnson, *Joining Together: Group Theory and Group Skills* (Englewood Cliffs, N.J.: Prentice-Hall, Inc., 1975), pp. 154-155.

24. Gerald M. Phillips, "PERT as a Logical Adjunct to the Discussion Process," *Journal of Communication* 15 (1965), pp. 89-99. Reprinted in Cathcart and Samovar, *Small Group Communication,* pp. 166-176.

whether or not you study and apply PERT be sure that your decisions will be converted into observable events, that definite actions are taken by designated members of the group, and that some procedure for monitoring is arranged to be sure that the solution is carried out as intended and that the desired state of affairs is achieved.

Specific Patterns for Group Problem Solving

With these general principles and guidelines for organizing effective problem-solving discussions, we now turn to specific patterns for guiding a group's thinking and talking. The outlines of questions below are suggestive: *the wording should be modified to fit the specific problem.* Each of these patterns is for a full-fledged, problem-solving discussion, which may actually take place over the course of more than one meeting of a group. If a group has only part of the total problem-solving process to engage in, it may need only a truncated version of one of these patterns. For example, a special committee may be asked to determine if a serious problem exists, not to find the solution. A group assigned to evaluate and choose from a list of alternatives would need to make only a limited analysis of the problem if that had been done by a prior group, but would need an outline to guide the setting of explicit criteria, evaluating the list of ideas, and arriving at a final decision. A group assigned to implement a detailed plan might follow the PERT procedure.

The Creative Problem-solving Sequence

The creative problem-solving sequence was developed as a discussion procedure for applying research findings about human creativity. It is based on the work of Alex Osborn, Sidney J. Parnes, and others associated with the Creative Problem Solving Institute. The pattern is most fittingly applied to problems for which there are many possible solutions, such as how to improve some product, alternative uses for idle buildings or tools, or any situation where imagination is called for.

I.   What is the nature of the problem facing us (present state, obstacles and causes, goals)?
   A.   What are we talking about?
      1.   Is the question or assignment clear to us?
      2.   Do we need to define any terms or concepts?
   B.   What is our area of freedom?
      1.   Are we to plan and take action, advise, or what?
      2.   What sort of end product should we produce through our discussion?
   C.   What has been happening that is unsatisfactory?

1. What is wrong? How do we know?
2. Who or what is affected, and under what conditions?
3. How serious do we judge the problem to be?
4. Have any corrective actions previously been tried that did not work?
5. What additional information do we need to adequately assess the extent and nature of the problem?

D. What is the desired situation or goal we hope to achieve?
E. What factors seem to have caused this problem?
   1. Are there any causative conditions of which we can be certain?
   2. What obstacles must we remove to achieve the desired situation?
F. How can we summarize the problem to include the present situation, the desired situation, the difference, the causes, and the obstacles?
   1. Do we all agree on this statement of the problem?
   2. Should we divide it into any subproblems?
      a. If so, what are they?
      b. In what order should we take them up?

II. What might be done to solve the problem (or first subproblem)? (Here the group brainstorms for possible solutions.)

III. By what criteria shall we judge our possible solutions?
   A. What absolute criteria must a solution meet?
   B. What relative standards shall we apply? (List and rank these values and standards by group agreement.)

IV. What are the relative merits of our possible solutions?
   A. What ideas can we screen out as unsupported by uncontested facts?
   B. Can we combine and simplify our list of possible solutions in any way?
   C. How well do the remaining ideas measure up to the criteria?

V. How will we put our solution into effect?
   A. Who will do what, when, and how?
   B. Do we need any follow-up or check procedures?

The creative problem-solving sequence could, of course, be repeated from II to V for each set of subproblems.

The Reflective Thinking Sequence

This pattern could be employed if there is only a very limited range of possible courses of action. There is considerable research casting doubt on its efficacy as an outline for guiding a problem-solving group discussion. It is based on the model of individual problem-solving thinking presented by John Dewey, with modifications espoused in numerous textbooks on discussion and small group communication. You will notice that the major difference between this outline and the creative problem-solving sequence is the order in which criteria and possible solutions are taken up by the group. The criteria-solutions sequence is likely to produce less ideas and less innovative ones, for criticism of ideas is encouraged even before they are verbalized.

I.   What is the nature of the problem facing us?
     (Here the outline is the same as for creative problem solving.)
II. By what criteria shall we judge our possible solutions?
III. What are feasible solutions, and what are their relative merits?
     (Each idea can be evaluated as it is presented, or there can be two distinct steps: A. Listing possible solutions; and B. Evaluating them.)
IV. What will be our solution?
V.   How will we put our decision into effect?

Ideal Solution Pattern

This pattern is especially suited to discussion of problems which will affect different groups of people with different interests, or which must have the support of various types of people with different concerns and values. For example, a change in traffic law would be of real concern to motorists, police officers, insurance companies, and businesses, at least. If the success of a policy or solution will be determined in large part by how well people with different frames of reference will accept it, the "ideal solution" model of problem-solving is the procedure that should be followed. The second major step (II) in the procedure is to explore the desires of people who would be directly affected by any change from the present situation. Thus, the discussants are urged to consider what *other* people want, would accept and make effective in achieving the goals of the group. The prohibitionists who succeeded in getting the United States Constitution amended to outlaw beverage alcohol may well have had a medically sound idea, but they failed to consider what the outcome would be when a large segment of the public rejected the solution. As a result, prohibition was not enforceable, and may have contributed directly to the growth of organized crime of other types. To understand the types of problems that the ideal solution pattern may be helpful with, consider the following problem questions:

Where should we five members of the Lamas family go for vacation next summer?

What courses should be offered by our department next semester?

What should be the law governing gambling in Idaho?

I.   What is the nature of the problem? (The rest of this section of the analytic outline would be very much like that for creative problem solving.)

II.   What would be an ideal solution from the point of view of each interested person or group? (A separate question, then, for each group, as:)
    A.   Merchants?
    B.   Customers?
    C.   Manufacturers?
    D.   Others?
III. What *can* be changed in the present situation?
    (That is, what solutions are possible? What *could* be done?)
IV.   What solution best approximates the ideal?
    (Here the group synthesizes and decides on the final solution to apply or recommend.)
V.   How will we put this solution into effect?

Sometimes you may not want to use this entire procedure for problem solving but simply ask questions during the analysis of the problem to get the group to consider various points of view. You would then use the group's findings about these as criteria when evaluating possible solutions to determine if they are realistic. That, of course, is the purpose of the "ideal solution" model.

Still other pattern outlines are possible, with the simplest being: I. What is the nature of the problem facing us? and II. How will we solve it? Any such outline might include many subquestions, and should be modified and worded to fit the actual problem facing the group. Certainly a group needs some procedure to organize and coordinate members' thinking and talking while engaged in problem solving—any outline is probably better than none. After making a careful analysis of the problem, develop the type of outline that seems most likely to bring out the type of thinking needed in order to arrive at a high-quality group product that will be acceptable to all concerned. Thus, the outline for a problem-solving procedure might be an amalgam of parts from several of the outline models above, and not the same as any of them.

The Leader's Outline

A study outline may get very long and complex. The leader may get so involved in trying to follow it that she is unable to listen well and adapt to what is happening in the group. What the leader needs is a short, simple outline based on the pattern for problem solving which the group has decided to use for organizing its thinking and talking. Such an outline, in abbreviated form, can be put on a chart for all to see and follow, or perhaps duplicated and given to each member of the group. Such a visual model was felt to be most helpful by the subjects in one investigation.[25] Study carefully the following example of a

25. John K. Brilhart, "An Experimental Comparison of Three Techniques for Communicating a Problem-Solving Pattern to Members of a Discussion Group," *Speech Monographs* 33 (1966), pp. 168-177.

leader's outline for guiding a group through the process of creative problem solving on a specific problem. Notice how the general questions from the model outlines above have been worded in terms of the specific problem. The leader, in actually using this outline, further revised his questions to fit the group's findings. He kept notes on his copy of the outline, modifying it as the group proceeded.

Problem Question. How might theft and mutilation of materials in the university library be reduced to a minimum?

I. What is the nature of the theft and mutilation now occurring in the library?
   A. Is the question clear to all of us?
   B. What limitations must we consider in our discussion?
      1. We can only recommend and advise; we are to draw up a proposal to be offered to the library committee.
      2. Do we want to place any other limits on our discussion of the problem at this time?
   C. What has been happening?
      1. What has been stolen or mutilated?
      2. How extensive and serious is this loss?
      3. What factors seem to contribute to the problem?
         a. In the library;
         b. In the classroom;
         c. Students and society at large;
         d. Other.
      4. Have any steps been taken to reduce the loss? If so, how did they work?
   D. Can we summarize our findings and formulate the goal we want to achieve?
II. In view of the findings, what *might* we do to reduce theft and mutilation of library materials?
   A. Types of materials (books, periodicals, etc.)?
   B. Any rearrangements?
   C. Additional facilities or staff?
   D. Publicity or campaigns?
   E. Other ideas?
   (Notice that the leader does not have any proposed solutions on this outline, but only general headings to encourage the group to think up solutions.)
III. By what criteria shall we judge our ideas for reducing theft and mutilation?
   A. Are there any absolute standards by which to judge them?
   B. What features should a solution have?

  IV.   How well does each idea measure up to our criteria?
- A.   Can we now combine or synthesize any ideas?
- B.   Are there any ideas which we can reject at face value as being unrelated to the facts or causes we have identified?
- C.   How does each remaining idea measure up to our criteria?

  V.   What will we recommend to the senate library committee?

 VI.   How will we prepare and present the report?
- A.   Who will write our actual report?
- B.   How will we present it?
- C.   Do we want to check up on what the librarian does with our recommendations?

Next is a much simpler leader's outline following the reflective thinking sequence:

  I.   What sort of written final exam should we have for our class?
- A.   How much authority (area of freedom) do we have?
- B.   What facts and feelings should we take into account as we seek to answer this question?

 II.   What are our objectives (criteria) in deciding on the type of exam?
- A.   Learning objectives?
- B.   Grades?
- C.   Type of preparation and study?
- D.   Fairness to all?

III.   What types of written final exam might we have?

IV.   What are the advantages and disadvantages of each?

 V.   What will be the form of our written exam?

Effective problem-solving discussion has been explored in depth in this chapter. We have considered a variety of ways in which decisions are made by and for small groups, and outcomes of each: expert, leader, averaging, chance, majority vote, and consensus. The research on group problem-solving procedures was reviewed, and from it a number of guidelines were derived: begin with a problem question rather than one that contains a solution; map out the problem in detail before talking about solutions, including what is unsatisfactory, contributing causes, and the exact goal; usually separate thinking up possible solutions from evaluating them; be sure the group members have agreed on criteria based on shared values before trying to reach a decision among varied possible solutions; evaluate all ideas thoroughly and critically before making a final decision; and work out specific plans to implement and follow up on solutions. Three alternative models or general procedural outlines for group problem solving were explained. Now it is up to you to put these guidelines and procedures into effect. Often you will have to "teach" a group of which you are a member to follow any outline if they are to proceed both efficiently and wisely. Effective group discussion is not common in untrained groups, nor is effective problem-solving behavior something we do naturally or intuitively. It is the result of much learning about groups and about problem solving, and of consciously applying acquired skills. May all your horses be swift and beautiful; may it never be said that your committee produced a camel for its entry in the Kentucky Derby!

Bibliography

Dewey, John, *How We Think,* Boston: D.C. Heath & Company, 1933.

Janis, Irving L., *Victims of Groupthink,* Boston: Houghton Mifflin Company, 1973.

Johnson, David W., and Johnson, Frank P., *Joining Together: Group Theory and Group Skills,* Englewood Cliffs, N.J.: Prentice-Hall, Inc., 1972, especially Chapter 3.

Kepner, Charles H., and Tregoe, Benjamin B., *The Rational Manager,* New York: McGraw-Hill Book Company, 1965.

Lee, Irving J., *How to Talk with People,* New York: Harper & Row, Publishers, 1952.

Maier, Norman R.F., *Problem Solving and Creativity in Individuals and Groups,* Belmont, Calif.: Brooks/Cole Publishing Company, 1970.

———, *Problem-Solving Discussions and Conferences,* New York: McGraw-Hill Book Company, 1963.

Osborn, Alex F., *Applied Imagination* (rev. ed.), New York: Charles Scribner's Sons, 1957.

Rubenstein, Moshe F., *Patterns of Problem Solving,* Englewood Cliffs, N.J.: Prentice-Hall, Inc., 1975, especially Chapter 1.

Key Concepts

Brainstorming—a procedure for releasing the creative potential of a group of discussants in which all criticism is ruled out for a period of time, the group works for a large number of ideas, and building on each other's suggestions is encouraged.

Consensus decision—a choice among alternatives, which all members of a group agree is the best they can make, that will be acceptable to all members.

Creative problem-solving sequence—a procedure for organizing and guiding group problem-solving discussion in which brainstorming is used to find possible solutions before discussing criteria.

Criterion—a criterion is a standard for judging among alternatives, often stated as a question; plural is "criteria."

Decision making—choosing among alternatives.

Groupthink—conformity of lower-status members to the beliefs and opinions of a high-status member or majority of a group.

Ideal solution sequence—a procedure for organizing and guiding group problem-solving discussion which puts emphasis on the acceptability of the solution to those persons who will be directly involved with it; after analysis of the problem the discussion concerns what would be an ideal solution from the point of view of all affected persons or groups.

Majority decision—decision made by vote, with at least 51 percent voting for the chosen alternative.

PERT—acronym for "Program Evaluation and Review Technique," a procedure for planning the details involved in implementing the solution to a complex problem in which many persons and resources are coordinated.

Problem—an undesired state of affairs, or the difference between what is expected and what is actually happening at some point in time; included are conditions (causes) producing the undesired state, obstacles, and some goal (desired state).

Problem question—a question calling the attention of a group to a problem without suggesting any particular type of solution.

Problem solving—procedure or series of steps through which an individual or group proceeds through time from a state of dissatisfaction to a plan for arriving at a satisfactory condition.

Reflective thinking sequence—a procedure for organizing and guiding group problem-solving discussion which puts emphasis on criteria and quality as opposed to quantity or innovativeness of possible solutions; criteria are discussed before proposing solutions, and solutions may be evaluated as soon as proposed.

Solution question—a formulation of a problem question in which is contained a solution or type of solution to the problem.

Values—deep-seated beliefs about what is good; priorities, or rank order of related things, experiences, relationships, etc.

Exercises

1. First, *rank* the following ways of making decisions in a group from 1 (most preferred) to 7 (least preferred). Second, compare your rankings with those of several other persons in a small group. Be sure to explain your reasons for the rankings you made, and listen to understand the reasons of other persons.

    ———— A. Let the leader of the group decide because she should have the right to make the decision. After all, she has the responsibilities.

    ———— B. Find out who is most expert on the topic, and let him decide what is best for the group.

    ———— C. Decide by chance, such as flipping a coin, rolling a die, or drawing straws.

    ———— D. Determine the average of what group members think.

    ———— E. Wait it out. A decision will finally emerge, or maybe if you wait long enough a decision will not be necessary.

    ———— F. Take a vote, and the majority rules. This is the American way to decide after the issues have been discussed.

    ———— G. Keep talking until you can arrive at a basic agreement from everyone as to what the decision should be. Everyone should participate in discussion until all agree you have arrived at the best possible decision the group can reach.

2. *Decision making by consensus.* Rank the following statements according to the degree to which you agree with them. Thus rank 1 is the statement you most agree with, and 5 is assigned to the statement you most disagree with. Now compare your ranks with those of several friends or classmates

in a small group. Try to arrive at a ranking for the group. In discussing your rankings, follow the guidelines for decision by consensus as outlined on page 122 as closely as possible.

_____ Sex is an expression of love and belongs in a close, enduring relationship, with or without marriage.

_____ Sex is simply a biological function; there is no reason not to experiment with it. Sex can be for showing liking, for fun, or simply for learning how to handle it.

_____ Sex is a natural expression of friendship or love.

_____ Sex apart from marriage violates the law of God. We believe people should remain virgin until married.

_____ Sex in and of itself is not bad, but it can lead young people into situations they are not ready for and cannot handle.[26]

Postdecision Reaction Sheet. On a sheet of paper record your answers to the following questions; then give the answers to your group's co-ordinator who will record them on one sheet of paper, compute the averages, and report them to your instructor who may record them on a chalkboard for discussion by the entire class.

1. How much chance to influence the group decision do you feel you had?

   1   2   3   4   5   6   7   8   9

   (none)   (a great deal)

2. How satisfied are you with the result of your group's decision-making discussion?

   1   2   3   4   5   6   7   8   9

   (very dissatisfied)   (very satisfied)

3. How well do you think other members of the group listened to and understood you?

   1   2   3   4   5   6   7   8   9

   (not at all)   (completely)

4. How much commitment do you feel to your group's decisions?

   1   2   3   4   5   6   7   8   9

   (none)   (very much)

5. What adjective best describes the atmosphere in your group during the discussion? _____

(Note: you will complete this same form after each of the next 3 exercises.)

---

26. Adapted from Johnson and Johnson, p. 63.

3.   *Decision making by majority vote.* A serious issue in a course on small group communication and discussion is whether student participation in classroom discussions should be evaluated in determining final course grades. Three alternatives are presented below. Divide the class into different groups from those used for exercise 2, with 7 or 9 members in each group. Discuss these alternatives for not more than 10 minutes, then vote for one by a show of hands. If none gets a majority, vote again between the two alternatives with the most votes.

   A.   The instructor should grade each student on participation during classroom discussions.

   B.   Students should grade each other on class participation, then each gets the average of all grades received from classmates.

   C.   Participation during classroom discussions in a course such as this should not be graded, for that makes for too much phoniness and competition.

   Now complete the Postdecision Reaction Sheet.

4.   *Decision by the group expert.* Look over the following alternatives. Then spend not more than 5 minutes deciding who in your group of 7-9 members is most expert on the subject. That person will rank the following 4 alternatives from 1 (best) to 4 (poorest), and announce the decision for the group when each group is called on to report its decision to the entire class. Meanwhile, you should also rank them in private. When your "group" decision has been announced, complete the Postdecision Reaction Sheet; your coordinator will tabulate and announce the results.

   _____   Women should have the right to an abortion on demand.

   _____   Abortion should be permitted only when both father and mother sign a statement requesting it.

   _____   Abortion should be illegal.

   _____   Women should be allowed to have an abortion only if a panel of physicians agrees that the pregnancy will be dangerous to the mother's life, or if the pregnancy resulted from rape.

5.   *Decision by the leader.* The class should be divided into new groups. One person in each group is appointed "leader" by the instructor. Each group is to observe some other group (on or off campus) during one of its meetings and make a record of each decision made and how it is made. Then the group will write a report based on their observations as a group. The instructor will list several groups you might observe. After a brief discussion about which to observe, the leader must announce to the other members of your group which of the possible groups you will observe, analyze, and describe in your report. Also, the leader will state when you will meet to write the report. The leader should explain why his or her decision is the best possible for your group. As soon as this has been done complete the Postdecision Reaction Sheet.

6.   Your instructor may want to tabulate the results from several methods of decision making in groups, obtained from the Postdecision Reaction Sheets. These can be tabulated as shown on p. 154, with all group averages (computed by the coordinators) and an average of these averages shown in each cell.

Decision Method	1. Degree of Personal Influence	2. How Satisfied with Decision	3. How well Listened to	4. How Committed
Consensus				
Majority				
Expert				
Leader				

Your instructor may also want you to try decision making by other procedures, and tabulate reactions to them. Compare your results. What do you learn from them?

7. Write three problem questions which might be discussed by a small group from your class. Present these either to your instructor or to a group of classmates for evaluation in the following areas: clarity, problem or solution, area of freedom of the class, competence of class.

8. Select problem questions obtained through exercise 7. Write leader's outlines for guiding discussion of a problem for which the creative problem-solving pattern, the ideal solution pattern, and the reflective thinking pattern are appropriate. Compare your outlines with those done by three or four classmates, then construct one outline acceptable to all of you.

9. With an observer to report how orderly the discussion appears to be, actually discuss the problem, following the outline agreed upon by your group.

6
Leading Discussions

The idea that leaders are important in discussion groups is virtually unquestioned. But many of us have feelings of ambivalence toward serving as leaders ourselves, and toward the leaders of groups to which we belong. Although almost everyone likes to be recognized as a leader, many people hesitate to learn the skills required or to take on the responsibilities of the leader role, perhaps for fear of failing or looking foolish. We may both respect and resent our leaders in a sort of love/hate relationship. As Cathcart and Samovar said,

> There is no lack of leaders or leadership and apparently no successful groups without leadership. Even when some members of a group consciously avoid leader roles, others arise to fill the void. The question then becomes not one of whether there should or should not be leaders but what constitutes the most effective and desirable leadership for a given group.[1]

Before you proceed further with the reading of this chapter, complete the following scale of leadership philosophy developed by Sargent and Miller.

SARGENT AND MILLER LEADERSHIP SCALE

We are interested in the things that are important to you when you are leading a group discussion. Listed below are several pairs of statements. Read each pair of statements and place a mark in the

1. Robert S. Cathcart and Larry A. Samovar, *Small Group Communication: A Reader,* 2nd ed. (Dubuque: Wm. C. Brown Company Publishers, 1974), p. 350.

one you believe to be of greater importance. On reacting to the statements, observe the following ground rules:

1. Place your check marks clearly and carefully.
2. Do not omit any of the items.
3. Never check both of the items.
4. Do not look back and forth through the items; make each item a separate and independent judgment.
5. Your first impression, the immediate feelings about the statements, is what we want.

1. a. _____ To give everyone a chance to express his opinion.
   b. _____ To know what the group and its members are doing.
2. a. _____ To assign members to tasks so more can be accomplished.
   b. _____ To let the members reach a decision all by themselves.
3. a. _____ To know what the group and its members are doing.
   b. _____ To help the members see how the discussion is related to the purposes of the group.
4. a. _____ To assist the group in getting along well together.
   b. _____ To help the group to what you think is their best answer.
5. a. _____ To get the job done.
   b. _____ To let the members reach a decision all by themselves.
6. a. _____ To know what the group and its members are doing.
   b. _____ To let the members reach a decision all by themselves.
7. a. _____ To get the job done.
   b. _____ To assist the group in getting along well together.
8. a. _____ To help the members see how the discussion is related to the purposes of the group.
   b. _____ To assign members to tasks so more can be accomplished.
9. a. _____ To ask questions that will cause members to do more thinking.
   b. _____ To get the job done.
10. a. _____ To let the members reach a decision all by themselves.
    b. _____ To give new information when you feel the members are ready for it.

Figure 6.1. The Sargent and Miller Leadership Scale. (F. Sargent and G. Miller, "Some Differences in Certain Communication Behaviors of Autocratic and Democratic Group Leaders," *Journal of Communication* 21 [1971], pp. 233-252.)

Now go to page 185 to score your scale and locate your position on the autocratic-democratic dimension of discussion leadership. With this in mind, you should get more out of your reading of the rest of this chapter.

The style and method of leadership have been matters of increasing concern to small-group researchers and theorists since the early 1940s. Prior to that time it was widely believed that leaders were specially gifted people who were "born to lead," and that there was little anyone could do to develop leadership skills. John Stuart Mill, the famous English philosopher, popularized this view over a hundred years ago. Even today, despite research findings to the contrary, we often act as if we believe there is some mystical quality of leadership which, if possessed, makes one a leader in virtually any situation. Generals are assumed to be capable of supplying effective leadership in education or government; football captains are elected to class offices; great teachers are made chairpersons of committees—and all too often the results are dismal.

People who keep abreast of research in leadership—and there has been a vast amount of it in recent years—know better. Leadership is not *a* quality or personality trait; leadership skills can be learned. Training people to diagnose and supply the changing leadership functions needed by a group has made many organizations more productive. Businesses and government agencies constantly look for people able to work with and lead others, then give them further specialized training in management theory and practice, human relations, listening, conference leadership, group dynamics, and speaking. The armed forces conduct training and retraining programs in leadership skills for officers of all ranks. Community action groups develop grassroots leadership through elaborate training programs. Unions conduct leadership training programs, often in conjunction with universities, to develop skills in their rank and file. In short, there is a great demand for people skilled at leading, and to develop such people a lot of money is spent on training.

Money and time spent on developing discussion leadership skills are invested wisely. As we have seen, discussion is fundamental to democratic organization and cooperation. No discussion group can be effective without appropriate leadership—and that means skilled leaders. Whenever a group has a designated leader (either elected or appointed), that person can almost literally "make or break" the group. In my own research studies I found that the degree of success in goal achievement and member satisfaction by adult study groups was so closely related to the leader's behavior that I often said: "Let me watch the leader for fifteen minutes and I will predict whether or not the group will be successful." Countless committees and task groups have faltered and accomplished little when the chairperson did not know how to perform as leader. I once watched a dramatic change occur among faculty members of a high school when the principal was replaced. Academic departments of a university are greatly affected by the way the chairman or head functions as a coordinator and administrator of faculty efforts. Recently a group of personnel in a university drew up a bill of particulars to support a vote of no confidence in their administrator; they charged that "He is singularly inept in conducting our meetings." Yes, leaders make a great difference in how effectively small groups function.

In this book we are not concerned with leadership in all types of groups, but only with leadership of discussion groups. What is expected of the designated discussion leader? What should be the leader's relationship to the rest of the group members to maximize satisfaction and productivity? In this chapter, we will first consider the concepts of leader and leadership; second, principles of effective leadership in discussion; third, a philosophy of leadership style; fourth, the special responsibilities of a discussion leader, and techniques for meeting these responsibilities.

As a result of reading and studying the issues raised in this chapter, you should:

1. Be able to distinguish among the concepts of "leadership," "leader," "designated leader," and "head."
2. Formulate a theoretical definition of discussion leadership that is situational, task-oriented, and accounts for behavioral characteristics.
3. Be able to describe behavioral characteristics usually found in the performances of effective discussion leaders.
4. Develop a personal philosophy of facilitative democratic leadership, and be able to cite research studies in support of this philosophy.
5. Be able to list and define the responsibilities and duties usually expected by a group of a designated discussion leader.
6. Be able to explain at least two or three techniques for managing each of a variety of problem members.
7. Be able to explain the process by which leaders emerge in initially leaderless task groups.
8. Respond appropriately as leader in the presence of disruptive member behaviors, disorganization, miscommunication, groupthink, unimaginative thinking, or other discussion inadequacies requiring specific leader techniques and skills.

LEADERS AND LEADERSHIP

It is possible for a discussion group to have no designated leader and yet to have excellent leadership. It is also possible for a discussion group to have a leader and yet be woefully lacking in leadership. If these statements seem paradoxical, it is only because the terms *leader* and *leadership* are confusing due to overlapping meanings.

Leadership refers to any behavior which helps a group clarify and achieve group goals. Social scientists are virtually unanimous in defining leadership as *influence.* The definition given by Tannenbaum, Weschler, and Massarik is typical: "We define leadership as *interpersonal influence, exercised in situation and directed, through the communication process, toward the attainment of a specified goal or goals.*"[2] Only that influence which is directed toward *group*

2. Robert Tannenbaum, Irving R. Weschler, and Fred Massarik, *Leadership and Organizations: A Behavioral Science Approach* (New York: McGraw-Hill Book Company, 1961), p. 24.

goals will be called group leadership, thereby excluding behavior in which one member influences another to work apart from or contrary to the good of the group. Excluded would be influence irrelevant to group goals, such as one member emulating the mannerisms of another or getting another to join him for refreshments after a meeting (unless that act is to achieve greater harmony in the group). Likewise, the use of force, threat, or power to influence another to comply will not be called group leadership. Leadership is not exercised when a follower has no choice but to obey or be harmed; that is compulsion.

When formal organizations appoint persons to positions of control and dominance over others, have they made group leaders? For example, does hiring a person as supervisor make her the leader of the workers? The answer depends partly on how you define "leadership." Gibb chose to call *all* influence from such an appointed position *headship* rather than *leadership*, and made these two concepts mutually exclusive. To be a head, to Gibb, meant to dominate, whereas to be a leader meant to gain the volunteered consent of those influenced. When one is appointed head, Gibb claimed, there could not be a group at all; the group goal is determined by the head in his own self-interest, and there is inevitably a wide social gap between the group members and head.[3] However, Gibb's definition of "headship" is almost the same as that usually provided for "autocratic leadership" by other writers. And very often a person in a "head" position influences both by positional domination and by democratic leadership, varying his style from task to task, moment to moment, as the situation facing him and the group changes. The "head" can clearly indicate when she is making the decisions, when she (or someone above her) is determining the goals, etc., and when these are in the area of freedom of the group. In short, Gibb greatly oversimplified by stating that a head cannot *lead*, and that a leader does not at times use positional influence (*headship*). Knowing the skills of leadership can be very important to the head who wants to build the teamwork, creativity, and cohesiveness that is possible when members of production work groups participate in decision making as much as feasible.

Discussion leadership is the responsibility of all members of a small group; it will usually be shared by several of them. It is now believed the tasks which were considered to be the sole responsibility of the leader (introducing the problem, guiding the discussion, probing, spreading participation, clarifying, resolving disagreements, asking questions, etc.) can better be handled by many members of a group. Some people may have more skills at certain leadership tasks, have special knowledge, or sensitivity to what the designated leader has missed. If so a *leadership team* emerges. Even though the leadership functioning may be dif-

3. Cecil A. Gibb, "The Principles and Traits of Leadership," in Robert S. Cathcart and Larry A. Samovar, eds., *Small Group Communication: A Reader* (Dubuque: Wm. C. Brown Company Publishers, 1970), p. 373.

fused within a group, the management of a business or governmental organization will hold the designated leader responsible for the productivity of the group. Nor are leaders of small groups in civic and church groups exempt from such responsibility: ". . . group members and outsiders tend to hold the leader accountable for group beliefs, proposals, actions, and products."[4]

The term *leader* is used in this book to refer to any person who is viewed by group members as a leader or any person who is designated (by appointment or election) as such and who as a consequence becomes a coordinator of the efforts of group members. Most discussion groups are more efficient and democratic if there is a designated leader, provided that leader has the support of the group and behaves as a member among equals. The Minnesota Studies of discussion groups showed clearly that "leaderless" groups are unproductive unless a leader (as perceived by the group members) emerges. But a designated leader is wise to encourage other members to also lead (in the sense of exerting influence) according to their skills and the needs of the group. Supporting this point, Bales found that task and social leadership are rarely performed equally well by the same person.[5] In a group there may be several people who lead: one who gets the group oriented and keeps talk coordinated and directed toward the goal, some who supply needed information, others who take the lead in finding and testing possible solutions to problems, and others who harmonize and reduce tensions. But there should be one *primary leader* as perceived by both members of the group and outsiders.

A designated leader has a special responsibility to maintain perspective and to see that all needed leadership services are performed. In this regard, Schutz described the function of a leader in a group as a *completer:* ". . . the best a leader can do is to observe what functions are not being performed by a segment of the group and enable this part to accomplish them."[6] As Schutz says, the prime requisites to being a leader are: knowing necessary group functions; sensing unfulfilled group functions; performing and getting others to perform needed functions; and being willing to take necessary action, even if personally displeasing. This concept of the "leader as completer" is a powerful guide to anyone who wants to be an effective discussion leader, and emphasizes again the importance of having some image of optimal group discussion such as was presented in Chapter 2.

The ideal, then, is a group in which most leadership functions are shared, with the designated leader doing whatever no one else can do as well. The proportion

4. Ernest Stech and Sharon A. Ratliffe, *Working in Groups* (Skokie, Ill.: National Textbook Company, 1976), p. 201.

5. Robert F. Bales, "Task Roles and Social Roles in Problem Solving Groups," in E.E. Maccoby, T.M. Newcomb, and E.L. Hartley, eds., *Reading in Social Psychology,* 3rd ed. (New York: Holt, Rinehart and Winston, Inc., 1958), pp. 437-447.

6. William C. Schutz, "The Leader as Completer," in Cathcart and Samovar, eds., *Small Group Communication,* p. 400.

of the total leadership which he or she supplies will vary greatly, depending on the way in which the group was formed, the expectations of the members, and other variables. Leadership at any moment is determined by an interaction of the external situation facing the group, the expectations and desires of the members, and the personalities and skills of the members. The *leader's* role is in part a result of interaction between the leader and other group members.

One-meeting groups should almost always have designated leaders. In a one-meeting group the designated leader will likely do most of the organizing, clarifying, summarizing and other procedural tasks; concomitantly, he or she will probably do little suggesting or evaluating of ideas. In a continuing group, routines will develop with members taking on specialized roles; after a time, the designated leader may be able to participate very much like any other member. As members take on tasks of leadership and develop skill in them, the designated leader's proportion of leadership will decline. However, the designated leader will always be expected to serve as coordinator and spokesperson for the group.

CHARACTERISTICS OF EFFECTIVE DISCUSSION LEADERS

What are the characteristics of an effective leader of discussion groups? The answer depends on many factors. From research it is possible to identify many factors which determine the leadership of a discussion group. There is no single trait or characteristic of "leadership," but by developing certain skills and behavior patterns discussed in the following paragraphs you can learn to serve well as a designated leader, chairperson, or moderator.

Although leadership depends on the complex field of forces and personalities in each different group, certain people do tend to emerge again and again as small group leaders.[7] Bird, in 1940, attempted to identify traits of leaders, but found little consistency from study to study, perhaps due to inadequacy of measurements, the variety of tasks and groups, or other uncontrolled variables.[8] He suggested that personality traits of a leader may be functions of the situation. Stogdill surveyed the literature bearing on leader traits, with only slightly more encouraging results than Bird: leaders as a group tended to be superior in intelligence and scholarship, responsibility, activity and social participation, and sociometric status.[9]

A very comprehensive set of studies of leadership covering fifteen years of research was reported by Fiedler, who developed the "contingency" theory of

---

7. Edgar F. Borgatta, Arthur S. Couch, and Robert F. Bales, "Some Findings Relevant to the Great Man Theory of Leadership," *American Sociological Review* 19 (1954), pp. 755-759.

8. C. Bird, *Social Psychology* (New York: Appleton-Century-Crofts, 1940).

9. Ralph Stogdill, "Personal Factors Associated with Leadership: A Survey of Literature," *Journal of Psychology* 25 (1948), pp. 35-71.

leadership—the type of leader who will function best in a particular situation depends on the type of problem facing the group and the members of the group. His groups included athletic teams, business management groups, crews of bombers and tanks, surveying teams, and policy-making committees. Fiedler concluded that the effectiveness of a group is dependent upon how appropriate the leader's style is to the group situation, that socially distant leaders are more productive in groups having such highly structured tasks as winning a game or surveying, and that a human-relations or group-centered style of leadership is most effective when the group is engaged in such relatively unstructured tasks as decision making and problem solving. Thus the typical committee chairperson would need to be ". . . considerate of the feelings and opinions of his members . . . permissive and nonthreatening."[10]

A productive approach to the study of leader characteristics, especially in discussion groups, was undertaken by John Geier at the University of Minnesota. Initially leaderless groups were questioned regularly to determine which members were perceived as exerting leadership and if a consensus leader had emerged. Both directly observable behaviors of persons who emerged as leaders and traits perceived by fellow group members were examined. In the successful groups, definite consensus leaders emerged; in all groups much energy was spent on a struggle for leader status. A clear pattern of leader emergence was found with two phases to it. During the relatively short and conflict-free first phase of leader emergence, participants with three types of characteristics were eliminated from a bid for the leader spot: the uninformed members (on the problem facing the group); the infrequent participants; and the rigid or dogmatic members who expressed their opinions categorically and were not subject to the influence of other members. The second phase in the struggle for the leader position could be either relatively short or prolonged with approximately forty percent of the group members still competing for preeminence. First, those who were authoritarian and manipulative in their methods were eliminated in favor of the more democratic. The final characteristic of behavior eliminating remaining contenders was called "offensive verbalization" by Geier, and included such behaviors as "incessant talking and stilted speech." It is also important to note that in the majority of groups where a leader emerged, another person who had contended for the leader post emerged as a "lieutenant."[11]

However, outside of classrooms or university laboratories the emergence process is seldom allowed to operate naturally. Leaders are either designated by

10. Fred E. Fiedler, "Situational and Personality Determinants of Leadership Effectiveness," in Dorwin Cartwright and Alvin Zander, eds., *Group Dynamics: Research and Theory,* 3rd ed. (New York: Harper & Row, Publishers, 1968). pp. 362-380.
11. John C. Geier, "A Trait Approach to the Study of Leadership in Small Groups," *Journal of Communication* 17 (1967), pp. 316-323.

a parent organization to a small group or selected by the members very early in the history of the group. Then the appointed leader undergoes a period of testing. If the selected leader would have emerged naturally, the group is able to get to its major business quickly and efficiently. But if the new leader comes to be perceived by the group as ineffective, he will be ignored or deposed, and the process of emergence will proceed, now delayed and impeded by the presence of an unsatisfactory designated leader.

From these findings and others cited below we can now form some definite suggestions for the behavior of small group discussion leaders.

Effective discussion leaders have a good grasp of the problem facing the group. They are informed (Geier), good at analysis, and have promising ideas for solving the problem. Maier, for example, demonstrated that leaders who have worthwhile ideas, if skilled in group techniques, produce better group outcomes than those who do not.[12] Larson discovered that emergent leaders initiated more themes or issues which were discussed by the group than did nonleaders.[13] Knutson and Holdridge found that leaders were more likely than nonleaders to engage in "orientation" behaviors, which are "message behaviors which reflected an attempt . . . to resolve conflict, facilitate achievement of the group's goal, make helpful suggestions, or lessen tension. . . ."[14]

Effective discussion leaders are skilled in organizing group thinking. Wilson found that persons who emerged as effective problem-solving discussion leaders had a much better than average grasp of the process of reflective thinking.[15] Brilhart found that study discussion leaders selected by participants as future leaders were unusually skilled in organizing discussions.[16] Maier demonstrated the value of leaders skilled in organizing group thinking.[17] To be an effective leader of discussions, you need to become familiar with patterns for group thinking, be able to suggest an appropriate pattern for any problem, be skilled at detecting tangents during discussion, and be able to bring the group back on track.

12. Norman R.F. Maier, "The Quality of Group Decisions as Influenced by the Discussion Leader," *Human Relations* 3 (1950), pp. 155-174.

13. Charles U. Larson, "Attention Span and the Leader," paper presented to Central States Speech Association Convention, April, 1969.

14. T.J. Knutson and W.E. Holdridge, "Orientation Behavior, Leadership, and Consensus: A Possible Functional Relationship," *Speech Monographs* 42 (1975), pp. 107-114.

15. Carl L. Wilson, "An Experimental Study of Selected Correlates of Emergent Leadership During Problem-Solving Discussion" (D. Ed. dissertation, Pennsylvania State College, 1953).

16. John K. Brilhart, "An Exploratory Study of Relations Between the Evaluating Process and Associated Behavior of Participants in Six Study-Discussion Groups" (Ph.D. dissertation, Pennsylvania State University, 1962).

17. See Norman R.F. Maier, *Problem Solving and Creativity in Individuals and Groups* (Belmont, Cal.: Brooks-Cole Publishing Company, 1970), pp. 253-277.

Effective discussion leaders are active in participation. They are above average for group members in frequency of verbal participation, yet not excessive talkers. They are never reticent in a small group, implying that such emergent leaders have a favorable self-concept, nor overly defensive or "sensitive" about being criticized or disagreed with. Morris and Hackman, like Geier, found emergent leaders to be among the most frequent participants in discussion groups (not necessarily the *most* frequent).[18] To be relatively quiet in a group is to have no chance to emerge as a leader, and to maintain the position of leader a member must be verbally active.

Effective discussion leaders speak well. Ability to speak clearly has been shown to be important to success in all social contexts. The able discussion leader speaks to the group as a whole in clear, impartial terms. His remarks are concise, organized, and pertinent. As Geier found, chosen leaders are *not* tactless, chattering, offensive speakers. Russell found that leaders of problem-solving groups were distinguishable from other members by higher degrees of communicative skill.[19] Lashbrook also found that leaders were perceived as speaking more clearly and fluently than were other group members.[20] Discussion leaders are most certainly characterized by special facility in verbalizing the goals, values, ideas, and ideals of their groups.

Effective discussion leaders are open-minded. I found that study-discussion leaders chosen by participants as future leaders were much more conditional in the way they expressed judgments than were leaders not chosen as future leaders. Maier and Solem demonstrated that a leader who suspends judgment and encourages full consideration of minority viewpoints is more effective than one who does not.[21] I have repeatedly given "dogmatism" and "authoritarianism" tests to students in discussion classes, and found that students most often chosen as leaders by classmates tended to score much better on these measures of open-mindedness. Haiman reported similar findings for his classes when using these scales and an "open-mindedness" scale which he devised.[22] The picture is clear: effective discussion leaders are more open-minded than average participants and can encourage open-minded consideration by participants.

18. Charles G. Morris and J.R. Hackman, "Behavioral Correlates of Perceived Leadership," *Journal of Personality and Social Psychology* 13 (1969), pp. 350-361.

19. Hugh C. Russell, "Dimensions of the Communicative Behavior of Discussion Leaders," paper presented to Central States Speech Convention, April, 1970.

20. Velma J. Lashbrook, "Gibb's Interaction Theory: The Use of Perceptions in the Discrimination of Leaders from Nonleaders" (Paper presented to Speech Communication Convention, December, 1975).

21. Norman R.F. Maier and A.R. Solem, "The Contributions of a Discussion Leader to the Quality of Group Thinking: The Effective Use of Minority Opinions," *Human Relations* 5 (1952), pp. 277-288.

22. Franklyn S. Haiman (From a paper given at the Annual Convention of the Speech Association of America, December, 1964).

Effective discussion leaders are democratic and consultative. Recall the findings of Geier and Fiedler supporting this advice. Likewise, Solem found that ideas suggested by designated leaders tend to be accepted or rejected uncritically rather than on their merits, pointing to the need for a "head" leader to be especially consultative and democratic when leading problem-solving discussion.[23] Rosenfeld and Plax found that democratic leaders asked more questions, attempted to answer less, and were more concerned with encouraging other members to participate than autocratic leaders. These democratic leaders were egalitarians, "feeling equal to both superiors and subordinates . . . people are equals with whom they work, the rewards, and the punishments are to be shared."[24]

Effective discussion leaders have respect for and sensitivity to others. In the kinds of relatively unstructured tasks facing most problem-solving groups, Fiedler reported that the most productive groups were led by people skilled in human relations who took a group-centered approach. In another study, leaders were found to be more empathic than other members of a variety of types of small groups. To be truly democratic, a discussion leader must trust the group and believe in its collective wisdom. Such leaders have been found to have a high opinion of all group members as people. They are careful not to attack or cause others to lose face, but to accept members as they are, keeping the critical comments centered on issues. Rosenfeld and Plax found that democratic leaders of discussion groups made more positive socio-emotional responses than did autocratic leaders, and that autocratic leaders were less sympathetic than democratic.[25]

The skilled leader is especially aware of how others are reacting, for example when a hesitant member wants to speak or the group is approaching consensus. That implies, of course, that able discussion leaders are *excellent listeners,* patient, able to summarize accurately and respond relevantly to what was said and meant.

Effective discussion leaders can take on distinctive roles. Many studies have shown that effective discussion leaders can take on roles distinctively different from those of other group members.[26] I found the most effective study-discussion leaders were those who asked more questions, gave more procedural guidance, and expressed fewer personal opinions than other members. Berkowitz

23. Arthur R. Solem, "An Evaluation of Two Attitudinal Approaches to Delegation," *Journal of Applied Psychology* 22 (1958), pp. 36-39.

24. Lawrence B. Rosenfeld, *Now That We're All Here . . . Relations in Small Groups* (Columbus, Ohio: Charles E. Merrill Publishing Company, 1976), pp. 75-76.

25. *Ibid.*

26. A. Paul Hare, *Handbook of Small Group Research* (New York: The Free Press of Glencoe, 1962), Chapter XI.

found when task pressures were not urgent, conferees preferred a chairman whose role was distinct, characterized by strong procedural control.[27] The concept of the "leader as completer" indicates the need for role flexibility, as does Fiedler's "contingency theory of leadership." You are well advised to practice and develop skill in as many of the task, procedural, and maintenance functions of group interaction as possible.

Effective discussion leaders share rewards and give credit to the group. They readily praise the group for successes, not taking credit or glory to themselves. They stress teamwork and look for ways to make members feel important to the group.

Still more terms could be used to characterize the behavioral style of effective democratic discussion leaders in groups of peers, but the major findings that have shown up with some consistency in recent research have been described sufficiently for you to form an image of the ideal small group discussion leader: informed, egalitarian, organized, knowledgeable, a skilled problem solver, active and outgoing, democratic, respectful and accepting of other persons, non-manipulative, articulate without being verbose, flexible, and group-centered.

TOWARD A PHILOSOPHY AND STYLE OF DISCUSSION LEADERSHIP

How one acts as a discussion leader depends in large part on his or her philosophy of leadership. A large number of writers have described the differences between the styles of autocratic and democratic leaders. These styles rest on distinct philosophies of leadership. Under normal conditions the discussion group leader will be most effective if democratic (group-centered) in style, controlling procedures with the consent of the group and helping the group reach consensual decisions based on thorough understanding and analysis of problems, creativity in solution finding, and hard-nosed critical thinking in reaching decisions.

A highly illuminating analogy to the function of the group-centered discussion leader is provided by Maier in his comparison of the starfish to a human problem-solving group. The leader is likened to the central nerve ring of the starfish, and the members to its rays. When the nerve ring is intact, it connects and coordinates the rays, and the starfish is very efficient in its movements. If the ring is severed, the rays can influence each other's behaviors to a degree, but internal coordination is missing. If one ray is stimulated to step forward (perhaps to seize a clam), the adjoining rays sense the pull on them and also begin to step forward, showing coordinated behavior based on external control. But if opposite rays are stimulated simultaneously, the animal becomes locked in position as each ray tries to move in opposite directions; this can even tear the starfish in

---

27. Leonard Berkowitz, "Sharing Leadership In Small, Decision-Making Groups," *Journal of Abnormal and Social Psychology* 48 (1953), pp. 231-238.

two and destroy it. The central nerve ring does none of the moving, but it coordinates the behavior of all the rays. Thus we get the coordinated behavior of a higher type organism rather than the summed efforts of five rays physically together but not coordinated unless one dominates the others. The ring does not do the work, but collects the information from all rays and produces an organismically unified response rather than a collection of individual responses which may or may not be interrelated. Maier likens the function of a group-centered discussion leader to that of the central nerve ring: "Thus the leader does not serve as a dominant ray and produce the solution. Rather, his function is to receive information, facilitate communication between the individuals, relay messages, and integrate the incoming responses so that a single unified response occurs."[28] Coordinating is acknowledged by virtually all writers to be the primary function of designated discussion leaders, but **how** it should be performed is a central question in small group leadership philosophy.

An autocratic discussion leader seeks to impose his will, belief, or solution on the group. The result is a pseudodiscussion during which the group goes through the motions of discussion but the end result is predetermined by the leader. Under an autocrat, no one speaks unless permitted by the leader. Everyone's ideas are judged by the leader. He decides on the exact order of events on the agenda and the sequence in which a problem will be discussed. He may listen to advice but when he has made up his mind, the "group decision" has been made. Power resides in this one person rather than in the group. He acts like the dominant ray of a nerve-severed starfish rather than as a coordinating leader. Such a leader rarely announces the agenda of a meeting in advance, nor does he often help inform members. Armed with a private agenda and as the only fully prepared person, he can readily dominate the other discussants. For example, an autocrat in the classroom decides just what questions will be discussed, and the "right" answer to each. When such hard-sell tactics fail to gain support, the autocrat may turn on the group, calling the members lazy, stupid, uncaring, or irresponsible.

If an autocratically inclined leader lacks the power of an absolute head, she may use all sorts of "soft-sell" manipulative techniques to seduce agreement. She is interested in whatever will advance her ideas and purposes; she may interrupt and ignore or argue with anything contrary, often without trying to understand the other speaker's point of view. A "divide and conquer" approach may be tried, by setting up a one-to-one communication network with a lot of "sweet talk" and politicking with promises of personal rewards to members who give support. Such an autocrat distorts summaries toward her purpose and states ideas with highly emotive language. Sometimes she coerces an agreement by preventing the group from making a decision until time for the meeting has

28. Norman R.F. Maier, "Assets and Liabilities in Group Problem Solving: The Need for an Integrative Function," in *Problem Solving and Creativity . . .,* pp. 438-439.

almost run out, then pressuring others to accept her solution. She may coerce participation from a member who prefers not to speak by saying something like "Tim, what do you think of that?" or "Mary, don't you agree?"

On what assumptions would you base your personal style of leadership? An autocratic style rests on the beliefs that a few select people (of which the autocrat is one) are specially endowed, that the majority are incapable or irresponsible, that the way to get people to act is to give them personal rewards and punishments. Such premises underlie the governing techniques of dictators, paternalists, and discussion leaders who predetermine the result which their groups should reach.

A democratic style of leadership is based on the belief that the collective wisdom is greater than that of any single member. In the words of Thomas Jefferson: "I know of no safe depository of the ultimate powers of society but the people themselves."[29] Fundamental to democratic leadership is the belief that all persons affected by a decision should have a voice in making the decision. In a democratic climate, any attempt to coerce or manipulate is both immoral and impractical. Immoral because manipulation destroys the human capacity to reason and decide for one's self. Impractical because manipulation when sensed leads to apathy, resistance, or even counterforce. A democratic leader participates with the group in making decisions concerning both the procedure and substance of discussions. He or she serves the group rather than making it a servant to self-serving ends.

The democratic discussion leader, in contrast to the autocratic leader, seeks to discover the group's will and facilitate its achievement. A discussion of this sort can never be predetermined by anyone, but will be the result of interaction. With democratic leadership, discussants speak when they want to, at least within the procedural norms adopted *by the group*. All ideas are treated as group property, and judgment of them is the responsibility of the entire group. All authority for decision making resides in the group. Influence comes primarily from information, ideas, and skills in doing what is needed to achieve mutually acceptable goals. When discussion leadership is democratic, everyone has equal opportunity to prepare himself for discussion. Even establishing the agenda and the pattern for discussing a topic or problem is the prerogative of the group, not a single member (or leader). All power exercised by the designated leader is granted by the group for the group's good. Such a leader may suggest and encourage, but will not compel, coerce, or manipulate. Ideally, a designated leader's approval is no more important than that of any other member. Such leadership is facilitative rather than restrictive in regard to the group's area of freedom.

29. Saul Padover, ed., *Thomas Jefferson on Democracy* (New York: Appleton-Century-Croft, 1939), p. 162.

In practice, a democratic leader will suggest procedures, but will not impose them. He may suggest a plan or solution, but will be quite ready to follow any procedure or accept any solution which the group, by consensus, prefers. For example: "What do you think about . . .," rather than, "We will. . . ."

Both autocratic and democratic styles of discussion leadership are in stark contrast to what is often called a laissez-faire style. It is not leadership, but an abdication of responsibility for leading. The laissez-faire "leader" does virtually nothing. In practice, he or she may open a discussion by saying: "It's about time we started our discussion," then sit back, exert no influence, and do virtually nothing to organize, clarify, or promote a solution. Into the void someone must step, or the group will flounder aimlessly. The usual result is either anarchy or a struggle for status. A group of skilled discussants, given this kind of appointed leader, may proceed fairly well, but all too often they waste time or else an autocrat takes over. Apathy and frustration are common.

Many times a designated discussion leader is in a headship position as part of a larger organization, and so may need to exert bureaucratic leadership. For example, a foreman is charged by his superiors with seeing that certain tasks are accomplished by the work group. A study-discussion leader is partly responsible to the organization sponsoring the study-discussion program (often a university, public library, or great books foundation). The chairperson of a committee appointed to carry out a task or to make recommendations is responsible to the parent body. A department head is bound by regulations and responsibilities which cannot be ignored. Such a bureaucratic leader must make clear the area of freedom of the group, and the limits placed on him and the group. It is essential that a "head" make clear when the decision will be made by the group and when she is only seeking information and advice on which to base a decision. Some of the topics to be discussed, the procedures to be followed during discussion, and specific recommendations or solutions to be applied can be determined by the group as a whole.

Designated task leaders (heads of departments, foremen, officers, even committee chairpersons) seeking a group decision often find the group waiting for the leader's analysis of the problem and solution to it, which the group members then tend to accept or reject apart from its merits in fact and logic. For this reason designated leaders are generally well advised to refrain from suggesting solutions, at least until after group members have suggested a number of them.

A remedy may be for a head to adopt a nondirective style of leading which puts responsibility on the group for directing their activities. The leader must exercise great self-control, withholding leadership at critical junctures, even letting the group flounder at times, so that participants will develop their own skills and motives. The nondirective leader will call attention to problems facing the group, whether of task or group maintenance, but will not solve them. On some occasions he or she may suggest and invite other alternatives, but will still leave the decision to the group. This is not an abdication of leadership. Whereas the laissez-faire "leader" does nothing, a nondirective leader works very hard, listens intently, and reflects her observations back to the group. He may clarify a problem, supply information, or summarize what he has noticed, but he always asks the group if they agree. He will ask many questions and will rebound to the group questions calling for his judgment or opinion. In time she can lead democratically and still discharge all responsibilities to a superior or parent body by making clear to all group members what must be done. Once members are accustomed to accepting responsibility for making decisions which affect them, they will not often want it any other way.

FUNCTIONS AND RESPONSIBILITIES OF THE DISCUSSION LEADER

A designated discussion leader cannot evade the responsibility for certain tasks and functions. Most adults are members of many small groups, and have neither the time nor the resources available to keep abreast of all details, regulations, and changes in the groups. Often we come rushing into a meeting, literally out of breath, with our minds still occupied by other matters. In this condition we try to orient ourselves to another discussion. If our leaders (or teachers) greet us with, "Well, what shall we do today?" we are likely to be irritated and to get nothing done. Students with five classes a day and businessmen with several conferences a day must place special responsibilities on designated discussion leaders. The leader in such cases has a special job to do, and doing it well will foster group cohesiveness, acceptance of solutions, and responsibility for the group's success by members. The group still retains the power to decide within its area of freedom, and can act more wisely because the leader has served it well.

If an appointed discussion leader is to coordinate the activities of members of a group, he or she must decide on the *amount and kind of procedural control* to exercise. There are times when strict control of content, organization, or other aspects of the discussion is necessary in order to bring about cooperative and efficient problem solving. From a study of problem-solving conferences in business and governmental agencies, Berkowitz found that there was a consistent tendency for members to prefer that the chairperson exercise the function of coordinating group process and procedural control without sharing these with other members, except that in matters of extreme involvement and urgency this norm was suspended in favor of sharing leadership.[30] Heyns and others have confirmed this finding in subsequent research.[31]

---

30. Leonard Berkowitz, "Sharing Leadership in Small Decision-Making Groups," *Journal of Abnormal and Social Psychology* 48 (1953), pp. 231-238.

31. Roger Heyns, "Effects of Variation in Leadership on Participant Behavior in Discussion Groups" (Unpublished doctoral dissertation, University of Michigan, 1958).

When working with peers, many leaders err because of too little control. When rank, status, or age creates a gulf between a designated leader and the rest of the group, the tendency is to exert too much control. Each designated leader must decide his own course, but he should be constantly reviewing it for needed changes. In short, while developing a unique role the leader must experiment to find out what most helps a particular group achieve its goals.

Normally, it is necessary to exert more control on procedures in the early part of a discussion or in the early life of a group than later. It is *wiser to supply too much procedural control than too little.* Once initial order has been established it is easy to relax controls. To bring order out of chaos is most difficult. A few guidelines may help the designated leader determine what to do:

1. *Group expectations* should be determined and adapted to. At least initially, a group leader will need to conform to what the members expect in this role.
2. *Group purpose* affects leader control. Learning, cathartic, or value-sharing groups usually need far less structure and control than groups facing complex problems.
3. *Group methods* vary in the amount of control needed. Brainstorming, buzz group procedures, a problem census, or the RISK technique require strict procedural control, whereas a less complex pattern for organizing group thinking will take far less procedural control from a designated leader.
4. *Membership skills and maturity* must be taken into account. Members with training and experience in discussion are much more able to share in leadership than are members with little or no training in discussion techniques.
5. *The leader's skill and confidence* should determine how he or she acts. It is decidedly more difficult to share tasks of procedural leadership than to monopolize them. Democratic leadership calls for skills in listening, organizing, summarizing, and timing that may take a long time to develop.
6. *Time urgency* may be a factor. Occasionally a decision must be made in a hurry, in which case a group will welcome strict control on its procedures. When time is not limited and members are vitally affected by what they decide, they will need less control.
7. *Highly involved groups require less control.* When members perceive the task is important to them personally, they will often resist procedural control by a leader. The implication is clear: the designated discussion leader should do all possible to help members realize the importance of their task, and become involved and concerned.

This brings us to the specific functions of the designated discussion leader, and ways in which they may be performed effectively. Any member can, of course, perform any of these functions, but the designated leader has the responsibility to see they are done. He or she should do them only to the degree necessary for efficiency and group cohesiveness. First, we will consider functions and responsibilities which may fall on any discussion leader, followed by tasks needed only in special types of discussions.

General Functions of Designated Discussion Leaders

Planning and Preparation for Meetings

Planning and preparation for discussion have been described in detail in Chapters 4 and 5. Designated discussion leaders have special responsibilities for the tasks described there: gathering information, agenda preparation, drawing up tentative outlines for guiding group thinking, notifying members of meetings, preparing and distributing reports, and having all physical facilities in readiness. Too, such a leader needs to be certain that a meeting is needed and that the purpose of it is clear and specific, understandable by all members. If several topics or problems must be dealt with, an agenda should be drawn up and circulated to members before the meeting.

Here is a checklist which you should find useful when preparing to lead discussions:

1. Have I a clearly defined purpose for this meeting? (Never hold a meeting unless it is necessary.)

2. What are the outcomes which should emerge from this meeting? (Information? Plans to gather information? Shared understandings? A goal for the group? Possible courses of action? A solution to a problem? A policy statement? A definite plan of action? Or what?)

3. Who will participate? How will they be notified of the purpose, agenda, time, and place of the meeting?

4. What is the best time and place for the meeting?

5. How much time is likely to be needed? For how long should the meeting be scheduled?

6. What physical arrangements do I need to make? (Room reservation? Audiovisual aids? Smoking? Pencils and paper? Refreshments? Other?)

7. How will the report of the discussion be made and distributed?

8. Will applications of decisions be made, and will we need to arrange for any follow-up?

9. Should the group discussion process be evaluated by the group? If so, how will this be done?

Functions expected of designated leaders during actual discussion can be classified into categories of initiating, organizing, spreading participation, stimulating both creative and critical thinking, facilitating understanding, promoting cooperative interpersonal relationships, and developing the group and members. Figure 6.2 summarizes these functions.

—Call Meetings—
—Arrange Facilities—
—Gather Information and Disseminate to Members—
—Prepare Agendas and Problem-solving Outlines—
—Initiate Discussion—
—Make Introductions, Resolve Primary Tensions—
—Suggest Procedures—
—Keep Discussion Organized, On Track—
—Spread Opportunity to Participate—
—Stimulate Creative Thinking—
—Stimulate Critical Thinking, Idea Testing—
—Facilitate Mutual Understanding—
—Promote Cooperative Relationships—
—Facilitate Cohesiveness and Teamwork—
—Handle Conflicts, Secondary Tensions—
—See that Records are Written and Kept—
—Serve as Contact with "Outsiders" or Parent Organization—
—Help Group and Members Develop to Potential—

Figure 6.2. Functions expected of designated discussion leaders.

Initiating the Discussion

1. Reduce primary tensions. See that all members are introduced to each other, and put at ease. This may be done with some icebreaker activity, a coffee hour, or other social activity for a new group. Use name tags or tents if members do not already know each other.
2. Announce the topic or purpose of the discussion and its importance. Make sure the area of freedom is clear to all members.
3. Distribute any outline for guiding the discussion, fact sheets, case problems, or other materials that will be needed.
4. Attempt to establish an informal atmosphere in which members feel secure, yet responsible enough to contribute. Sometimes a "ventilation" period of a few minutes may help get the discussants acquainted with each other's values, beliefs, backgrounds, and attitudes on the problem. This is a period of totally free, unstructured, unorganized talk usually related to the problem or task facing the group, but which serves primarily a socio-emotional function. The designated leader who senses a need for ventila-

tion and encourages it may later find the job of keeping talk organized, relevant, and objective much easier than if no ventilation of feelings and positions had occurred. It is important that ventilation not go on so long that members begin to feel that time is wasted, but long enough for them to want order and organization. Any open conflict is a good sign that it is time to get the discussion organized.

5. Announce any rules of procedure. You may want the group to set these up, but be prepared to suggest procedures.

6. Present an outline for organizing the group's talking, unless you have already done so. Ask the group to consider this pattern, and to accept or modify it.

7. If needed, get a group recorder. If any other special leadership services are needed, see that someone is prepared to supply them.

8. Keep all these opening remarks *as brief as possible* to accomplish the job of initiating structure into the group and getting discussion underway.

Keeping the Discussion Organized and Orderly

1. Once the group has adopted some pattern or outline for coordinating the members' talk and thinking it can be put on a chalkboard or chart. You may need to distribute a guide sheet for any new procedure to be followed by the group (e.g., brainstorming or the RISK technique).

2. Keep the group oriented toward its goal. Be sure the goal is clearly understood by all and is the goal towards which the group wants to move. From time to time you may need to ask, "How will this help us to achieve our purposes?" or "Are we losing sight of our objectives?" When asked to do so, discussants frequently write down very different statements of the group's objectives, showing how very important it is to see that all members of a group understand and agree on the goal, and keep it always in mind.

3. Watch for any extended digressions. When you notice one, you can point it out and ask the group what to do about it. If a discussant offers a solution prematurely, ask him to hold it until the group has finished "mapping" the problem. If someone changes topics in a learning discussion, you might ask if the group has finished with the previous topic.

4. In a problem-solving discussion, see that all findings, ideas, criteria, and possible solutions are accurately recorded.

5. If you notice a lot of repeating with nothing new being added, ask if the group is ready for the next topic. The findings by Schiedel and Crowell and by Fisher (previously cited) indicate that a group will not follow the steps in a problem-solving pattern in a strictly linear way as does a computer. Groups will cycle on each point, and sometimes backtrack. The leader must decide if the diversion is needed "kicking around" of ideas or

a waste of time—and if the latter, bring the group back on track. A group which resists following a definite outline of procedure at the opening of a discussion may do so gladly after confusion and disorganization have set in.

6.   Summarize, or see that a summary is made of each major part of a problem-solving discussion. Be sure the summary is complete and acceptable to the entire group. Sometimes a summary can be made by reviewing what is on the chart or board.

7.   Make a clear transition to each new question or step. This can be combined with a summary. For example, "We have found that time pressure, high cost of duplication, and lack of policing contribute to theft and mutilation. Are we ready to consider possible solutions? (pause) Okay, what might we do to reduce theft and mutilation?"

8.   See that all major topics or phases in the process of problem solving are thoroughly discussed. Point out anything of importance that is being overlooked.

9.   Keep track of time, and remind the group of any time limits so they can consider all aspects of the problem.

10.   Bring the discussion to a definite conclusion. Too often a discussion ends without any sense of closure. Members suddenly remember they have to be elsewhere, and dash off amid chaos. Any plan for the future is left unfinished. The conclusion might include any or all of the following: a summary of all progress made by the group; a statement of how reports of the meeting will be distributed to members and other interested persons; comments about preparations for the next meeting; assignments for follow-up and implementation; commendations to the group for a job well done; an evaluation of the meeting to improve the group's future discussions (Chapter 9 discusses in detail how to do this).

Equalizing Opportunity to Participate

1.   Point out in your opening remarks that part of your role will be to see that everyone has an equal opportunity to get the floor and be heard, that you will be primarily a coordinator, and that the substance of the discussion must come from the group as a whole.

2.   Address your comments and questions to the group, not to individuals, unless you want to elicit a specific bit of information.

3.   See that all members have an equal chance to participate. While no one should be forced to speak, neither should anyone be prevented from speaking by other members.

4.   Make a visual survey of all members every minute or two, looking for any indication that a member may want to speak. If you see such a reaction from a discussant who has had little to say, "gatekeep" him into the

discussion by saying something like, "Joe, did you want to comment on that idea?" Encourage him to speak, but do not embarrass him if he has nothing to say by asking a question like, "Joe, what do you think about that idea?"

5. Be sure to listen with real interest to what an infrequent participant says, and see that other members are also listening to him or her. Perhaps this member can be assigned to investigate and report on special information. If you learn his or her personal interests, these may give you clues for bringing a quiet member into the conversation.

6. If the group contains compulsive talkers who make long speeches or who speak so often that others get little chance, try to control them for the benefit of the group. A number of techniques for doing so are listed next. Use the less overt and obvious techniques first in order to avoid having a dominant but valuable member lose face. If these techniques do not work, then use the blunter methods of controlling the dominators and interrupters.

   a. When feasible, seat talkative members where you can easily overlook them.

   b. When you ask a question of the group, let your eyes meet those of members who have spoken infrequently and avoid those of highly vocal members.

   c. When a compulsive talker has made a point, cut in with, "How do the rest of you feel about that idea?"

   d. Restate briefly what has been said at length.

   e. Ask each person to make only one point per speech.

   f. Have one member keep a count of frequency of participation, then report his findings to the group.

   g. In private, ask the frequent talkers to help you get the quiet members to speak more often.

   h. Point out the problem and ask others to contribute more. For instance, "We have heard a lot from Peter and Marion, but what do the rest of you think about. . . ?"

7. If a member asks for your opinions on a controversial issue or what you as leader think the solution should be, as a rule you should bounce such questions back to the group unless other members have already expressed their opinions and suggestions. For example, if when asked for an opinion you might reply: "Well, let's see how other group members feel about this."

8. Don't comment after each member has spoken; it is all too easy to get into a wheel network of verbal statements (L-M-L-M-L-M and so on).

9. React with acceptance and without evaluation, showing only that you understand or need clarification. If evaluation seems necessary, invite it

from others with a question such as, "How well does that agree with other information we have?"

10.   React nonverbally. It is important for you to nod or otherwise show you heard and understood, especially when an infrequent participant speaks.

Stimulating Both Creative and Critical Thinking

It has already been pointed out that creative and critical thinking do not mix well. However, someone must ask questions at appropriate times to spark imagination or to promote critical thinking by group members. A hypercritical atmosphere may stop the flow of information and ideas, or a sweetness-and-light atmosphere may develop in which nobody feels free to challenge faulty evidence or ideas. Janis, concerned about the phenomenon of conformity and consensus at any price which interferes with critical thinking, came up with a number of preventatives against faulty decision making.[32] These preventatives are incorporated into the suggestions below.

To encourage **critical** thinking, try the following techniques:

1.   Keep asking for information and analysis of the problem if the group gets solution-minded.

2.   See that evidence is tested for reliability and not accepted at face value. You might do this by asking questions which will encourage the group members to test and evaluate it. For example:

To check the relevance of evidence, you might ask, "How does this apply to our problem?" or "How is that like the situation we are discussing?"

To evaluate the source of evidence, you might ask such questions as, "What is the source of that information?" "How well is _____ recognized in his field?" "Is this consistent with his other pronouncements on the subject?"

To check on the credibility of information, you might ask: "Do we have any information which is contradictory?"

To test a statistic, you might ask how it was derived or how an average was computed.

Bring in outside experts to challenge the views of the group and its central members.

3.   See that all group members understand and evaluate all standards, criteria, or assumptions used in making value judgments. For example, you might ask, "Is that criterion clear to us all?" "Is this something we want to insist upon?" or "Do we all accept that as an assumption?"

There are a number of procedures you can follow to insure that a

32.   Irving L. Janis, "Groupthink," *Psychology Today* 5 (Nov., 1971), pp. 43-46, 74-76; and *Victims of Groupthink* (Boston: Houghton Mifflin Company, 1972).

proposed major policy is thoroughly and critically tested before it is adopted:

a. The RISK procedure (see Chapter 7);
b. Ask all members to discuss tentative solutions or policies with people outside the group;
c. One or more members can be asked to take the role of critical evaluator and challenger of all ideas, with high priority in speaking to see that all doubts are aired openly;
d. Subdivide the larger group into two subgroups under different leaders to evaluate all alternatives, then rejoin to iron out differences;
e. Before reaching a binding decision on a policy of far-reaching consequence, hold a "second-chance" meeting at which all doubts, moral concerns, or untested assumptions can be explored before a final conclusion is reached by the group.

4. See that all proposed solutions are given a thorough testing before they are accepted as group decisions. Encourage the group to apply the available facts and all the criteria. Some questions you might ask:

"Do we have any evidence to indicate that this solution would be satisfactory?" "Unsatisfactory?"

"Are there any facts to support this proposal?"

"How well would this idea meet our criteria?"

"Would that proposal get at the basic problem?"

"Is there any way we can test this idea before we decide whether or not to adopt it?"

Encouraging **creative** thinking is equally important. The description of the problem is an especially rich source of ideas, so keep the group on the problem until it has been thoroughly described. A few special techniques:

1. Apply the principle of deferred judgment even when not brainstorming, and try to get as many alternative solutions as possible. Perhaps you can use some of the following questions:

"How *might* we . . .?" (rather than "How *should* we. . .?)

"What other ideas can we think of?"

"Can we recall any solutions used elsewhere that might be used to help solve this problem?"

2. An effective device is to take up each major characteristic of the problem and ask how it might be modified, solved, or eliminated.
3. Watch for possible solutions which suggest whole new areas of thinking, and then pose a general question about the new area. For example, if a member suggests signs in the library to warn about the cost of theft, you might ask, "How else might we publicize the cost of losses to the library?"

Facilitating Mutual Understanding

A designated discussion leader has a great opportunity to serve as a model of effective listening. Only when discussants listen to understand each other can they think together. Occasional summarizing will help promote mutual understanding and clear communication, but there is much more the leader can do.

Try to reduce the expression of ideas and judgments in biased, loaded, or emotive language. Aside from being a model, you can often rephrase or question a biased statement. For example:

Member: "Such socialistic ideas will ruin our country."

Leader: "You feel that governmental control would somehow do more harm than good. How do the others feel about this?"

Member: "The cops are brutal to blacks."

Leader: "You believe that the police use undue force when arresting a black? What evidence do you have that this is so?"

Whenever a statement is unclear to you or when you see a discussant showing signs of not listening or of being confused (such as a frown or puzzled look), check for understanding. You might say something like, "I'm not sure I understand that. Do the rest of you?" "Let me see if I got your meaning. I think you said that. . . ." "I'm not sure we all understood your point. Could you give us some examples, or describe how it would work?" "Joe, you seem puzzled by what Marcia said." "Is that point clear to us all?" Especially watch for minority points of view, and insist that they should be at least understood by all participants. Novel and unusual ideas are often ignored or rejected without being considered.

Promoting Cooperative Interpersonal Relations

Many things can interfere with the ability of members to cooperate with each other. An important responsibility of leadership is sensing the climate of interpersonal relations and member feelings, then doing whatever may be needed to promote satisfaction and harmony within a group. Clear communication, acceptance, orderly procedures, and a sense of accomplishment will do much to promote good interpersonal relations and cohesiveness. However, discussion is not an entirely rational and logical process. People have feelings and are motivated for many different reasons. The designated leader can do many things which may help bring unity out of a conflict over values or ideas:

1. Watch for indications of hidden agendas at variance with the group objectives. Call these to the attention of the group. The group can usually solve a problem of conflicting purposes if the members are fully aware of it.

2. Emphasize the importance of seeking mutually acceptable solutions. Stress the unity of purpose which brought the group into existence by using the word *we* often.

3. Keep conflicts focused on facts and issues, stopping at once any attacks on a member's personality or character.

4. Don't let the discussion get so serious that people cannot enjoy themselves. Humor may help reduce the tensions that are generated when people work hard together at the job of hammering out ideas. Good task leaders may have trouble with humor. Lee observed that many of the most efficient leaders were lacking in human warmth.

> When men are driven, they lose spontaneity and the zestful interest in what goes on. . . . There is a very real danger that our concern with improving human communication may lead members to forget the human part of the matter. . . . We need efficiency *and* satisfyingness. One may try to rig a discussion in the image of a belt line; if he succeeds he may find that those who attend become as inert as machines without the capacity (or will) to create. [To maintain a balance in discussion, Lee suggested that designated leaders] listen with lessened tension when the bent to comedy or diversion or personal release is being manifested . . . [and] pick up the problem *after* the camaraderie or tension has been spent.[33]

> Secondary tensions build, and they must be released or interpersonal friction will grow. Effective discussion is characterized by a constant shifting between the serious and the playful, the relevant and remote, kidding and criticism. Certainly you will want to let the group chain out fantasies which lead to the establishment of shared beliefs and values. The result of such tension-relieving activity is much more concerted action by group members. If you are not skilled at relieving tensions, welcome the leadership of members who are. Then bring the group back to the task outline when the fantasy chain is completed or secondary tensions have been reduced to a level where productive problem-solving discussion can again resume.

5. When a group seems to be deadlocked, look for a basis on which to compromise. Perhaps you can synthesize parts of several ideas into a consensus solution. Conferees may represent points of view which they cannot abandon or sell out, but eventually a decision must be made. For example, labor and management negotiators must eventually agree on a contract if the company is to work. To handle the problems presented by conferees representing diverse interests, we can use techniques employed by mediators of bargaining conferences. The mediator seeks to find a common ground, a *compromise* solution which all parties can accept as the *best*

---

33. Irving J. Lee, *How to Talk with People* (New York: Harper & Row, Publishers, 1952), pp. 158-160.

achievable solution. Each partisan yields something in order to obtain something. In common parlance, "half a loaf is better than none." A complete surrender by one of two or more partisans will only postpone the settlement of a basic issue.

To encourage compromise, you may first need to point out that compromise need not be a sellout or dirty word. As Edmund Burke put it, "All government,—indeed every human benefit and enjoyment, every virtue and every prudent act,—is founded on compromise and barter."[34] Second, insist that the interests and needs of each participant are clearly understood by all other participants. Find the minimum conditions which are acceptable to every conferee, and then suggest a solution which will meet these minimums. Of course, this may take a great deal of discussion.

6. If a role struggle is going on, try suggesting suitable roles for members (e g , "Joe, would you summarize what we've said on this?"). If necessary, bring an extended role struggle out into the open and ask the group to talk about the social problems of a role and status struggle and how to cope with them.

Developing the Group and Its Members

The need for personal and group development will vary widely from person to person and group to group. A continuing group, such as a college class, a standing committee, an engineering staff, or a study-discussion group should definitely allow time for feedback and evaluation of meetings. A one-meeting discussion group, on the other hand, may have no reason to spend time evaluating the group process.

Sometimes the impetus for growth can be given by asking the group, after a discussion has ended, to examine its discussion. For example, a designated leader might ask, "How well did we do in our discussion?" or "What might we do to make our next meeting more profitable than this one?" If a group is having trouble, the leader might interrupt the discussion with some comment such as this: "We seem to be making little headway. What's wrong? How might we get more accomplished (or, relieve this tension, or make the discussion more interesting)?" The specific question should be in reaction to what the leader senses is wrong.

A class studying discussion techniques should have at least one observer for almost every discussion. The observer may break into the conversation to point out what he sees is hampering the group, make a brief report after the discussion, fill out rating forms which the group can discuss, or raise questions pertinent to the group's procedures. Any continuing group will benefit by doing this occasionally. A member can serve the group as an observer by focusing her

34. *Ibid.*, pp. 90-91.

attention for a period of time on the process instead of on the content of the interaction. Periodic evaluations of the group's performance and procedures should be made. Interpersonal feedback sessions in which members air any negative or positive feelings not previously cleared up may help a group. Advice on how to do this is provided in the final chapter. However it is done, a definite leadership service is made to a continuing group when members are made more aware of how they are participating and interacting together. In Chapter 9 the role of observer and procedures for group evaluation are explained in detail.

The preceding list of leadership functions and techniques is at best a partial one. Whatever his techniques, the leader must be flexible, adapting to the specific group. The main tools of the discussion leader are carefully laid plans, questions, skillful listening, clarifying comments, effective summaries, tension-relieving humor, and appropriate observations which are fed back to the entire group. Democratic, shared leadership, even when one person has been designated the leader, contributes most to group success and member development. Even "heads" can function as group-centered leaders much of the time during discussions by groups for which they are assigned responsibility.

Bibliography

Bormann, Ernest G., *Discussion and Group Methods: Theory and Practice,* 2nd ed., New York: Harper & Row, Publishers, 1975, Chapter 11.

Cathcart, Robert S., and Samovar, Larry A., eds., *Small Group Communication: A Reader,* 2nd ed., Dubuque: Wm. C. Brown Company Publishers, 1974, Section IV.

Fiedler, Fred E., *A Theory of Leadership Effectiveness,* New York: McGraw-Hill Book Company, 1967.

Lee, Irving J., *How to Talk with People,* New York: Harper & Row, Publishers, 1952.

Maier, Norman R.F., *Problem-solving Discussions and Conferences,* New York: McGraw-Hill Book Company, 1963.

Tannenbaum, Robert; Weschler, Irving R.; and Massarik, Fred, *Leadership and Organization: A Behavioral Science Approach,* New York: McGraw-Hill Book Company, 1961.

Key Concepts

Autocratic leader—person who dominates and controls a small group, using positional power or manipulative strategies, usually for self-serving ends.

Completer, leader as—leader who determines what functions or behaviors are most needed for a group to perform optimally, then attempts to supply those behaviors.

Democratic leader—person who coordinates and facilitates discussion in a small group by consent of the group, thus helping to achieve group-determined goals.

Designated leader—person appointed or elected as leader of a small group.

Discussion leader—leader of a group's verbal interaction; coordinator of discussion process and procedures.

Emergent or "natural" leader—member of an initially leaderless group who in time is named as "leader" by all or nearly all members.

Head—person with positional power over other members of a small group, assigned to that position by a larger organization; e.g., foreman, supervisor.

Headship—influence or control over the behavior of members of a group based on power of position, such as the right to hire, fire, and determine income.

Leader—a person who exercises goal-oriented influence in a group; any person so named by the members of a group.

Leadership—any influence exercised through communication process which helps a group clarify and achieve goals.

Exercises

1. Select a case problem, preferably from your own experience, for which you do not have a solution. Prepare and distribute copies of this case to all members of your discussion group. Be sure you present all information the discussants will need to understand what is wrong in the present situation, and to decide what would be the desired situation. During the discussion a classmate should serve as observer, rating you as a leader. Following the discussion (20-30 minutes as assigned by your instructor), the observer will guide your group in a brief evaluation of the discussion. At the class meeting after the discussion you should hand the following to your instructor: (1) a copy of the case; (2) a copy of your leader's outline; (3) a report of the discussion following the format on page 94; (4) the observer's rating sheet evaluating your leadership; (5) a brief essay in which you evaluate your functioning as leader of the discussion. You may want to make a recording of the discussion for later analysis. As you listen, make a list of:

   a. The functions you performed, how effectively you performed them, and how appropriate each was to the need of the group at the moment;

   b. Points during the discussion where you failed to supply some needed leader intervention, and what happened as a result. Did someone else eventually provide the needed function? If not, how was the group process and/or productivity hurt?

2. Select a short poem and make copies to distribute to half of your class. Then conduct a discussion of this poem. Two or more groups may be discussing simultaneously, each with one or more observers.

3. Buzz groups should draw up lists of topics, problems, or value questions about which all members would like to learn more. Select the subject of most interest to the group, and compile a bibliography of pertinent materials. Each discussant should then do the required reading, making study notes and a tentative leader's outline. Then the group can discuss the topic, with the designated leadership rotating every fifteen to twenty minutes. One or more observers should report their findings before each new designated leader takes on his responsibilities. Some possible questions:

   "What can religion contribute to the life of twentieth century man?"

"What control should government exercise over the production and distribution of pornographic material?"

"How might the family structure be made more stable and enriching to the lives of members?"

4. Select a problem. Then have each class member prepare and deliver a leader's opening remarks for initiating a discussion of the problem. Have the class evaluate each introduction.

5. After a brief discussion, have each participant write a summary of what was said. Compare the summaries. What can you conclude?

6. Plan and conduct a panel discussion, based on previous closed-group discussions in class. While one group is presenting its panel, the rest of the class will serve as an audience. The entire class can then evaluate the moderator's techniques, the organization of the discussion, the spread of time and participation among the participants, and the handling of the forum following the panel discussion.

7. Role play some problem-solving discussions (preferably using case problems presented by your instructor). Two or three problem members should be planted in each group, doing such things as pleading personal interests, sidetracking and introducing irrelevant issues, making cutting personal criticisms, talking incessantly, remaining silent, and so forth. Experiment with various leader techniques for handling these problem members and evaluate the results.

8. Practice applying the various techniques for critically testing and evaluating ideas on a proposal of broad significance to your college or university which has strong support from members of your class. You might consider the following proposals for new policies (if new to your school): elimination of all grades; elimination of all course requirements for a degree; publication of student evaluations of all faculty members; elimination of one or more intercollegiate athletic programs.

    What effect does application of the technique have on the decision of the group? What did you learn from this experience in taking a "second look?"

9. In small groups discuss three different case problems in turn, with rotating designated leaders who move from group to group as the cases change. Each leader will role play a very different style (viz., autocratic, group-centered, do-nothing or laissez faire), as explained and assigned by your instructor. Discuss the impact on the group of each style or philosophy.

10. In small groups compile lists of guidelines for democratic discussion leaders under the headings "DO" and "DON'T."

11. In a project group, plan and conduct an experiment to test the effectiveness of various leader techniques for equalizing opportunity for participation, promoting creative or critical thinking, keeping a discussion organized, and so forth.

12. Engage in four discussions of case problems supplied by your instructor.

Alternate between having a designated leader and no designated leader. What differences do you observe? What are some implications of these differences?

13. Each class member should obtain one or more charts of the organization of clubs, businesses, agencies, or schools of which he or she is a member. Compare several of these organizational charts. Invite persons holding positions of headship at several levels in two or more different types of organizations to attend your class. Ask them to describe their concepts and techniques of leadership, and what is expected of them in their positions.

14. Scoring and interpreting the Sargent and Miller Leadership Scale. The scale you filled out on p.156 had ten items. A maximum score of 10 means you are very democratic in your responses to this test; a minimum score of 0 means you are very autocratic. Put a (1) after each item you checked as indicated in the key:

KEY:

1. a	2. b	3. b	4. a	5. b
6. b	7 b	8. a	9. a	10. a

Now read on in the chapter, and you will find some of the research that has been done on this scale. You may want to discuss your choices with several of your classmates.

7
Organizing and Leading Learning Discussions

Learning groups of all types, at all age and educational levels, formal and informal, sponsored and spontaneous, in and out of classrooms, exist not to reach concensus decisions, or produce advice or resolutions. Learning discussions have as a general objective only the growth, enlightenment, and increased personal understanding, perspective on life, and satisfaction of the members of the group. Thus the group exists as a resource or means to a personal end for each member. There is an old saying to the effect that if two people each having one idea apiece give them to each other, then each is twice as rich in ideas as before—this is the very gist of learning discussion. In learning groups there is no need to reach accord on values, beliefs, or courses of action. What is sought is a fuller understanding, a wider grasp of information pertinent to a topic, or consideration of a problem from as many points of view as possible. With no need to reach accord on issues, a wholly different pattern of discussion is often called for than in problem-solving groups.

From years of observing learning groups as a researcher, conducting them as a teacher, participating in them as student and interested discussant, conducting training programs for teachers and study-discussion leaders, reading widely in the literature of learning discussion, and both participating in and facilitating several types of encounter groups, I have attempted to distill some principles and techniques for planning and leading learning discussions. That is what this chapter is about. As a result of your reading, study, and guided applications of this chapter you should be able to:

1. Describe how discussion can be used to achieve learning objectives of persons at all ages and educational levels.
2. Explain the purpose of and procedures for leading groups in a

variety of learning discussion techniques: case discussion, problem census, affective discussion, problem exploration, and fine arts discussions.

3. List the steps in a discussion of an artistic creation, such as a poem, short story, painting, dress design, music, or building, and prepare an appropriate outline for leading a discussion of such things in which you are interested.
4. Identify types of questions for focusing learning discussion, and ask each in appropriate places during discussions.
5. Explain the Johari window as a model of areas of discussion between two or more persons, and how encounter discussion can increase the "public area" of participants.
6. List, explain, and apply eight guidelines for making encounter feedback supportive and productive of personal growth.

There are innumerable settings in which learning discussions take place. For example, last evening, during what was primarily a social gathering of four couples, I enjoyed an impromptu discussion of how homes might be made more energy efficient. The host (an engineer), a statistician, a business professor, and I spent nearly two hours sharing our knowledge and ideas about alternative ways to insulate, heat, and cool houses. We soon discovered that each of us had a strong interest in the topic and considerable knowledge; we spontaneously set out to share it. I left with many new ideas for a "dream" house. Likewise, after watching dogs perform at field trials I have often gotten into informal discussions of their merits, resulting in a gradual change in my criteria in breeding and training. When an informal social group discovers a common interest, "chit-chat" can often become a deeply satisfying learning discussion.

In recent years, much more classroom attention has been given to discussion as a means of sharing knowledge, beliefs, and feelings. Many colleges and universities have in-service programs for helping their faculty members learn to lead classroom discussions. Workshops are held frequently in schools for teachers who want to become better discussion leaders. Even kindergartners are learning from each other in teacher-stimulated interchanges about how the pupils feel, things they saw on a field trip, differences in reactions to new foods, likes, and dislikes. Much use is made in some schools of committee groups to study a variety of sources on a topic, distill the information, and present it to the class in some type of report. In continuing education outside the usual collegiate structure, much noncredit learning goes on in discussion groups sponsored by universities, libraries, churches, and other organizations. For example, the Faculty Women's Club of the university where I teach sponsors a book discussion group and several hobby clubs in which the members discuss what they are doing. Many university extension programs use a format of some type of planned presentation, followed by small group discussions in which participants share their reactions and evaluations of the formal program.

Encounter and other experiential "growth" groups of all types can be found in most large and some smaller communities. In these groups members learn about themselves. They learn new ways of relating and communicating, and how to cope with various personal problems. Highly specialized experiential groups exist to cope with problems of alcohol, drugs, weight, and mental health.

Guidelines for learning group discussion are presented in a wide range of guide sheets, leader's manuals, and books. Some of these are listed in the bibliography for this chapter; others can be located in your local library or obtained from sponsoring agencies.

Why this great expansion of learning through discussion? For one thing, we have come to view learning as much more than the acquisition of factual information and skills. "Learning" has come to mean any *change* which comes about in a person due to experience; "education" as the structuring of situations in which change will be facilitated. Learning objectives have been organized and classified into 3 types: (1) "cognitive" or intellectual, ranging from recognition and recall of specific information to abilities in combining and creating; (2) "affective" having to do with values and feelings; and (3) "psychomotor" which are primarily about physical skills. Extensive research has shown that active participation in discussion groups is often more productive of higher mental skills and changes of beliefs and values than is any type of lecture, video, or individualized instruction format.[1] There is no clear evidence of the superiority of either lecture or discussion in increasing retained and applied knowledge. The older person," largely committed to what he is and what he does" and with extensive experience, needs the opportunity to ". . . *think about what he already knows* . . ." which the ". . . informal study-discussion process attempts to give him."[2]

Extensive use of group discussion formats has been made to bring about changes in personal values and actions. Reserach by Kurt Lewin and associates during World War II showed that the presentation of information followed by discussion was much more likely to get housewives to use kidneys and other organ meats than was a strictly persuasive speech approach. Weight Watchers, Alcoholics Anonymous and allied groups, and efforts to get heart patients to take care of themselves have all found discussion to be productive of change.

Many studies have shown that cooperative group interaction is superior to competitive learning structures in reducing racial stereotypes and increasing ac-

---

1. See D.W. and R.T. Johnson, *Learning Together and Alone*, (Englewood Cliffs, N.J.: Prentice-Hall, Inc., 1975), pp. 191-192, for a summary of some of this research. Also see W.J. McKeachie, "Recitation and Discussion," in O.E. Lancaster, ed., *Achieve Learning Objectives*, 3rd ed. (University Park, Pa.: The Pennsylvania State University, 1963), Section F.

2. John W. Powell, *Research in Adult Group Learning in the Liberal Arts* (White Plains, N.Y.: Fund for Adult Education, 1960), p. 3.

ceptance of people of different types, provided the discussion is not a one-shot affair. For example, Witte found that members of interracial groups of students who met over the period of a semester increased more in the amount of inter-racial peer tutoring, racial acceptance, and interracial contact outside of class than did students not in such groups.[3] Cooperative classroom discussion groups were found to increase cross-racial friendship, helping, and attraction in such courses as English and math. Ability to take the social perspective of other persons (as opposed to ego- and ethnocentrism) may well result from discussion in heterogeneous groups.[4] That educational innovations such as individualized instruction, computer-assisted instruction, nongraded and open classrooms, team teaching, and "new" math are not helpful if the quality of interaction in the classroom is not given proper consideration was demonstrated by Hunter.[5] The cooperative relationships established in a discussion *group* approach to learning may be essential if many learning objectives are to be achieved. Haines and McKeachie showed that competitively structured discussions produced an in-crease in anxiety, less self assurance, and more self-oriented behavior, whereas cooperative discussions produced a decrease in anxiety, an increase in task-oriented behavior, and higher-level intellectual functioning by students.[6] The following quotation from Johnson and Johnson summarizes well the need for cooperative interstudent relationships:

> Beyond all doubt, cooperation should be the most frequently used goal structure. The conditions under which it is effective and desirable are almost too many to list. Whenever problem solving is desired, whenever divergent thinking or creativity is desired, whenever quality of performance is expected, whenever the task is complex, when the learning goals are highly important, and when the social development of students is one of the major instructional goals, cooperation should be used. When a teacher wishes to promote positive interaction among students, a facilitative learning climate, a wide range of cognitive and affective outcomes, and positive relations between himself and the students, cooperative goal structures will be used.[7]

GUIDELINES FOR ORGANIZING AND LEADING COOPERATIVE LEARNING DISCUSSIONS

Based on the preceding survey of research and philosophy about learning at

3. P.H. Witte, "The Effects of Group Reward Structures on Interracial Acceptance, Peer Tutoring, and Academic Performance" (Unpublished doctoral dissertation, Washington University, 1972).

4. Johnson and Johnson, *Together and Alone,* pp. 193-196.

5. Elizabeth Hunter, *Encounter in the Classroom* (New York: Holt, Rinehart and Winston, Inc., 1972), pp. 1-15.

6. D.B. Haines and W.J. McKeachie, "Cooperative versus Competitive Discussion Methods in Teaching Introductory Psychology," *Journal of Educational Psychology* 58 (1967), pp. 386-390.

7. Johnson and Johnson, *Ibid.,* p. 66.

all levels, some general guidelines can now be established for setting up coopera-tive learning discussions.

Always establish a cooperative group goal. The outcome to be achieved should be presented as a **sharing** of individual knowledge and perspectives, never as competing for status by giving "good" or "correct" answers. Whatever is stated or listed by a member of the group becomes the property of all members. The pooling of information and ideas is a group accomplishment, not a matter of individual performance. Members should be encouraged to help each other with all that is said and done, and to look on each other as partners rather than as competitors in learning.

Give rewards to the group, not individuals. This means that praise for good work is directed to the group, not to individual members. Such comments as "I thought we had a very interesting discussion," "I got a lot from all of you," or "That was a really fine discussion we had" are group oriented, and stress the cooperative relationship. On the other hand, comments like "Joe, you really helped us out" stress the competitive individual.

Keep the focus on common experience. Effective learning discussion grows out of a common body of experiences. All discussants should be reading the same articles or books, looking at the same painting or movie, observing the same group of children, or perhaps studying the same problem. Meaningful enlightenment discussions evolve from differing perceptions of such phenomena, supplemented by events or data experienced by one or a few group members. Each will see the same events somewhat differently, and each will differ in interpretations and evaluations.

The secret of productive learning discussion is to focus on what has been observed by all discussants. It has been found that members of study-discussion groups were more satisfied with the leadership and with the discussion and learned to qualify their judgments more often in groups which discussed topics most closely relevant to the assigned readings. Members of groups which dis-cussed many topics peripheral to the readings did not show as much satisfaction or as much learning.[8]

Sometimes it will be productive to divide up the work of reading and research in a committee-type learning group among subgroups and have them report to the rest of the small group. Generally avoid one-person assignments, for too much then depends on the interpretations of one reader or observer. The inter-pretation of individual or subgroup reports should always be the responsibility and right of the entire group, not an "expert" who made the report.

Limit the number of issues or topics. Greater learning and more satisfaction

---

8. John K. Brilhart, "An Exploratory Study of Relationships Between the Evaluating Process and Associated Behaviors of Participants in Six Study-Discussion Groups" (Ph.D. dissertation, Pennsylvania State University, 1962), pp. 283-293.

were also found in groups where the average number of distinguishable topics per two-hour discussion was less than eleven than in groups where the average was more than fourteen topics per meeting.[9] Jumping rapidly from topic to topic should be avoided. In general, it is unwise to plan to discuss more than three or four basic issues per hour. Of course, several subquestions might be discussed under each of these broader issues.

Plan a variety of open-ended questions. Open-ended questions are those which do not call for a specific, brief answer, but encourage a variety of answers from different points of view. The contrast between "closed" or specific-answer questions and open-ended questions is indicated by the following pairs in which the open-ended question occurs first.

O—Are there any types of acts now classified as crimes which we think should be decriminalized?
C—What acts does the Chief of Police say should be decriminalized?

O—What does the fifth stanza mean to you?
C—What is the meaning of the fifth stanza?

O—How safe do current nuclear generating plants appear to be?
C—Are nuclear power plants safe?

O—What good is membership in the U.N. to the United States?
C—What did the United States pay into the U.N. last year?

This is not to say that no questions asking for specific items of information should be asked, but they should be used to garner evidence and as follow-up questions to the broad issues of the discussion. Such "memory" questions as "What is the name of the Muslims' bible?" may bring out needed facts, but the answer itself is not discussable if accepted as correct by the group.

Numerous classifications of types of general questions have been developed. The list of types below may help you in planning questions to stimulate and facilitate learning discussion.

1. Translation—asking the discussants to change information or statements into their own language. Examples: "How else might we say that?" "What does _____ mean to you?"

2. Interpretation—the question asks the respondent to determine relationships among facts, generalizations, values, and so on. Discussants are challenged to give meaning to a body of information by such questions. Examples: "How serious is the problem of alienation among students at _____?" "Why might the settlers have slaughtered the buffalo?" "What might have motivated Luther to defy the Church?"

9. *Ibid.*, pp. 275-282.

3. Analysis—the group is called on to divide an issue or problem into major components or contributing causes. Examples: "What factors determine the total amount of money you earn on a savings account?" "What other things may have contributed to the rate of illiteracy in the United States?" "When do you most enjoy discussing?"

4. Value—the respondents are asked to make statements of evaluation, judgment of degree of goodness, rightness, or appropriateness. Examples: "What is the best way to respond if someone calls you a honky or nigger?" "Is it ever right to pollute the air?" "Is capital punishment justifiable as a deterrent to murder?"

5. Prediction—the discussants are called on to use information in predicting some future trend or condition. Examples: "What energy sources do you think we will be using to heat our houses twenty years from now?" "What do you think will happen to Willy if he doesn't change his behavior?"

6. Synthesis or problem solving—discussants are asked to engage in creative thinking that incorporates information, analysis, prediction, and values in arriving at a conclusion. Examples: "What should you do if you discover a close friend has been shoplifting?" "What should we do to reduce drunken driving?"

(For more information about questions, see pages 85 to 91.)

Be guided by the nature of the subject. The pattern for a learning discussion is usually inherent in the subject of discussion and the group purpose in discussing it. Thus if a group desired to understand and appreciate poetry, the pattern would emerge from that purpose and the poem. A group discussing a film might well discuss such characteristics as the truthfulness of the theme, the acting, the staging, the photography, and their enjoyment of the film. A group seeking to understand differences in conceptions of God might discuss Catholic beliefs, various Protestant beliefs, and Jewish beliefs. Or, they might compare each major religion by focusing on images of God, beliefs concerning divine purpose, and man's relation to God. A group seeking to understand the problems of open and fair housing for all citizens might use a problem-solving outline (even though the discussants would not necessarily seek a solution).

Focus on how the subject relates to interests of the members of the group. To do otherwise, of course, is not to have a *group* goal but an autocratically determined one. One procedure useful for organizing learning discussion of materials previously examined by all members of a group is to poll the group for questions each wants to explore, writing them all on a board or piece of large paper where all can see. Each person can then vote for 3-5 topics of greatest interest. These questions are then discussed in the order of most to least interest (votes).

It is especially important to plan questions relating a topical discussion to personal concerns and experiences of members of a discussion group. For example, compare the following two sets of questions for guiding a discussion of reactions to Arthur Miller's *Death of a Salesman*. The first set is all too typical of what teachers do to turn students off: ask questions reflecting the interests of the teacher, closed questions, and those which have no connection to the personal lives of the students. The second set encourages the student discussants to relate the play to their personal lives.

1. What method of character introduction is used?
2. Which point of view does the author use?
3. What are some figures of speech used by Miller?

versus

1. What is unhealthy about Willy's inability to face reality?
2. Do we think it was wrong for Biff to quit trying after he surprised Willy in the hotel in Boston? Why?
3. What should we do when someone else fails us, like a teacher we don't like?
4. What does Miller seem to think of the American business world?
5. Should an employee ever take second place to the good of the company?

PATTERNS FOR OUTLINING AND ORGANIZING LEARNING DISCUSSIONS

Sometimes there should be no attempt to organize a learning discussion such as an "affective" discussion or an encounter session. But discussions for many classes and study-discussion groups should be organized somewhat, with a designated leader being responsible for developing a set of organized questions that can be raised to focus and give some order to the group interaction. Many of the same logical patterns used to organize informative public speeches can be applied to discussions.

Topical or Major Issues

This is the most common pattern for learning discussions. The group discusses a set of topics or issues, each of which can be phrased as a question. These should be the basic issues which must be understood for members to gain an overall view of the subject matter under study, and to share their differing reactions to it. While a designated leader should prepare a set of questions and subquestions to guide exploration of the major issues, he should never insist that the group discuss all of his questions or only his questions. The group must decide what issues will be discussed; the leader can suggest the issues and ask if the discussants want to omit any of them or add others.

Three examples will be presented to show this pattern of organization. The first is from a group that was discussing motion pictures. After seeing each film they used the following outline:

I.   What was the reaction to the theme of the picture?
II. How good was the acting?
III. How well was the picture staged and costumed?
IV. How effective were lighting and photography?
V.   Would we recommend this picture to our friends?

Following a viewing of the movie "The Poseidon Adventure," a class was divided into small groups for discussion of the following topical outline:

I.   How did Scott establish himself as leader of the group that escaped?
II. What role did each person play in the group which contributed to their successful escape?
III. How were these roles established by member and group?
IV. How does this movie relate to leadership in our class?

After reading about the United States and communism, a group studying American foreign policy discussed the following issues during a two-hour meeting:

I.   How feasible is a policy of coexistence?
II. How feasible is a policy of containment?
III. How feasible is a policy of liberation for communist-dominated countries?
IV. What should be the main tenets of American foreign policy toward communist states?

These questions were planned in advance by the designated discussion leader. A number of subquestions emerged from the members' reactions to the readings.

Chronological

When discussing a historical trend, the subject can best be dealt with in a time sequence. Consider the following typical outline:

I.   How did the United States treat Indians while the country was being settled?
II. How did it treat them during the heyday of the reservation system?
III. How are we treating them now?
IV. What should be done for the Indians in the future?

A series of subquestions were discussed under each of these general issues. They dealt with such topics as treaties, legal contracts, citizenship, finances, discrimination, health, and education.

Causal

The logic underlying this pattern of questions is cause-effect. Since the relationships between events are not so simple as "A caused B," the questions and outline should indicate the complexity of a field of forces leading to some subsequent event(s). If a group were discussing the social problem of sexual assaults, they might be encouraged to follow an outline of questions following a causal pattern.

    I.   How serious is the crime of sexual assault today?
        A.   What kinds of acts do we include as sexual assaults?
        B.   How frequent are these crimes?
        C.   Who commits them, and against whom?
   II.   What factors or conditions seem to produce sexual assaults?
        A.   Do we have any evidence of physical characteristics that might contribute to being an assaulter?
        B.   What personality characteristics may contribute to this crime?
        C.   What role do family relationships play in sexual assaults?
        D.   Do any social conditions seem to be contributory?
        E.   Are there any other factors which seem to us to be contributory?
  III.   Do we now have any opinions about what makes a rapist?

Comparative

A *comparative* pattern might be used to compare two or more policies, objectives, organizations, and so forth. The group might begin by discussing criteria and goals, or with the first of the topics to be compared. For example, a group of students could discuss the merits of various teaching-learning approaches they have experienced while using the following outline:

    I.   What are the advantages and disadvantages of lecturing?
   II.   What are the advantages and disadvantages of discussions?
  III.   What are the advantages and disadvantages of seminar or tutorial methods?
  IV.   What are the advantages and disadvantages of programmed instruction?

Organization for a Fine Arts Discussion

Many learning groups, both in and out of the classroom, have found enlightenment and pleasure in discussing such works of art as poetry, paintings, short stories, pieces of sculpture, or buildings. The staff of the Center for Continuing Liberal Education of the Pennsylvania State University worked out a basic sequence for such discussions. This format has proven to be helpful in countless discussions. Here is the basic format: (1) group examines the work of art together; (2) group discusses what they perceive in the work of art and what it means to them; (3) group again examines the work of art. Relatively little time will be spent discussing the artist, his motives, or his life. If artistic techniques are considered, they are left until near the end of the discussion.

Literature

The following set of questions may be used to guide the discussion of a poem. With modifications, the same questions could be used to discuss any other art form. With any specific work, some of the questions may be fruitless or meaningless, and others may be needed to open up avenues of perception and thought. Whatever questions are discussed you should be careful to relate talk to the actual work of art (e.g., "What do certain words of the poem contribute to what I perceive?"). Most of the time should be spent on ideas relevant to the work of art which the group finds fruitful to discuss; no previous beliefs about how one ought to react to a poem or painting should block discussion of meaningful, relevant approaches to the work.

Introduction: A member of the group reads the poem aloud.

I.   What situation occurs in the poem?
    A.   What is actually taking place? What do you see in the poem?
    B.   What other actions are described by the people in the poem?
II. How does the speaker in the poem feel about the situation he is discussing?
    A.   At the beginning of the poem?
    B.   In the middle?
    C.   At the end?
    D.   What is the nature and direction of the change of his feelings?
III. What kind of person does the speaker appear to be in the poem?
    A.   What kind of person would feel as he feels?
    B.   What kind of person would change as he does (or remain unchanged)?
IV. What broad generalizations underlie the poem?
    A.   What ideas does the poet assume to be true?
    B.   Does he arrive at any insights, answers, or solutions?
    C.   How do we feel about these generalizations?

Conclusion: A group member reads the poem aloud.

Some of the questions in the general outline above may not fit a particular poem. You must plan questions for the specific poem, depending on what it is about, how it is written, the reactions it evokes in you, and so on. This adaptation is illustrated in the following poem and outline for a discussion of it by a group of college students.

Invictus
William Ernest Henley

Out of the night that covers me,
    Black as the Pit from pole to pole,
I thank whatever gods may be
    For my unconquerable soul.

In the fell clutch of circumstance
    I have not winced nor cried aloud.
Under the bludgeonings of chance
    My head is bloody, but unbowed.

Beyond this place of wrath and tears
    Looms but the Horror of the shade,
And yet the menace of the years
    Finds, and shall find, me unafraid.

It matters not how strait the gate,
    How charged with punishments the scroll,
I am the master of my fate;
    I am the captain of my soul.

I.   What do you think this poem is about?
    A.   What might "night" refer to in the first line?
    B.   The black pit?
II.   What sort of person does the speaker appear to be to you?
    A.   What does the second stanza tell you about him?
    B.   What do you think is his attitude toward dying?
    C.   What do you understand about his view of life and afterlife?
    D.   What do you make out of the last two lines?
III.   What beliefs or assumptions underlie the poem?
    A.   What does the poet assume to be true?
    B.   How do we feel about these beliefs?
IV.   Do you like this poem? Why?

A group might discuss a short story, essay, or even a novel in a similar fashion. The following outline was prepared to guide a discussion by a group of people who had all read *Jonathan Livingston Seagull*.[10]

10. Richard Bach, *Jonathan Livingston Seagull* (New York: Macmillan, Inc., 1970).

I. What does the story mean to you?
 A. Is it more than the story of a gull?
 B. Do we find any religious themes in the story?
 C. What do you feel was the high point of the story?
II. What do the leading characters mean to you?
 A. How would you characterize Jonathan?
  1. Is he like anyone you know?
  2. How do you feel about such a character?
 B. What sort of character is Chaing?
  1. What does he represent to you?
  2. Why do you think Bach gave him an oriental name?
  3. Do we have any personal "Chaings?"
 C. What do you think of Fletcher?
  1. What significance do you attach to his crashing into the wall?
  2. What sort of person does he remind you of?
 D. Do any other characters stand out for you? Who and why?
III. What impact do you think Jonathan and his friends would have on the flock?
 A. What do you think happened to the Breakfast Flock after Fletcher's miracle?
 B. How might this affect other gulls?
 C. How does our society view the purpose of life?
 D. How do we view it?
IV. What are our personal feelings in response to *Jonathan*?
 A. Would you want to be like Jonathan in any ways?
 B. Would you have joined his school?
 C. If you had been Jonathan, would you have returned to teach the rest of the flock?[11]

Visual Objects

An outline of questions to guide a discussion of a visual object such as a painting, sculpture, clothing, building, or photograph should focus on various characteristics of features of the object, not the whole. The discussants are led to shift the visual focus in this way, and to describe what they see from each new perspective, such as shape, color, lines, texture, areas, and so on. As part of her work in one of my classes, a student prepared the next outline to lead discussion of an abstract painting.

11. Adapted from John Hasling, *Group Discussion and Decision Making* (New York: Thomas Y. Crowell Company, 1975), pp. 95-96.

Introduction: Painting is hung in front of group seated in a semicircle, and group asked to examine it silently.

I. What different elements do you see?
   A. What do you notice about the texture?
   B. What colors do you notice?
   C. What do you notice about the shapes?
   D. Do you observe anything in the lines?

II. Overall, combining the different elements, what do you perceive?
   A. Does it seem to portray any specific object, idea, or event?
   B. Do your personal experiences or ideas affect your perceptions in any way?

III. What feelings do you experience from looking at the picture?
   A. What emotions does it arouse?
   B. Does it move you to want to take any action?
   C. What seems to be evoking your reaction or arousal?

IV. What does the painting seem to say to you?
   A. Does it have any specific message or theme for you?
   B. What might be the purpose of this painting? Strictly aesthetic?

V. How do you evaluate the painting?
   A. Do you think the artist said what he wanted to say?
   B. Do you feel it was worth saying?
   C. How did the artist achieve this, or what prevented him from achieving it?
   D. Has the painting or our discussion of it revealed anything new or important to you?
   E. Does it have any universality or significance?[12]

Studying Problems

A group wanting to learn as much as possible about a particular problem could use one of the problem-solving patterns without coming to any decisions or solution as a group. The purpose is for each member to achieve a better understanding and have a number of alternatives available. If the members are quite heterogeneous in backgrounds and values, all will learn from the knowledge, perspectives, beliefs, and ideas of each other.

Regardless of the pattern used to organize thinking and talking in a learning discussion, it should reflect the basic purpose, which is learning, reflect the basic issues of the topic or question being discussed, and reflect the particular interests and needs of the group members. To get a better understanding of these principles and how they are applied in a given situation, you may want to prepare a set of leader's outlines on problems and topics to which each type of organization is appropriate, then engage in such discussions with your friends or classmates.

12. Adapted from outline of Ms. Connie Chatwood; April, 1973.

Each discussion and outline should be followed by observer and group evaluation.

SPECIAL TECHNIQUES FOR LEARNING GROUP DISCUSSION

The literature of learning discussion contains many special formats and techniques, some of which can be applied in a wide variety of situations, and some of which have very limited usefulness. Some would be most useful with small children, some with young adults, some with continuing education groups, and some with almost any age level or type of learning group. The techniques presented in this chapter were selected for their adaptability to a wide range of situations.

Case Discussion

Often discussion seems desultory when talking about a vague or abstract problem area. Rather than beginning with the general problem, the leader presents the group with a specific case as a point of departure. First, this case is discussed as if the group were trying to actually solve it, and then the group is asked to generalize from the specific case problem to similar situations they have faced or may face in the future. The following two cases, prepared by students in my classes from their personal experience, may be used for case discussions in your group or class, or you can use them as models in writing your own case problems.

THE TEACHER'S DILEMMA

An English teacher in a consolidated, rural high school has had extensive dramatic experience, and as a result was chosen by the principal to direct the first play in the new school. The play will be the first major production for the school. Its success may determine whether or not there will be future plays produced at the school, and if well done can bring prestige to both teacher and the school. As a result, the teacher (a friend of mine) is exhausting every means available to her to make the play an artistic success. She has chosen the cast except for the leading female part. The principal's daughter wants the part, and the principal told the teacher he really wants his daughter to have it. But—she is a poor actress, and would jeopardize the success of the show. Tentatively, the teacher has chosen someone who should do an excellent job in the role, but the principal has implied that if his daughter is not selected, he will appoint another director.

What should I tell my English teacher friend to do?

THE RELATIONSHIP

A close friend of mine recently became engaged to a girl I introduced him to a couple of years ago. Soon after the engagement his fiancée began making extensive plans for the wedding, which is to take place in a few months. She has purchased a gown, groom's ring, and household items. But my friend now feels he is being pushed into a marriage he no longer wants. At the time of engagement he felt deeply in love, but now he says he does not feel ready for the responsibilities of marriage. He told me in confidence that the only attraction he now feels for the girl is a physical one; he does not feel friendship. But he is afraid to reveal his true feelings to her; he thinks she is much in love with him and doesn't want to hurt her. Also, he says it would be hard to end their physical relationship, though they are both afraid she might become pregnant. He says he would be glad to break off the engagement; however, his fiancée reminds him that if he was willing to take her virginity he should be man enough to marry her. His parents are somewhat opposed to the marriage; hers are encouraging it.

My friend feels confused, guilty, and trapped. He has come to me for advice. What should I tell him?

Problem Census

This technique, explained in detail in the next chapter, can be used for learning groups to draw out lists of issues, feeling and belief statements, concerns, and goals for a unit of study. The target question on which the census is conducted must be of real interest to the participants, imply that many answers are possible, and be focused and clear to the participants. I once used this technique to great advantage in teaching high school biology. I posed the question "What would you like to learn about human inheritance?" to the class before beginning a unit on genetics. We posted all questions presented by the class. Then, to get answers to as many of these questions as possible, we planned our unit with readings, special reports, investigative committees, and guest speakers. Students learned a great deal about genetics, using library resources, cooperating, and themselves. Every member of the class seemed exceptionally interested and involved. I later used this technique with other high school subjects: biology, physics, and speech. Since then it has proven most valuable in the conduct of classes in communication skills, graduate seminars, and adult study groups. This is useable as a special discussion technique at every level of age and sophistication.

Epstein gave some examples of the kinds of target questions she has found most useful in getting into vital concerns of high school students:

What would you like to know about race?

What do you want to know about sex?

What do you want to know about drugs?[13]

It takes great honesty, fairness, and objectivity on the part of a leader to use such a technique. The issues that are raised meet the concerns of the group rather than the needs of the leader.

13. Charlotte Epstein, *Affective Subjects in the Classroom: Exploring Race, Sex, and Drugs* (Scranton, Pa.: Intext Educational Publishers, 1972), pp. 12-13.

Affective Discussion

This term, coined by Epstein, refers to a ventilation of feelings among several students in a class, but the technique can be used with any learning group at almost any level.[14] The purpose is to express and explore "feelings" of members of a group, often necessary before people can make objective and intelligent responses to factual information, ideas, and beliefs different from those they currently hold. The group should consist of 6-10 persons seated in a tight circle. In a traditional classroom the teacher can seat a part of the class in front of the room for affective discussion while other students work at their seats. A rotation system assures that every student has equal time to be in such a group. A college class can be divided into small groups, instructed in the procedure, and each group then allowed to work with the teacher as consultant or observer. I have used it with graduate students in a research class before entering into the study of statistics. These adults get deeply involved in a catharsis of their fears about statistics, and many have testified that ventilation of their feelings with me and classmates made it possible for them to learn "math" which they had been sure they could not learn. Fears of speaking up in groups or serving as spokesperson for a group in conference or before a large group meeting ("stage fright") can be dealt with through affective discussions in speech classes.

An affective discussion begins with the beliefs (assumptions) that all persons have feelings and that any feeling is "okay" to have. The technique is based on the assumption that we need to express our feelings without apology and have them accepted without criticism in order for adequate intra- and interpersonal communication to occur. Yet many teachers and would-be discussion leaders avoid the expression of feelings—they just want the "cold facts." The vital issues remain hidden agenda items which are never brought up, and block rational consideration of the surface agenda.

In conducting such a discussion the learning facilitator plays little active part, and even sits outside the circle. Present the opening question, then *listen*, perhaps making an occasional facilitative comment showing understanding and acceptance, but *no* evaluation, critical arguing or disagreement, weighing, or questioning of any kind. Here the leader is for once advised to be *laissez faire*. In the classroom this is learner-learner interaction; the teacher is largely an outsider to the affective discussion.

Epstein developed a game to help teachers in training learn what to say and what not to say as facilitators of affective discussions. This game applies the principles Gibb discovered to increase trust and reduce defensiveness. In general, avoid doing anything that remotely smacks of evaluation, control, strategy, superiority, certainty, or lack of concern for other participants. Epstein put a number of statements on cards, each with a number indicating whether the

14. *Ibid.,* Chapter 2.

impact of the statement would be positive or negative and to what degree (from +30 to −30). Then the cards are read aloud one at a time. Each student records a guess as to its value; next the real value is read from the card, and the student is awarded error points based on the difference between her guess and the number on the card. Here are some examples from her lists:

That's right. −25

That's wrong. −25

Don't you mean . . .? −25

That's not a very nice thing to say. −25

Gasp! −25

Look that up in your textbook. −15

We don't use such language here. −25

I know you didn't mean that. −25

The fact is that. . . . −25

What do you think? +25

How do you feel about that? +30

Let him finish his thought. +15

Let's discuss that point for a few minutes. −25

Don't say such things unless you really know. −30

It's all right to say what you feel. +30

I don't know. +30

I won't answer questions during this discussion. +30[15]

I hope these examples have helped you to understand the nonevaluative, totally accepting role of the leader or facilitator of affective discussion.

Questions can be on any issue about which group members have shown strong feelings. These issues might come from a problem census, inability to come to consensus on a problem, fantasy chains, or issues raised in a textbook. For example, in a course on small group communication an affective discussion might be generated from such questions as: "How do we feel about members of project groups who are undependable?" or "How do we feel about autocratic leaders?" A lively interchange is likely on any question involving a subject on which students talk a lot:

"How do we feel about parking penalties on campus?"

"How do we feel about interracial dating?"

"How do we feel about having to wear seat belts?

15. *Ibid.*, pp. 31-34.

Out of the exchange of feelings and beliefs the participants are likely to learn how very differently some people feel, yet at the same time that they are not alone. The one is broadening, the other comforting. We need both.

There are many other special discussion techniques for learning groups, such as role playing, agree-disagree guides, and the incident technique. You may want to read about some of them, and perhaps even demonstrate one in your class. But those reported here are adaptable to all types of discussion groups, and are likely to involve us on the affective level.

LEARNING BY ENCOUNTER

The encounter process as a means to personal growth and group development has been described, developed, and employed extensively over the last two decades. The T-Group process (T for training) created by workers in the National Training Laboratories has been greatly elaborated and modified by various other approaches to "sensitivity" training through encounter among group members. Prominent among the authorities on this type of discussion are Carl Rogers, George S. Bach, Leland Bradford, Jack Benne, Joseph Luft, and Gerard Egan. The student interested in gaining extensive personal insight and interpersonal skills might want to participate in a group laboratory led by a skilled "facilitator" or "trainer." There are diverse objectives and approaches for encounter groups, described in such books as those by Egan, Golembiewski, Howard, and Rogers listed in the bibliography at the end of this chapter. The interested reader should consult these works.

"Encounter" means that members explore their reactions to each other, describing what they feel openly and honestly. This should be done in a supportive way to help participants understand how they are being perceived and responded to by other people. Such feedback is then a means to gaining self-insight and self-acceptance. A high degree of trust is essential if encounter discussions are to be productive. You will recall Gibb's findings about ways of communicating during encounter discussions (T-Groups) which increased trust, as opposed to ways of communicating which increased defensiveness (see pp. 69-71). The purpose of encounter discussion was explained by Luft in a model of interpersonal communication developed by him and Ingham. This diagram, called the Johari Window for its originators, divides one's awareness into four areas, using the dimensions "known to self" and "known to others."[16] Figure 7.1 presents a simple version of this diagram. The Public Area is the area of free communication which person A can talk about and others can talk about with him. The Hidden Area represents what person A knows about himself which he spends

16. Joseph Luft, *Group Processes: An Introduction to Group Dynamics* (Palo Alto, Cal.: Mayfield Publishing Company [formerly National Press], 1963), pp. 10-15.

energy in keeping from others, and the Blind Area represents what others know, think, or feel about A which they do not tell him. The Unknown Area represents A's potential for behavior which has never been perceived or experienced by himself or the others in a group relationship. Through self-disclosure A can reduce the Hidden Area, and through feedback the others can reduce A's Blind Area, leading to a better understanding of self. Sudden and unexpected insights during an encounter discussion may even lead to a reduction of the Unknown Area. Encounter discussions focus on enlarging each participant's Public Area, thus making for better understanding of self, and more open, honest, and complete communication. When A reveals some of what had been kept hidden, he will have more energy freed up for constructive work. As some of the mask is slipped aside, others can respond to him as he sees himself. If they accept him, and find some identification with his feelings, fears, and needs, he can thus come to a greater acceptance of self and greater positive assertiveness. As others

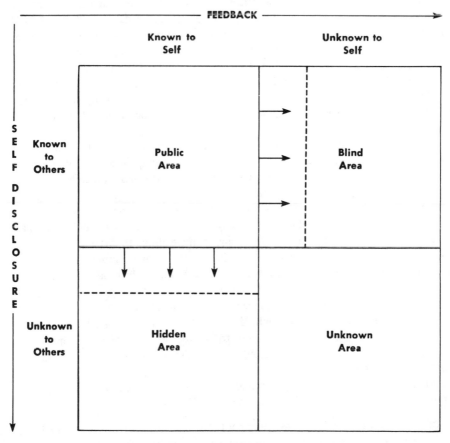

Figure 7.1. The Johari Window.

describe their reactions to his behavior more completely, he can now adjust his behavior, if he so chooses, to get different responses. In a full encounter, nothing of import is left in the Hidden or Blind Areas as "unfinished business" among the group participants. As the Public Area is increased for all members, the potential for both individual and group problem solving is enhanced.

Certain types of limited interpersonal feedback and interpersonal encounter can be used by any group studying small group discussion and/or enrolled in a speech communication, social psychology, group dynamics, or other course concerned with discussion and small group communication. In this context, *feedback* is defined as information given to a person by another (or others) about how the other has perceived and been affected by him or her. This permits the recipient of feedback to compare the responses of others with the responses expected. Feedback lets you compare your self-image with the image others hold of you; others may see you very differently from how you see yourself. Like a mirror, feedback lets one see how he or she is judged on such dimensions as active-passive, agreeable-disagreeable, dependent-independent, warm-cold, and helpful-harmful. You may think of yourself as warm and friendly, but discover that others feel you are cold and aloof, or everyone may perceive you differently. Since self-images are based on what we *think* others think of us, such feedback can modify your self-concept, perhaps increasing your confidence, reducing dogmatism and so forth. If so, you are more likely to disclose your feelings and responses, making possible still greater openness and trust among the members of your group.

In feedback sessions among members of a class in group discussion or a working group, comments should be limited to what happens among members of the group while it is in session, excluding talking about other situations members have been in, topical issues, or theorizing—a "here and now" focus, excluding talking about "then and there." Participants should state their remarks as *their personal* reactions and feelings, describing how they feel or felt and what they were reacting to. They should avoid any name-calling, theorizing about why someone acted as he did, accusing, or telling another how he should behave.

Any extensive period of feedback or encounter in interpersonal relations should be conducted in the presence of your speech instructor or some experienced group trainer. If no experienced trainer is available, you can still benefit from limited interpersonal feedback. Many variations are possible. The important thing is for each member of the group to be free to invite or not to invite the reactions of others. Comments should be limited almost entirely to what has happened in the class.

The following guidelines should make a feedback discussion more helpful to the discussants:

1. *Describe* rather than pass judgment. No one should feel condemned as a
    person. A description of one's own reactions and feelings leaves the re-

ceiver of feedback free to react as he sees fit. Avoiding the use of evaluative, emotive, or stigma terms reduces the need for the recipient to react defensively. For example, rather than saying, "You were nasty," one might say, "I felt myself growing very angry when you. . . ." And don't forget to express positive feelings which are sincere.

2. *Be as specific as possible.* To be told he or she is dominating may do a discussant more harm than good. Rather, the recipient should be told what was perceived as an attempt to dominate. Give details, describing what was done and your reactions to it. For example, "When we were talking about how to proceed, I thought you refused to consider anyone else's ideas, so I felt forced to accept your suggestions, face an attack from you, or leave the group."

3. *Consider the needs of the receiver.* What can the receiver hear, accept, and handle at this time? A lambasting to relieve your own tension may do much harm if the needs of the receiver are not sensed and responded to. Usually you should balance negative reactions with any favorable ones you may have.

4. *Deal only with behavior the receiver can change.* For example, you would not tell a stutterer that such hesitations annoy you, or a person with a tic in his cheek that it drove you nuts! However, you might let him know that you feel he has been sulking and you don't like it when he withdraws after his suggestion has been turned down.

5. *Don't force feedback on another.* Let the recipient invite comments (unless you respond immediately after something is said or done). If she indicates she wants to hear no more, stop. She is not likely to accept what you say anyway.

6. *Check to see if your feedback is understood.* Did the receiver understand what you mean? Watch for reactions, perhaps asking him or her to restate your point.

7. *See if the others agree with you.* You may find that other participants do not respond as you did to a particular participant. Questions like, "How do the rest of you feel about that?" should be asked often. When no one else agrees, try to find out why!

8. *Expect slow moments.* At times there will be a lot of hesitation and fumbling. A group may be very hesitant to express its feelings openly. It may take a long time for frank feedback to develop.

Feedback can be especially useful after discussion of a problem directly involving the group, such as, "What should be the date and type of our final exam?" or "By what policy should this class be graded?" Feedback can be especially helpful between friends and within families, sometimes under the heading of a gripe session. Indeed, no close interpersonal relationship can develop without interchange of this sort.

It is possible to set up a few general categories to guide the evaluation of each other in a feedback discussion. These criteria should not be applied ritualistically to everyone, nor should comments be limited to them. For example, on the chalkboard might be written *leadership, attitudes, preparation, speaking, accept-ance of others*, and *warmth*.

In this chapter we have considered how to organize, participate in, and lead many types of discussions, all of which are aimed at the learning and growth of the individual members rather than the creation of some group product such as a recommendation or solution to a problem. A cooperative relationship among participants, such as is required for any discussion group, usually leads to more individual learning than does a competitive relationship. The *sharing* of informa-tion, perceptions, and responses to each other—rather than decision making—characterizes the content of such discussions.

Bibliography

Egan, Gerard, *Face to Face: The Small Group Experience and Interpersonal Growth*, Monterey, Cal.: Brooks/Cole Publishing Company, 1973.

Epstein, Charlotte, *Affective Subjects in the Classroom: Exploring Race, Sex, and Drugs*, Scranton, Pa.: Intext Educational Publishers, 1972.

Golembiewski, Robert T. and Blumberg, Arthur, *Sensitivity Training and the Laboratory Approach*, Itasca, Ill.: F.E. Peacock Publishers, Inc., 1970.

Hock, Louise E., *Using Committees in the Classroom*, New York: Rinehart and Company, 1958.

Howard, Jane, *Please Touch*, New York: McGraw-Hill Book Company, 1970.

Hunter, Elizabeth, *Encounter in the Classroom*, New York: Holt, Rinehart and Winston, Inc., 1972.

Johnson, David W., and Johnson, Roger T., *Learning Together and Alone: Co-operation, Competition, and Individualization*, Englewood Cliffs, N.J.: Prentice-Hall, Inc., 1975.

Luft, Joseph, *Group Processes: An Introduction to Group Dynamics*, Palo Alto, Cal.: National Press, 1963.

Powell, John W., *Research in Adult Group Learning in the Liberal Arts*, White Plains, N.Y.: Fund for Adult Education, 1960.

Rogers, Carl R., *Carl Rogers on Encounter Groups*, New York: Harper & Row, Publishers, 1970.

Shaw, Marvin E., *Group Dynamics: The Psychology of Small Group Behavior*, 2nd ed., New York: McGraw-Hill Book Company, 1976, Chapters 10 and 11.

Stevens, John O., *Awareness: Exploring, Experimenting, Experiencing*, Moab, Utah: Real People Press, 1971.

Key Concepts

Affective discussion—members of a small group express and explore their feel-ings, especially fears, in relation to some topic or concept, requiring total acceptance and positive facilitation by leader or teacher of the group.

Causal pattern outline—sequence of questions for organizing a learning discussion based on the assumption of a cause-effect relationship among events.

Case discussion—learning discussion beginning with consideration of a specific problem or "case" about which group members exchange perceptions, ideas, and possible solutions.

Chronological pattern outline—a series of questions for organizing a learning discussion in which issues are taken up in a time series, such as first, second, and third.

Comparative pattern outline—a set of questions asking the discussants to compare two or more things, institutions, or other concepts on certain criteria or characteristics.

Encounter discussion—open expression of feelings and reactions of members of a group to each other and the group as a whole.

Feedback—description by member of a group of her reaction "here and now" to behavior of another member of the group.

Fine arts pattern outline—a sequence for discussing some product of human creativity beginning with examination of the object, discussion of perceived features, interpretation of the whole, evaluation, and ending with reexamination of the object.

Johari window—diagram (resembling a drawing of a window) representing the state of interpersonal communication between two or more persons, divided into Public, Hidden, Blind, and Unknown Areas.

Problem census—technique for getting questions from members of a group, ranking them, and creating a long-term agenda for the group based on member interests in relation to some topic.

Exercises

1. Select a subject of interest to the entire class, then write a detailed leader's analysis outline for a learning discussion on this subject. Compare with those done by your classmates. What do the differences in your outlines indicate?

2. Plan a strategy for leading discussion of a short poem of your own selection. If there is time, have three or four poems discussed by subgroups of classmates. In each discussion evaluate orderliness, enjoyment, and learning. Do the same with a piece of music, sculpture, design, a painting, a dress, or some other visual artistic production.

3. All members of your group or class may view a film or TV program. Together prepare an outline of questions, then discuss the film or show.

4. Each member of your group should prepare a "three-dimensional collage" on a grocery bag or cardboard box. On the outside fasten things such as pictures, objects, statements, and drawings to represent various aspects of your "Public Area" self (Johari window) which you are willing to talk about with others with whom you are acquainted. On the inside put things to represent facets of your self which you would keep hidden from all but your very closest friends (or from all other persons). Bring this to your meeting or class.

    First, put your three-dimensional collage where everyone can look it over for a few minutes prior to any discussion. Then go around the group, focusing on first one collage and then another in some order, such as clockwise. Describe what you interpret the things on the outside of the collage to mean about the creator of each collage except your own: What sort of personality characteristics does the collage indicate? What interests does the person seem to have? What is most and least prominent? What seems to be missing from the person's interests? What does the arrangement indicate? (Do *not* evaluate how well it is constructed!) This assignment must not be graded—everyone's collage is okay.

After the group has systematically examined and responded to each collage, discuss how the members of your group feel toward each other and toward the group compared to when the session began. Do you feel more or less trust? Cohesiveness? Liking?

Now see if anyone wants to take some of the contents from inside (the Hidden Area) and trust the group to see and respond to them. This must be strictly voluntary—no one has a right to pry inside another's collage. What happens to your feelings toward participants who reveal some of the Hidden Areas of self and make them public?

5. Conduct a problem census on some question, possibly "What do we want to know about small group discussion techniques?" or "What would we like to know about different religions?" After the agenda has been completely rank ordered, have a planning committee develop a schedule to deal with each of the questions, topics, or issues recorded.

6. Write a list of responses you think would be dampening and facilitating of an affective discussion. In a group of 5 or 6 persons combine and discuss your lists into a list you can all agree upon, rating each item (response) from +30 to −30 in 5-point intervals.

7. Conduct an affective discussion either with a group of classmates or some other group, and report the results in a short essay. The target question might come from a previous problem census, or the following list:

    "How do we feel about classmates who don't talk up?"

    "How do we feel about interracial marriages?"

    "How do we feel about capital punishment?"

8. Following a series of discussions, have a "feedback" session. On a chart or chalkboard write a set of terms for guiding the feedback. These should be selected by the group, possibly including some of the following: attitudes, preparation, speaking, supportiveness, acceptance of others, self-acceptance, personal insight, openness, warmth.

9. Engage in an encounter session or laboratory, with a trained facilitator to conduct the session(s). Use the guidelines on page 206 as a contract for the members of the group.

8

Special Techniques for Discussion in Public and Organizational Settings

Moderators of public discussions and leaders of small groups within larger organizations are frequently confronted by situations which require special discussion and leader techniques. A wide variety of such techniques has been developed, several of the most helpful of which are presented in this chapter. As a result of your study and practice in connection with this chapter, you should:

1. Know how to select participants for a public discussion.
2. Be able to plan and moderate an effective panel discussion or public interview program.
3. Know how to keep a forum period orderly and fair to all.
4. Know when and how to plan and conduct a Nominal Group Technique session.
5. Be able to conduct a problem census in which the participants feel secure enough to express any concern.
6. Be able to conduct buzz group discussions at appropriate points in large group meetings.
7. Be able to lead a RISK technique session in a way that every significant concern of each member is aired and dealt with to the group's satisfaction.
8. Be able to react with acceptance as leader of a problem census or RISK session to any item proposed by a participant.
9. Understand the purpose of parliamentary procedures when used in committees of larger organizations.

10.   Be able to use parliamentary procedures appropriately when leading discussions of small committees.

PUBLIC DISCUSSIONS

All public discussion is conducted for the enlightenment of an audience, not primarily for the sake of arriving at a decision among the discussants or for their learning. Thus all public discussion is a form of public speaking by a group, no matter what format is employed or whether the audience is physically present or listening to a broadcast. As in all public speaking, special concern must be given to planning, organization, and adaptation to the audience. Very precise timing is essential for broadcast discussions, and highly advisable for any public discussion. The cycling, restating, and socializing of a private discussion may tend to bore or confuse an audience. A blend of planned performance and spontaneity is combined in effective public discussions.

The purpose of a public discussion is usually determined by the program committee of some organization, the producer of a broadcasting station, or a group before whom the presentation will be made. A *moderator*, a special designated leader, needs to be appointed. In the case of a broadcast discussion, the moderator will almost always be a regular employee of the station or network. To plan and organize the discussion, the moderator would contact the hoped-for participants and ask each to agree to be a part of the program, telling them the general topic or issue, the purpose of the discussion, the reasons he or she was selected as a participant, who the other participants will be, and who is likely to compose the audience.

Participants in a public discussion should be selected on criteria of expertise, fluency, and diversity. They should be experts on the topic or knowledgeable representatives of special points of view, and able to state their information clearly and concisely. An audience will benefit little from ignorant, misinformed, or incoherent discussants!

A variety of types of public discussions have been described, but only three are used frequently. Therefore, the rest of this section will be devoted primarily to how to plan and organize these types: panel, group interview, and forum.

Panel Discussion

As you will recall, a panel discussion involves a group of specialists interacting informally in front of and for the benefit of an audience. A panel group should represent a variety of points of view, or "sides" or a major issue. For example, if you were to have a televised panel discussion on how to reduce traffic congestion and air pollution in a city, yet improve transportation, you might want such people as the following: (1) a city planner who had investigated rapid transit systems; (2) an air pollution control expert; (3) a highway engineer; (4) an urban businessman; and (5) an automotive designer. For a panel on the pros and cons of hunting as recreation before a conservation class you might have: (1) an antihunting lobbyist; (2) a professional game biologist; (3) an articulate sport hunter; and (4) a spokesman for the National Wildlife Federation.

Public discussions call for special physical arrangements. When staging a live audience public discussion, it is important that all discussants be in view of each other and of the audience at all times. Only with this arrangement can a sense of direct interaction occur. To accomplish this, seat the discussants in a semicircle, usually with the moderator at the center. The audience then faces the panel, and the panelists can alternately face the audience and each other. Panelists should be seated behind a table, preferably with some sort of cover on the front of it. Two small tables in an open "V" make an excellent arrangement.

A large name card should be placed on the table in front of each panelist. If the room is large and microphones are needed, they should be in sufficient number and so placed that the panelists can largely ignore them. Neck microphones can be used. If a chalkboard or easel is available, display the topic or question being discussed; sometimes the major issues or questions can also be listed. Such visual devices help auditors keep the discussion organized and clear in their minds.

In a very large assembly it may be necessary to have floor microphones for a forum discussion. If so, these should be strategically placed and their use clearly

Figure 8.1. A panel discussion is a form of public speaking.

explained to the audience before the forum begins. If not essential, do not use them. They will inhibit some people, and can lead to much confusion and delay.

The outline for a panel discussion could follow a problem-solving pattern or one of the enlightenment patterns suggested earlier. The moderator should ask each participant in the forthcoming panel to suggest questions for the discussion, then use these in preparing the leader's outline of three to five major questions, each with appropriate follow-up or subquestions. This rough draft outline should be sent to each of the participants so they have a chance to investigate and think of possible answers to each question.

The moderator prepares a special outline with an introduction, the pattern of questions to be raised, and a planned conclusion format. Of course physical arrangements need to be made by the moderator also, including name cards, possibly a poster with the overall topic or question, seating arrangements, etc. It is the moderator's job to see that the panel is kept organized when underway, summarizing each major topic or having the participants do so, and keeping it moving so that time is well distributed among the major topics on the outline and among the participants. A moderator's outline might look like this:

Introduction

I. Ladies and gentlemen, the question of whether or not the use of marijuana should be legalized and controlled by laws is of significance to all of us: young people, medical personnel, parents, law officers, and concerned citizens.

II. Our panel of experts represent different fields and points of view concerning marijuana:
   A. Dr. Robert Jones, at my far right, is Professor of Internal and Diagnostic Medicine at State University Medical College and author of *The Physiology of Marijuana Users*.
   B. Mr. George Ballou is Commissioner of Police for our city and former director of the division of narcotics.
   C. Ms. Robin Jones, a master's candidate in chemistry at State University, is a spokeswoman for the Society to Legalize Marijuana.
   D. Dr. Cedric Hoese is Professor of Sociology, specializing in social problems at State University and author of a recent article entitled "The Flow of Marijuana in an Urban Complex."

III. Our panel has agreed to discuss the question: "Should the use of marijuana be legalized and controlled by the government?" Four specific issues on which we will focus are:
   A. Does evidence indicate marijuana to be dangerous to the user?
   B. Are users ever dangerous to society?
   C. If it were to be made legal, by whom and under what conditions should use be permitted?

D.   Would legalization increase or decrease the problems facing our police and courts?

Discussion

I.   Does the evidence indicate that marijuana is dangerous to users? (Here would be the subquestions and the rest of the outline through the four issues mentioned in the introduction.)

Conclusion

I.   Let us summarize our agreements and differences on the four major issues: (A.; B.; C.; D.).
II.   We should all be better prepared to make our own choices about using marijuana and about what laws we want as citizens.
III.   We have time for a few questions from the audience.

Public Interview

A public interview, such as the familiar TV shows "Meet the Press" and "Face the Nation," has a group of questioners represent the audience in drawing out information and opinions from a spokesman or expert. Such a discussion may be held in a classroom, before any sort of organization which presents informational programs, or as a civic forum on a community problem or political issue. Although it may be largely unplanned, it is much fairer to both interviewee and interviewers to have them meet in advance and agree on the areas or topics to be explored, any subjects on which the interviewee would not want to respond, and some general pattern of topics, questions, or issues. This also permits everyone to prepare more specifically.

The interviewers should be chosen as representatives of various interests in the audience and/or because of their knowledge which will enable them to ask questions that will bring out the special knowledge and beliefs of the interviewee. Questions should not be designed to "trap" the respondent into embarrassing admissions or leading questions which make debater points for the questioner. The aim is to get straightforward, informed answers, not to put the respondent on the spot. The questioners should become very familiar with the work, writing, speeches, and experience of the respondent so that their questions are adapted to his specialization as well as the audience interests and knowledge.

This technique has great value in getting in depth into a subject or problem area, is more lively and interesting than most lectures if handled well, and if done properly is somewhat easier for the interviewee than preparing a formal speech. It is often superior to a general forum in that a panel of interviewers will be able to develop a line of questioning without skipping from topic to topic, can prepare questions carefully, and not ask irrelevant, long-winded, or con-

Courtesy United Press International Photo.

Figure 8.2. A public group interview—James McCord before the Senate Watergate Committee.

fusing questions. Also, this avoids the danger of guest baiting by a querulous audience member, or speech making by would-be orators.

Sometimes as many as three or four experts are interviewed at once, but most often one or two. The best arrangement is to put the guest expert or experts at one table, the moderator in a central position facing the audience directly, and the interviewers on the other side of the moderator at a different table so that everyone on stage can see each other and still face the audience as shown in Figure 8.3.

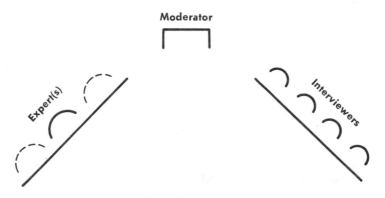

Figure 8.3.

To start the program, the moderator should mention the timeliness or importance of the subject to the audience, introduce the guest expert(s), then introduce the panel of interviewers. A very brief explanation of the format or procedures will help everyone, audience and participants, keep track of what is happening. Follow this by an invitation for the first question, which will usually have been agreed to in advance. But it is not wise to have a rehearsal or "dry run" of the program; spontaneity and surprise are features of a successful group interview.

After each interviewer has asked a main question, the others may follow up with requests for more detail, clarifications, etc., especially if they hear unexpected answers which have implications that need to be explored for the benefit of the audience. The moderator may also clarify, maintain order, see that all questioners have equal opportunity, rule out a question as irrelevant, and protect the interviewee from argument or harassment if such should occur. He will need to move the group on to new areas if they take too much time with one subtopic, select the questioner if two start to ask a question at once, and remind the questioners of their role if any of them start to make speeches. In closing, he may make a final summary, thank all the participants, and turn the program back to the chairman.

Forum

A forum discussion is often conducted following a speech, panel discussion, educational film, public interview, or symposium. To have a satisfactory forum discussion requires strict procedural control by a moderator who understands the purpose of the forum and has mastered techniques for keeping the discussion interesting and fair to all persons involved. A chairperson or moderator should control the forum following a speech, film, or other presentation; the moderator of a panel, symposium, or public interview also moderates any forum following such a group presentation. Follow these guidelines:

1. During the introduction to the panel (or other program) announce that there will be a forum or question-answer period. This allows listeners to be thinking of questions and/or remarks.
2. State whether only questions or both questions and comments will be permitted.
3. Just before allowing the audience to participate, announce definite rules to assure equal opportunity for all to speak, and insist that they be followed:
   a. Raise your hand and wait to be recognized before speaking;
   b. No one may speak a second time until each person who wants to speak has had the floor at least once;
   c. Comments or questions should be addressed to either a specific panelist by name or to the entire panel;

      d.   Remarks must be limited to not more than_____seconds;

      e.   Speak loudly enough to be heard by everyone (or, go to the floor microphone, if one is available).

4.   Tell the audience if there will be a definite length of time for the forum; then end it when scheduled.

5.   If the audience is large, recognize people from various parts of the room in a systematic pattern.

6.   Encourage different points of view by asking for them: "Does anyone want to present a *different* point of view from that which we have just heard?"

7.   If a questioner cannot be heard by all, restate the question clearly and concisely.

8.   If a question is unclear, or lengthy, restate it to the originator's satisfaction.

9.   When the alloted time is nearly up, state that there is just enough time for one or two more questions (or comments).

10.   If no one seeks the floor, wait a few seconds, then thank the panel and audience for their participation and either dismiss the meeting or go on to the next item on the agenda.

SPECIAL CONFERENCE AND UP-THE-LINE TECHNIQUES

There are a large number of special discussion techniques for getting small group involvement into a large group meeting and for up-the-line communication in large organizations, conferences, and workshops. The four selected for inclusion in this book are all discussional and group centered in nature, and of great value in a number of situations. Such techniques must be explained carefully by the coordinator of the meeting; often a special guide sheet of instructions is handed to participants explaining the purpose and steps or rules of the procedure.

Buzz Groups (Phillips 66)

This procedure is used to organize a large group meeting into many small groups which work concurrently on the same question. The purpose may be to get questions for a speaker or panel, to identify problems or issues, to compile a list of ideas or possible solutions, to develop a list of techniques for implementing and adapting a general solution to local conditions, to get personal involvement and thinking by members of a large class, etc. For example, the writer was a participant in a workshop of about 500 local education leaders in Kentucky who met to understand and work out techniques for promoting a "minimum foundation program" for public education in that state. Needed was a favorable vote of taxpayers in a special statewide election that would mean state tax support for local schools based on need. This would mean higher taxes overall and a flow of money from the wealthier districts to the poorer. Several times the entire group used the Phillips 66 technique to identify specific local problems, inexpensive advertising and promotional techniques, arguments for the program, etc.[1] These lists were processed in work groups of fifteen to eighteen members each and the final results distributed to all members. Even though the conference was large, every participant was active in discussions and the sense of enthusiasm and involvement was truly remarkable. The procedure:

1.   The chairman presents a "target" question to the entire assembly, which may be seated in rows in an auditorium or at small tables. This question should be very concise, limited, and specific. For example:

"What techniques could be used to publicize the MFP to citizens of each county or city?"

"What topics or issues should be dealt with in next year's convention?"

"What new projects might local unions undertake to help members with social problems?"

"What questions would you like to have Dr. Hanson answer about the effects of narcotics?"

Each question should be written on a card (4 x 6 or 5 x 8) with one card for each group of six members. It is a good idea to display it also on a large poster or blackboard in front of the assembly.

2.   Divide the large group into work groups of 6 by seating them at small tables, or in an auditorium by counting off by 3 in each row, then having alternate rows turn to face each other as shown in Figure 8.4.

Figure 8.4.

3.   Appoint a recorder-spokesman for each group based on seating, as: "The person sitting in the forward left-hand seat of each group will be its recorder. The recorder should write on the card *all* ideas presented, then have the group put them in rank order." An assistant or assistants then pass out the cards.

1. This procedure was developed and popularized by J. Donald Phillips, President of Hillsdale College in Michigan, who served as consultant for the Kentucky Conference. The Conference was held in 1954 at Eastern Kentucky State College.

4. Next, ask each group to record as many answers to the target question as they can think of in five minutes, then spend one minute evaluating the list to decide if any items should be eliminated and in what order to present them. Thus discussion occurs in groups of six members for six minutes—66!

5. When the five minutes are up, warn the groups and allow an extra minute if all seem involved. Then ask them to evaluate and rank the list.

6. At this point you may do any of several things, depending on the size and plan of the overall meeting.

   a. Collect the cards, which are then edited to eliminate duplications with a tally of the number of times each item was mentioned on cards. The total list is then duplicated and handed to the entire group at a subsequent meeting, presented to some special group for processing, or whatever is appropriate; or

   b. The chairman asks each recorder to report orally from his seat one *new* item from his card without explanation, or say "pass" if all his items have been presented. A secretary writes all the items on a chart or chalkboard in front of the room. The list is then processed as above or as under the problem census technique.

   c. The questions listed are presented in rotation to the speaker or panel.

This technique is also used by teachers in classes studying literature, social problems, political science, psychology, and so on. The buzz groups in a class may have more than six minutes and may even follow a brief outline prepared by the teacher. A number of reports have indicated very little or no difference in the amount of information learned from a more traditional lecture approach, and significantly more creative and critical thinking and modification of values by students involved in discussions. Variations of many types in the buzz group procedure are possible, limited only by the ingenuity of the chairperson or teacher.[2]

The Nominal Group Technique (NGT)

Some of the research into brainstorming showed that people working individually in the presence of others can generate more ideas for solving problems than will the same number of people interacting. Interacting groups deciding on a solution by consensus sometimes suppress divergence, producing a "groupthink" outcome. As an outcome of effort to codify the research on small group problem-solving interaction, Delbecq and Van de Ven developed a procedure they

2. For more details, see especially George M. Beal, Joe M. Bohlen, and J. Neil Rauda-baugh, *Leadership and Dynamic Group Action* (Ames, Iowa: The Iowa State University Press, 1962), pp. 191-199.

call the Nominal Group Technique. It is an alternative to conventional problem-solving discussions.[3] They found that NGT will usually produce more alternatives and a higher quality solution than will discussion in a conventional group session. A nominal group is one in which people work in each other's presence on the same task, but they do not interact verbally. NGT alternates between interacting verbally and working silently in the presence of others. It is *not* recommended for the typical problems which come up in the operation of any organization, but only for such major problems as planning a long-range program; it is not for routine meetings.[4] Delbecq claimed that the superiority of NGT for major program planning resulted from two things: (1) when a question is asked in a group, as soon as one person starts to answer it all others stop thinking; and (2) most people do not work hard in interactive meetings, but they will when acting individually in the presence of others.[5] As a result, he claimed that different angles, approaches, and possibilities are either overlooked or not brought up (you will recall that the prescriptive developmental outlines for problem solving were developed to offset this tendency). The NGT helps to reduce secondary tension and control conflict, and it virtually eliminates the chance for some members to make speeches to impress or represent outside constituencies rather than to help the group. On the negative side, NGT is not a complete problem-solving process, it does not enhance cohesiveness (and may reduce it), and produces far less member satisfaction than does problem-solving discussion.[6]

The essence of NGT is for several persons (six to nine) to work individually in each other's presence by writing their ideas down on paper, then to record these ideas on a chart as a group, clarify them, and evaluate them by a ranking procedure until a decision has been reached. The procedure may be varied somewhat, but should always involve members working silently, then discussion, then silent work, more discussion, and so on. Here are the steps for the leader as outlined by Delbecq:

1. State the known problem elements or characteristics of a situation which differ from what is desired. At this point there should be *no* mention of solutions, and no interaction. Members are seated at a table facing a chart easel. A large group can be divided into several small working groups, each with a leader.

3. Andre L. Delbecq, Andrew H. Van de Ven, and David H. Gustafson, *Group Techniques for Program Planning: A Guide to Nominal Group and Delphi Processes* (Glenview, Ill.: Scott, Foresman and Company, 1975), pp. 7-16.

4. *Ibid.*, pp. 3-4.

5. Andre L. Delbecq, "Techniques for Achieving Innovative Changes in Programming," a presentation at the Midwest Regional Conference of the Family Service Association of America; Omaha, Nebraska; April 20, 1971.

6. *Ibid.*

2. Ask the participants to generate a list of features of the problem, considering the emotional, personal, and organizational. Then give a clear definition of the problem. (1 and 2 can be one step, with no discussion as in step 2, with leader presenting the problem and moving group at once into step 3.)

3. Allow the group five to fifteen minutes to work silently. Each person is asked to write down all ideas he/she can think of on a sheet of paper.

4. In a "round robin" session the results are collected on a sheet of paper (chart) in front of the group where all can see the list.

    a. Ask each person in turn to give *one* item from his or her list. This item is recorded on the chart. No discussion is allowed at this time;

    b. Do not record who suggested the idea, or more than one idea from a person at a time;

    c. Keep going around the group until *all* ideas have been posted on the chart. Additional ideas may occur to members while this is going on; be sure they are stated and listed;

    d. If someone has the same idea as another, put a tally mark by the idea, but don't record it twice;

    e. The leader has also generated a list, and posts her ideas in turn just as for the other members.

5. Clarification interaction—anyone may ask another person for clarification of an idea or proposal on the list. Questions such as "What does item 6 mean?" or "Do you understand item 4?" are now in order for discussion. The leader should take the group through the list item by item, but only to clarify and elaborate, *not* to evaluate. At this point allow no lobbying, criticism, or argument for an idea.

6. Each person is now given a set of note cards, on which he writes the five or so items (all should have same number of cards, one item per card) he most prefers. These cards are now ranked (5 being highest, and 1 being lowest rank) and collected by the leader. Sum the ranks for each item, and divide by the number of persons in the group to get a value weight for each solution.

7. Now engage in an evaluation discussion of the several items having the highest average ranks. This should be a full and free evaluative discussion, with critical thinking, disagreement, and analysis encouraged.

8. If a decision is reached, fine. If not, revote, and then discuss further. This process can be repeated several times if necessary until a clear synthesis of a few ideas or support for one idea has emerged. The end result is submitted to the appropriate planners, executive, or other group for action.

This is a "supergun" technique, to be used only for major issues. Obviously you could use variations of this technique in many discussion sessions, by having quiet periods when discussants think silently and jot down their ideas on paper to enrich the ensuing discussion.

The Problem Census

This "posting" technique is useful for building an agenda for future problem-solving meetings, for program planning by an organization, or to discover problems encountered by a group of employees or students that might not be known by a supervisor or teacher. For example, a university department in which the writer was employed conducted a problem census which developed into the agenda for a series of future meetings. Different members of the faculty committed themselves to investigate the various problems and to prepare a presentation of information and an outline for each problem as it came up in turn. A group of salesmen for a feed company scattered over two states met with the sales manager to develop a list of problems and programs for a series of monthly meetings. A class in discussion developed a list of questions about how to handle various problems often encountered in committee leadership, and this became the agenda for a series of eight class meetings which included problem-solving discussions, reports, role-played demonstrations, a film, and some lecture. The graduate teaching assistants in the writer's department frequently use this technique to prepare agendas for a series of weekly seminars.

The problem census technique involves a series of distinct steps to be followed by the supervisor or other designated leader of the group:

1. Seat the group in a semicircle facing a chart or chalkboard.
2. Explain the purpose of the technique, which is to bring out all problems, concerns, questions, or difficulties any member of the group would like to have discussed.
3. The leader then asks each participant to present one problem or question, going around the group clockwise. Anyone not ready to present a new problem says "pass" and the next person has the floor. After one complete round, anyone who said "pass" may now add his question or problem. The group continues to do this until all problems have been presented.
4. The leader "posts" each problem as it is presented, writing it clearly on a chart or chalkboard where all can see. Each filled chart page can be fastened to the wall with masking tape. The leader must be totally accepting of whatever is presented, never challenging its validity or disagreeing. She may need to ask for clarification or elaboration, but always in a way that does not challenge the concern being expressed by a member. Often she will need to "boil down" a long question to the core issue, but should always rephrase it and ask if that is what the speaker intended before posting the rephrased question.
5. The group now evaluates the list for priority by voting, usually with each member voting for his top three or four choices. But all problems are included on the agenda—this merely gives order to the list.
6. The group may now find some of the questions can be answered or solved

at once by other members to the satisfaction of the presenter. Such questions are then removed from the list, and the remaining ones are now in order for future treatment.

7. Each problem is dealt with in turn. Some may call for a factual presentation by a consultant, some may be handled by a brief lecture or other informational technique, some by printed materials; but the core problems should be analyzed and dealt with by the entire group or a subcommittee of it, following one of the appropriate problem-solving patterns presented in Chapter 5.

A modification of this technique was used by Kenneth Hance in a number of plants of the United States Steel Corporation. He first taught supervisors in the Homewood Works to lead problem-solving discussions of how to reduce accidents and waste material. Participants were small groups of workers under each first-line supervisor. All the ideas, questions, and problems they came up with were presented to higher management by the supervisors, and a definite response to each item was returned from top management. The result was that this plant changed from the worst waste and accident record in the corporation to the best as production workers identified problems and recommended solutions which they *accepted.* Dr. Hance subsequently served as a consultant throughout the corporation.[7]

The "RISK" Technique[8]

This technique is useful in organizations to test out reactions to proposed changes in policy or procedures before final decisions are made, or to reduce misunderstanding, resistance, or problems from such changes when they are imposed from above. For example, the manager of a supermarket might suddenly be informed by the district manager of the chain of which the store is a part that a new type of inventory procedure will be installed, greatly modifying the work of many employees. Or, an insurance company might consider altering coverage in a fast selling line of policies. The RISK technique would be a useful small group procedure in such cases. It could help to reduce rumors and false impressions, to maintain morale in the face of change outside the supervisor or group's control, to retain group members who might otherwise quit because of unfounded fears, to reduce production robbing tensions and anxieties, and to harness productively the energies, knowledge, and creativity of people. Other-

7. Kenneth G. Hance (Paper presented to Central States Speech Association Convention, St. Louis, Missouri, April, 1969).

8. This technique was named and developed by Norman R.F. Maier, as described in *Problem-Solving Discussions and Conferences: Leadership Methods and Skills* (New York: McGraw-Hill Book Company, 1963), pp. 171-177.

wise, fantasy, sabotage, and immobilizing fear too often result from changes in routine, equipment, or policies. Not often needed, the RISK technique is invaluable in such situations.

To make it work, the leader-supervisor must be sincerely interested in airing *all* possible fears, risks, complaints, grievances, difficulties, and problems; and must be completely accepting of these even if they may seem to be factually or logically ridiculous; and able to refrain from *all* evaluative or critical responses— play a strictly procedural and supportive role. The technique can be of great value in helping an emotionally involved leader or middle level manager to listen, understand, and accept the fears of subordinates. The steps in the procedure:

1. Present in detail the proposed change of procedure or policy to the group.
2. Explain the purpose and procedures to be followed in the RISK technique, being sure to describe the leader's nonevaluative role.
3. Invite and post all "risks," fears, problems, doubts, concerns, etc. The leader should allow no evaluation and make none himself, verbal or non-verbal, much as in brainstorming. The leader or other members of the group may clarify or simplify a member's risk statement, but never modify its intent. It is essential that the wording of the "risk" as posted be fully acceptable to the presenter. Allow plenty of time. Often the most significant items, the most threatening and disturbing to members, do not come until late in the session, often after periods of silence. The leader should keep encouraging the members to think of more risks. Members will be feeling out the leader and each other to determine if it is safe to express these, or if they might be in some way ridiculed or retaliated against.
4. After the initial meeting, reproduce and circulate the list to all participants, inviting any additions that may have been thought of in the interim.
5. At the next meeting of the group, add any further risks mentioned.
6. Then, have the *group* decide if each risk is serious and substantive. No risk should now be considered as the property of its presenter, but of the entire group. Often the discussants can resolve many of each other's fears, doubts, and concerns at this point as they share experiences, ideas, and points of view. All such items should now be removed from the list.
7. Remaining risks are now processed into an agenda, much as with the problem census. Some can be resolved by obtaining information, but the problems remaining can now be dealt with one at a time in problem-solving discussions, solutions being worked out by the group.

PARLIAMENTARY PROCEDURE IN COMMITTEES

Some organizations require that their committees follow parliamentary procedures, usually specifying that the authority for the rules of procedure shall be

Robert's Rules of Order.[9] This section is based on the principles and rules laid down in that reference work for committees. Even Robert did not recommend that committees use any more of the elaborate framework of parliamentary law than was absolutely necessary to expedite their work or to make action by the committee legal under the constitution of a parent organization. A rather formal level of parliamentary rules is necessary and useful to accomplish the work of large deliberative groups of 25 or more members. Even in large groups, the amount of detail and formality in parliamentary procedure should be adjusted to the size, sophistication, and amount of conflict within the assembly. The member of a committee (or other small group) who keeps uttering "second the motion," "point of order," "question," or "I move to table the motion" may either be showing off or is ignorant of the basic purpose of parliamentary law and of rules of order that apply to small groups.

Some organizations have a special executive group known as a "board" or "executive committee," provided for in the bylaws of the society. Such a group has only the authority vested in it by those bylaws or a special vote of the assembly of the organization. A board is usually empowered to act for the assembly between its regular meetings so long as actions of the board do not conflict with those of the assembly of the society at large. Other committees have smaller areas of freedom than a board, usually to investigate, consider alternatives, recommend to the parent organization, or take action in a very limited scope of authority. There are two types of these committees in most large organizations: *standing* and *special.*

Standing committees are established to perform some continuing work or duty, so they exist "permanently" or as long as the assembly authorizes even though membership of the committee may be changed periodically. Members serve on standing committees until their replacements have been selected. Many organizations have such standing committees as membership, social, and facilities.

Special or *ad hoc* committees are appointed as need arises to carry out specific tasks. When the assigned task has been completed the special committee ceases to exist. Thus when a special committee to investigate and recommend a new meeting place for a large group has made a report to the assembly the committee no longer exists. Members may be elected to such a committee, or appointed by the president or board.

A committee meets on call of its chairperson or any two members. The quorum is a majority (minimum number of members required to be present to carry out business) unless otherwise specified by the parent organization. The

---

9. Henry M. Robert and Sarah C. Robert, *Robert's Rules of Order Newly Revised* (Glenview, Ill.: Scott, Foresman and Company, 1970), Chapter XVI.

chairperson usually acts as secretary of a small committee, but large committees may appoint a separate secretary. If a professional secretary who is not a regular member of the committee is asked to keep records, the chairperson is still responsible for the minutes or other records, and should sign them.

The specific rules governing meetings of boards and committees (as specified by Robert) are considerably less numerous and far more informal than those governing an assembly:

1. Members do not need to obtain permission from the chair by formal recognition before speaking or making a motion. They may speak up whenever they want, so long as they do not rudely interrupt another.

2. Motions do not need a second. A motion is a proposal to take some action as a group.

3. There is no limit on how many times a member can speak on an issue, and motions to limit or close discussion are never appropriate.

4. Informal discussion is permitted with no motion pending. In a parliamentary assembly a formal motion must be made before an issue can be discussed. In committee, usually no motion is made until *after* consensus or at least a majority has been achieved through extended discussion.

5. A vote is taken, often by a show of hands, to confirm a decision already sensed by the group. "Straw" votes can be taken at any time to determine if a majority or consensus exists before taking a binding vote. The leader might say: "Let's see how we stand on this. Would all who favor it please raise your right hand."

6. When a proposal is clear to all members, a vote can be taken and the outcome recorded as a decision even though no motion has been introduced.

7. The chairperson can ask if all members "consent" or agree with an idea or proposal. Then if no one objects, the decision has been made and is reported in the minutes—for example, "It was decided by consent that we should have Jean and Bob draft a resolution to present at the next meeting of the club."

8. Committee chairpersons can speak up in a discussion, taking a stand on a controversial issue, without leaving the chair. They can also make motions and vote on all questions as do all other members of the committee. (In some large committees it may be decided that the chairperson will act as if in a large assembly, and then he or she should do so *at all times*, voting only to make or break a tie, and not participating in the substance of the discussion.)

9. A motion to **reconsider** a previous vote can be made at any time, and there is no limit on how many times a question can be reconsidered. Unlike in a parliamentary body, any person who did not vote with the losing side can move to reconsider. Thus a person who was absent or who did not vote

can ask for the reconsideration of a previous decision or vote if the action has not yet been carried out.

10. Formal reports of committees should contain only what was agreed to by a vote of at least a majority of those present at a regular and properly called (notice given each member) meeting at which a quorum was present. Informal reports for in-committee communication were explained in Chapter 3.

11. Motions can be amended in committee, but this is best done informally, voting on the proposed change in a motion only if it cannot be decided by consensus in the time available for a meeting.

12. Many of the motions required in an assembly are irrelevant; a member can discuss virtually anything informally in committee sessions, so there is no need for points of order, motions to table, or matters of personal privilege. In short, the bulk of what is called "parliamentary law" is not needed and can even be obstructive to committee deliberations and actions.

Guidance on how to draft committee reports and resolutions was provided in Chapter 3. Usually the chairperson makes formal reports from a committee in writing. In a meeting of the parent body the committee chairperson may give an oral report, then hand the written report to the secretary of the assembly. Reports of less formal motions or work in progress can be made orally. When a committee report includes a recommendation for action by the entire assembly, the spokesperson for the committee presents it as a main motion. No second is required, for at least one other person has supported it within the committee. Robert recommended that the speaker say something like "I move to adopt the report of the _____ committee" when concluding a report which does not include a motion for action as a way of getting endorsement for the report. Such motions to "adopt" and resolutions for action are then treated as any other main motion on the floor of an assembly. Here are some ways of presenting committee reports:

"The Committee on _____ reports that. . . ."

"I move the adoption of the resolution just read."

"The _____ Committee moves that. . . ."

If a committee is unable to reach consensus and a minority of its membership wants to make a report or recommendation different from that of the majority, it usually is permitted to do so as soon as the "majority" committee report has been made. This is not a *right* of a committee minority, but of course during debate under parliamentary rules the members who did not agree with the majority position can speak their opposition. However, no one has the right to allude to what happened during the committee's private discussions unless the entire committee has agreed that this is to be permitted.

In summary, keep business in a committee informal, using only a very minimum of rules of order and precedence. Use votes to show that a legal majority supported all reported findings, recommendations, and actions, but not to shut off discussion or imply that majority is the preferred way of making decisions in a small committee. Write and present formal reports to parent organizations carefully and in good form. Have a spokesperson (usually holder of the chair) speak for the committee; no second is needed when that person speaks for the committee to the parent body. The committee members should be prepared to support the committee's resolutions, and refute arguments that may be made against the committee's well thought out recommendations.

The special discussion techniques presented in this chapter can be of great value in public presentations or to leaders of small groups in large organizations. But all of these techniques require strong procedural leadership and careful adherence to a format. The leader must be neutral at all times, accepting all points of view and feelings, and seeing that they are given a complete and fair hearing. Participants must understand the purpose of the discussion and all rules of procedure (norms). "Equal opportunity" could be the theme for leaders of such special techniques. Led correctly and in appropriate situations, these techniques can do much to inform audiences about diverse points of view, increase personal involvement and cohesiveness in large groups, facilitate up-the-line communication, and bring real but "risky" problems out in the open where they can be dealt with rationally. When in committee, adapt parliamentary law to the processes of a small democratically led group, keeping motions, formality, and voting to the very minimum essential to conform to bylaws and make for efficiency.

Bibliography

Beal, George M., Bohlen, Joe M., and Raudabaugh, J. Neil, *Leadership and Dynamic Group Action*, Ames, Iowa: Iowa State University Press, 1962.

Delbecq, Andre L., Van de Ven, Andrew H., and Gustafson, David H., *Group Techniques for Program Planning: A Guide to Nominal Group and Delphi Processes*, Glenview, Ill.: Scott, Foresman and Company, 1975.

Maier, Norman R.F., *Problem-solving Discussions and Conferences*, New York: McGraw-Hill Book Company, 1963.

Robert, Henry M., and Robert, Sarah C., *Robert's Rules of Order Newly Revised*, Glenview, Ill.: Scott, Foresman and Company, 1970.

Key Concepts

Ad hoc or **special committee**—committee created to perform a specific task, then disband.

Board—a standing committee empowered to act in behalf of a large organization when that organization is not meeting; often called an executive committee.

Buzz group session—large group meeting is divided into small groups of approximately six persons each, who discuss a target question for a specified number of minutes, then report their answers to the entire large group.

Forum—discussion within a large audience, controlled by a moderator, usually following some presentation such as a lecture, panel discussion, or film.

Moderator—designated leader of a public discussion such as a panel, group interview, or forum.

Nominal Group Technique (NGT)—special procedure in which six to nine persons work individually in silence to generate ideas, then interact to pool, clarify, and evaluate these ideas until a plan to solve a major problem has been adopted.

Parliamentary law (and procedure)—a codified body of rules and procedures governing deliberation in a large assembly such as a legislature or business meeting of a society. This must be simplified and streamlined if bylaws mandate it for a committee.

Problem census—technique in which a group is polled for problems which are posted, then ranked by voting to create an agenda for future problem-solving discussions (or other treatment).

Quorum—legal minimum number of members who can make decisions during a meeting on behalf of an entire group.

RISK technique—procedure for bringing fears, doubts, risks, or other misgivings members of a group have to a new policy or procedure out into the open where all these items can be discussed and dealt with objectively as problems.

Exercises

1. Conduct a census of problems that members of your class would like to discuss, or of problems in the operation of your class or project group.

2. Conduct a public interview with an expert on a problem or topic of interest to members of your class. Appoint a moderator and a group of interviewers who will research the topic thoroughly and prepare questions. Work out all arrangements with the guest expert, then conduct the interview before the class or some appropriate audience.

3. Plan in detail a panel discussion on a topic of national importance. Imagine that you can select whomever you want as panelists. Select them, giving a rationale for each panelist. Then prepare a moderator's outline.

4. The class can be divided into project groups, each of which will research a problem of interest to it and of importance to all the class. Then the group should prepare and present a panel for the benefit of the rest of the class.

5. Consider a possible new procedure for grading, or an extended assignment for your class. Then practice the RISK technique with this proposed procedure.

6. Conduct a Nominal Group Technique session in your class. Divide the class into small groups of six to eight persons, and seat each group at a table or in a semicircle facing a chart easel or wall on which are taped sheets of large plain paper for recording results. Your instructor will coordinate and time the exercise, but a student should be appointed to coordinate each working group. Work on some target question such as "How should registration procedures at our college (or university) be revised?" or "How might our highways be made safer?"

7. Form a society or club-like organization of your class. Select as presiding officer a student who has training and experience as a presiding officer (or, the instructor could do this). Then establish such committees as (1) *ad hoc* committee to plan an end-of-the-term party; (2) committee to devise a plan for calculating final class grades; (3) committee to recommend a type of final examination; and (4) committee to recommend a room designed for this course. Each committee should elect its own chairperson, then operate under Robert's rules for committees of an organization. Allow two weeks for committees to work and conduct meetings. Then hold a special parliamentary session of the class at which all committees present their reports and recommendations to be acted on by the entire class.

9
Observing and Evaluating Discussions

As many writers have pointed out, the old motto "practice makes perfect" should be revised to read "practice makes permanent." So it is in discussion. Unless practice is constantly evaluated, it may result in bad habits. The means to learning is practice with analysis and evaluation leading to change in future discussions.

Constructive evaluation depends on observation and feedback of information about how a discussion group is doing. Through reading this book, listening to your instructor, and practice, you are developing a participant-observer orientation. Even while you are participating in discussion, a part of your attention is given to observing how you and your group are proceeding. One cannot both observe and participate in the same instant, so attention must be shifted rapidly from the content of the discussion to the processes of the group. As skill is developed in being a participant-observer, a discussant becomes more and more able to supply both the functional roles needed by the group and feedback about what is going on. Evaluative feedback can be used by the group to change or correct any lack of information, attitudes, norms, or procedures which keep the group from being as productive as it might be.

Skillful as one may become at maintaining a participant-observer orientation, he will sometimes become so involved in the interaction over an important issue that he will lose perspective. Then a nonparticipating observer will be helpful. Any group learning the skills and attitudes of discussion (such as in a small group communication class) will benefit from the feedback of a nonparticipating observer. This chapter describes the role of the observer, suggests how he or she can be most useful to a group, and supplies forms for recording observations and evaluations. Some of the techniques and forms can be used by discussants even when a nonparticipating observer is not available.

As a result of studying this chapter and practice in using its contents, you should:

1. Be able to describe the role of a reminder-observer and a critic-observer.
2. Be able to prepare a specific set of questions which you would seek to answer as observer of any specific group to which you are assigned.
3. Be able to explain how to reduce defensive reactions to your observations.
4. Distinguish between process and content observations.
5. Be able to devise postmeeting reaction forms appropriate to any group of which you are a member, chart the flow and frequency of verbal interaction, and use group, member, and leader rating scales.

THE ROLE OF THE OBSERVER

Every student of discussion and group processes needs the experience of observing discussion groups at work. As students have remarked countless times, "It looks different when you are sitting outside the discussion." The observer can see clearly what he was only vaguely aware of while discussing. After observing other discussants, he may be motivated to change his own conduct as a discussant. It is therefore suggested that you observe as many discussions as possible. In the speech classroom, it is wise for you to change frequently from being a discussant in one group to being an observer of another.

A very useful technique is the "fishbowl" arrangement in which a discussion group is surrounded by a circle of nonparticipating observers. These observers may all be focusing on the same aspects of group process and/or content, or may be assigned to observe, evaluate, and report on different factors (e.g., leadership, patterns of group problem solving, use of information, roles of members, verbal and nonverbal communication). Observers can be assigned on a one-to-one basis to participants as "alter egos" who make whispered suggestions to the discussant behind whom they sit, or when asked to do so indicate how they think their discussant feels or what he or she means by some action or comment.

Do not try to observe everything at once. Limit your focus to a few aspects of the discussion, perhaps at first to only one. Later, with experience, confidence, and increased awareness of the dynamics of a group, you will be ready to observe without a definite focus. You will then be able to decide as you watch which characteristics of the group are most important to assess in detail. No observer can simultaneously chronicle the content and flow of interaction, take notice of various group and individual objectives, judge the information and logic of remarks, assess the atmosphere, and note the organization of the discus-

Figure 9.1. The fishbowl is a good arrangement for multiple observers.

sion. If the observer tries to do so, the result is sure to be confusion which will reduce both personal learning and ability to give feedback to the group.

The nonparticipating observer can do three types of things, sometimes all during a single discussion: learn from the example of others; remind the group of techniques or principles of discussion they have overlooked; supply critical evaluations of the discussion. Responsibilities as reminder and critic to the group will be discussed in the following pages.

The Reminder-Observer

Often group members need to be reminded of what they already know. During interaction they may fail to notice what has been happening or to remember useful attitudes and techniques. To help them, a type of reminder-observer role has been developed. The reminder helps the group without offering any criticism. Many of your classroom discussions will be improved by having one member participate only as a reminder-observer. The reminder role should be changed from one discussion to another in order to give everyone a chance to remind without depriving anyone for a long time of the chance to practice discussion skills. Once you have developed skill in maintaining a participant-observer orientation, you will be able to act as a reminder to nonclassroom discussion groups in which you are a participant. If you serve as a model, gradually you will notice that all members of a continuing group begin to remind.

Designated leaders of group, especially those in positions of headship, may benefit from the "coaching" of a reminder-observer. The parliamentarian to a presiding officer of a large assembly serves as an observer-coach. More and more large organizations are employing the services of communication "auditors" who study the flow of information within the organization, and devise ways to improve it. These persons frequently need to assess a large number of meetings and discussions.

Before serving as a reminder, the following guidelines for reminder-observers should be studied carefully. They are designed to reduce defensive reactions to your observations.

DO:

1. Stress the positive, pointing out what a group or leader is doing well.
2. Emphasize what is most important, rather than commenting on everything you may have observed.
3. Focus on the processes of the group rather than on the content and issues per se.
4. Put most of your remarks in the form of questions or suggestions, keeping in mind that all authority for change rests with the group. You have no authority except to remind, report, and raise questions.
5. Remain completely neutral, out of any controversy about either content or procedure. You can do this by asking questions in a deadpan manner, such as, "I wonder if the group realizes that we have discussed_____, _____ and _____ in the space of five minutes?" "Are we ready for the consideration of possible solutions?" "I wonder if John and Amy understand each other's points of view?" "I wonder if we all understand the purpose of our committee?" "Is everyone getting an equal chance to participate?" Such questions remind the group of principles of good discussion without leveling specific criticisms.
6. Show trends and group characterisitics rather than singling out individual discussants for comment (unless absolutely necessary).
7. Interrupt the discussion only when you believe the group is unlikely to become aware of what is troubling it. First give the group enough time to correct itself.

DON'T:

1. Play the critic-umpire, telling anyone he is wrong.
2. Argue with a member or the group. If your question is ignored, drop it.

3.   Tell the group what they should do, your only job is to remind the group members of what they know but have overlooked.

When serving as observer, there are many things you might look for. The content of this book can provide you with a sort of checklist for observing. Some specific things you might notice when serving as reminder are suggested by the following questions:

1.   Are the group goals clear? What helped or hindered in clarifying them?
2.   Are all members aware of their area of freedom?
3.   Is the group gathering information to define the problem fully, or has it become solution-centered too soon?
4.   Do members seem to be well prepared for discussing the topic?
5.   Is information being accepted at face value or tested for dependability?
6.   Has a plan for the discussion been worked out and accepted by the group?
7.   Does the discussion seem to be orderly and organized?
8.   Do discussants display attitudes of inquiry and objectivity toward information, issues, and the subject as a whole?
9.   To what degree does the group climate seem to be one of mutual respect, trust, and cohesiveness?
10. Do all members have an equal opportunity to participate?
11. Is the pattern of interaction open, or unduly restricted?
12. How sound is the reasoning being done by the group?
13. How creative is the group in finding potential solutions?
14. Is judgment deferred until all possible solutions can be listed and understood?
15. Does the group have a list of specific and useful criteria, and is it applying them to possible solutions?
16. While evaluating ideas, is the group making use of information from earlier parts of the discussion?
17. Are periodic summaries being used to help members recall and move on to new issues without undue redundancy?
18. Are there any hidden agendas hampering the group?
19. Are any norms or procedures hampering the group?
20. Are there any breakdowns in communication due to poor listening, bypassing, or stoppers?
21. Is the style of leadership appropriate to the group?
22. If a designated leader is present, is he or she encouraging the sharing of leadership by other members?
23. Is the discussion being recorded and charted accurately?
24. Is the degree of formality appropriate to the group size and task? Are parliamentary rules or other procedural techniques being used well?
25. What else seems to be affecting the group's attempts to achieve a goal?

In addition to serving as reminder during the discussion, afterward a reminder-observer may be able to help the group by leading a discussion of the discussion or by making a detailed report of his observations. At this point he can take either of two approaches, depending on what the group wants from him and his degree of expertise:

1. A reporter, who describes the meeting without judgment, diagnosis, or suggestions for future meetings.
2. A coach, who offers tentative explanations for the behavior of the group and suggests procedures the group might employ to advantage.

The Critic-Observer

A critic-observer may do considerable reminding, but the primary function is as a critic. Such an observer belongs only in the classroom or training group. In some cases the critic-observer is primarily an advisor, either to the group as a whole or to a designated leader. For example, your instructor may interrupt a discussion to point out what he feels is going wrong and to suggest a different technique or procedure. After you have become a proficient observer, you might take the role of critic-advisor for a small discussion group in another speech class or perhaps even for a group in your own class.

The critic-observer usually makes a more detailed report after the discussion than does the reminder-observer. In addition to describing and interpreting important aspects of the discussion, the critic will express opinions about weak and strong points of it. She may compliment the group, point out where and how it got into trouble, and even place blame or take an individual to task. This must be done cautiously and with tact. Many students hesitate to criticize the participation of others, and some balk at accepting criticism leveled at them. Discussants can be helped to give and accept criticism by reminding them of two points: (1) all criticism should be constructive, objective, sincere, and designed to help; (2) all critiques should include both positive and negative comments, with the good points being presented first.

The critic-observer, of course, will look for the same kinds of group behavior as will the reminder. In general, judgments should cover at least four basic general aspects of the discussion: (1) the group product, including how well it has been assessed, how appropriate it seems to be to the problem, and how well group members support it; (2) the group process, including patterns of interaction, decision making, problem solving, and communication; (3) the contributions and functional roles of individual members; and (4) leadership, especially if a designated leader is present. Different criteria will be needed for public and private groups, learning and problem-solving groups, advisory and action groups. Observation and rating forms can be developed by the student of small groups for various types of discussions and groups. The forms included in this chapter are suggestive general models which should be modified or used as guides for the preparation of specific forms and rating scales adapted to specific situations in your class or natural groups.

TOOLS FOR OBSERVING AND EVALUATING

Any group can improve its efficiency and atmosphere by taking time out for unstructured evaluation. The designated leader is in the best position to initiate such a bootstrap operation by suggesting the group take some time to study and discuss its activity. If this is not done on some periodic basis, there is danger of its being neglected. For this reason, regular times for assessment have been built into the operations of many business, government, and military groups. Also, a systematic review is likely to be more objective than one which is undertaken during a crisis. However, if group evaluation is limited to regular periods following scheduled meetings, much of importance may be forgotten. Also, taking a break for an unplanned evaluation may correct a damaging attitude or procedure before a serious breakdown can occur within the group; therefore, it seems advisable for a continuing discussion group to use both routine and spontaneous discussions of discussion (evaluation sessions).

Many tools for more formal observation and evaluation of both groups and individual discussants have been developed and reported elsewhere.[1] In this book a few of the more important tools are reported, especially those likely to be helpful for classes in discussion, leadership, and small group communication. Instruments for assessing a group are presented first, followed by those for evaluating individual participants and designated leaders.

Evaluating the Group

Postmeeting Reaction Sheets, or PMR's as they are called for short, are frequently used to get objective reactions from discussants. Since PMR's are anonymous, a participant can report personal evaluations without any threat to self. A PMR may be planned by a chairperson or other designated leader, by an instructor, by a group, or by the organizers of a large conference. The PMR's are distributed, completed, and collected immediately following the discussion.

A PMR sheet consists of a simple questionnaire designated to elicit frank comments about important aspects of the group and the discussion. Questions should be tailored to fit the purposes and needs of the person preparing the questionnaire. Sometimes the questions concern substantive items, sometimes interpersonal matters, and sometimes matters of technique and procedure. Two or more types of questions may be mixed on a PMR. Three illustrative PMR sheets are shown in Figures 9.2, 9.3, and 9.4. These can be used for almost any type of discussion.

---

1. See bibliography at end of chapter.

POSTMEETING REACTION SHEET

Instructions: Check the point on each scale that best represents your honest judgment. Add any comments you wish to make which are not covered by the questionnaire. Do *not* sign your name.

1. How clear were the *goals* of the discussion to you?

    _____

    very clear   somewhat vague   muddled

2. The *atmosphere* was

    _____

    cooperative and cohesive   apathetic   competitive

3. How well *organized and systematic* was the discussion?

    _____

    disorderly   just right   too rigid

4. How effective was the *style of leadership* supplied by the chairperson?

    _____

    too autocratic   democratic   weak

5. *Preparation for this meeting* was

    _____

    thorough   adequate   poor

6. Did you find yourself *wanting to speak* when you didn't get a chance?

    _____

    almost never   occasionally   often

7. How satisfied are you with the *results* of the discussion?

    _____

    very satisfied   moderately   very dissatisfied
                            satisfied

8. How do you feel about *working again* with this same group?

    _____

    eager   I will   reluctant

    Comments:

Figure 9.2.

POSTMEETING REACTION SHEET

1. How do you feel about today's discussion?

    excellent _____ good _____ all right _____ so-so _____ bad _____

2. What were the strong points of the discussion?

3. What were the weaknesses?

4. What changes would you suggest for future meetings?

(you need not sign your name)

Figure 9.3.

Specialized PMR forms for learning discussions are presented in Figures 9.5, 9.6, and 9.7. The first of these was developed to give evaluative reactions to the leader of a group discussing such products of human creativity as poetry, stories, music, paintings, or carvings. The second can be used to get feedback for almost any learning group; it can be modified quite readily to get any kind of responses you might want. Figure 9.7 is designed to be used during recesses of an encounter group.

REACTION QUESTIONNAIRE

Instruction: Circle the number which best indicates your reactions to the following questions about the discussion in which you participated:

1. *Adequacy of Communication:* To what extent do you feel members were understanding each others' statements and positions?

   0   1   2   3   4   5   6   7   8   9   10

   Much talking past each   Communicated directly with
   other, misunderstanding   each other, understanding well

2. *Opportunity to Speak:* To what extent did you feel free to speak?

   0   1   2   3   4   5   6   7   8   9   10

   Never had a   All the opportunity to
   chance to speak   talk I wanted

3. *Climate of Acceptance:* How well did members support each other, show acceptance of individuals?

   0   1   2   3   4   5   6   7   8   9   10

   Highly critical   Supportive and receptive
   and punishing

4. *Interpersonal relations:* How pleasant and concerned were interpersonal relations?

   0   1   2   3   4   5   6   7   8   9   10

   Quarrelsome, status   Pleasant, empathic,
   differences emphasized   concerned with persons

5. *Leadership:* How adequate was the leader (or leadership) of the group?

   0   1   2   3   4   5   6   7   8   9   10

   Too weak ( ) or   Shared, group-centered,
   dominating ( )   and sufficient

6. *Satisfaction with role:* How satisfied are you with your personal participation in the discussion?

   0   1   2   3   4   5   6   7   8   9   10

   Very dissatisfied   Very satisfied

7. *Quality of product:* How satisfied are you with the decisions, solutions, or learnings that came out of this discussion?

   0   1   2   3   4   5   6   7   8   9   10

   Very displeased   Very satisfied

8. *Overall:* How do you rate the discussion as a whole apart from any specific aspect of it?

   0   1   2   3   4   5   6   7   8   9   10

   Awful, waste of time   Superb, time well spent

Figure 9.4.

POSTMEETING REACTIONS FOR LEARNING DISCUSSION LEADER

Leader's Name _____

Instruction: Circle number on each scale which best indicates your reaction.

1. *Preparation* for leading the discussion seemed:

thorough and appropriate   very inadequate

| 7 | 6 | 5 | 4 | 3 | 2 | 1 |

2. *Organizing* and *guiding* the discussion were:

clear and orderly, not stilted   rigid or haphazard

| 7 | 6 | 5 | 4 | 3 | 2 | 1 |

3. *Spreading of participation* was:

just right   completely neglected

| 7 | 6 | 5 | 4 | 3 | 2 | 1 |

4. The *style* or philosophy of the leader was:

group centered stimulator   autocratic ("expert")

| 7 | 6 | 5 | 4 | 3 | 2 | 1 |

5. *Participating* in the discussion was:

satisfying and enjoyable   boring or frustrating

| 7 | 6 | 5 | 4 | 3 | 2 | 1 |

Comments:

Figure 9.5.

LEARNING GROUP PMR FORM

1.   What did you especially *like* or *dislike* about the discussion?

2.   What, if anything, do you believe you learned?

3.   What do you most *approve* and *disapprove* in the leader's behavior?

Figure 9.6.

PMR SHEET FOR ENCOUNTER SESSIONS

Instructions: Circle number indicating your reaction on each scale.

1. How well was discussion focused on the "here and now" experience of the group?

1	2	3	4	5	6	7

   little; mostly   totally on
   story telling   here-and-now

2. How open were members in describing feelings and reactions?

1	2	3	4	5	6	7

   no self-disclosure   open, much self-disclosure

3. How descriptive and supportive were members?

1	2	3	4	5	6	7

   evaluative and critical,   neutral   entirely descriptive
   a "hatchet job"   of reactions and
                                                  others' behaviors

4. How specific and clear were comments?

1	2	3	4	5	6	7

   vague, general and   clear, specific
   theoretical   and focussed

5. How much responsibility did members assume for the session?

1	2	3	4	5	6	7

   leader dominated, much   members assumed responsibility
   dependency behavior   for success of session

   Comments:

Figure 9.7

The results of the PMR questionnaires should be tallied and reported back to the group as soon as possible, either in printed form or by posting on a blackboard or chart. The results then become a guide for review of past practice and for planning new practices. The questions must be designed to produce data which can readily be tabulated, summarized, and reported.

Figure 9.8. PMR sheets can help you diagnose group problems.

Interaction Diagrams

A diagram of interaction made by an observer will reveal a lot about the relationships among members of a group. The diagram can reveal who is talking to whom, how often each member participates orally, and any dominating persons. A model interaction diagram is shown in Figure 9.9. Notice the data at the top of the sheet; the names of all participants are located around the circle in the same order in which they sat during the discussion. Each time a person speaks an arrow is drawn from his or her position toward the person to whom the remark was addressed. If a member speaks to the entire group, a longer arrow points towards the center of the circle. Subsequent remarks in the same direction are indicated by short cross marks on the base of the arrow.

Rating Scales

Rating scales can be used by critic-observers to record their judgments about any aspect of the group and its discussion, including group climate, cohesiveness, efficiency, satisfaction, degree of mutual respect, organization of discussion, adequacy of information, and the like. A five or seven point scale is sufficiently detailed for most purposes. Members of a class in small group communication

INTERACTION DIAGRAM

frequency and direction of
participation

Group _____

Time _____

    Begin _____

    End _____

Place _____

Observer _____

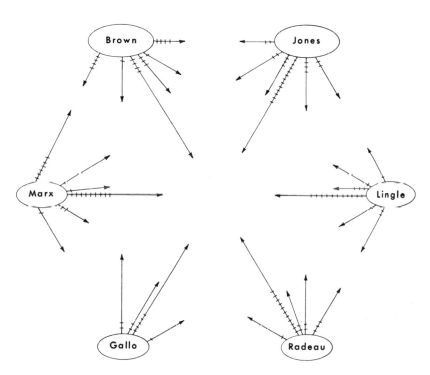

Figure 9.9.

can learn much by preparing their own scales to rate both groups and participants on various characteristics; deciding what to emphasize and rate will force
you to think through many issues on group process. A sample of the type of
instrument you might develop for rating a small group discussion is shown in
Figure 9.10.

DISCUSSION RATING SCALE

Date _____   Group _____

Time _____   Observer _____

Group Characteristic	5 excellent	4 good	3 average	2 fair	1 poor
Organization of discussion					
Equality of opportunity to speak					
Cooperative group orientation					
Listening to understand					
Evaluation of ideas					

Comments:

Figure 9.10.

Figure 9.11 is a scale for rating the problem-solving procedures of a group.
This scale was adapted from one developed by Patton and Giffin.[2] The group
should discuss any deficiencies pointed out by the scales, and how to overcome
them in the future.

2. Bobby R. Patton and Kim Giffin, *Problem-Solving Group Interaction* (New York:
Harper & Row, Publishers, 1973), pp. 213-214.

PROBLEM-SOLVING PROCESS SCALE

Instructions: On each scale indicate the degree to which the group accomplished each identified behavior. Use the following scale for your evaluations:

Poor	Fair	Average	Good	Excellent
1	2	3	4	5

Circle the appropriate number in front of each item.

1   2   3   4   5   1.   The concern of each member was identified regarding the problem the group attempted to solve.

1   2   3   4   5   2.   This concern was identified *before* the problem was analyzed.

1   2   3   4   5   3.   In problem analysis, the present condition was carefully compared with the specific condition desired.

1   2   3   4   5   4.   The goal was carefully defined and agreed to by all members.

1   2   3   4   5   5.   Valid (and relevant) information was secured when needed.

1   2   3   4   5   6.   Possible solutions were listed and clarified before they were evaluated.

1   2   3   4   5   7.   Criteria for evaluating proposed solutions were clearly identified and accepted by the group.

1   2   3   4   5   8.   Predictions were made regarding the probable effectiveness of each proposed solution, using the available information and criteria.

1   2   3   4   5   9.   Consensus was achieved on the most desirable solution.

1   2   3   4   5   10.   A detailed plan to implement the solution was developed.

Figure 9.11.

It often pays to have more than one observer filling in the same rating scale independently; you could even use a fishbowl arrangement with several observers. The observers can learn by comparing their ratings, and discussing those on which they differ by more than one point.

Evaluating Individual Participants

Almost any aspect of individual participation can be evaluated by preparing appropriate forms. An analysis of roles of members can be made by listing the names of all members in separate columns on a sheet on which the various functions described in Chapter 2 are listed in a vertical column at the left side of the sheet (Figure 9.12). Each time a participant speaks, a tally is made in the column after the role function just performed. If a member performs more than one function in a single speech, two or more tallies are made. The completed observation form will indicate what functions were supplied adequately, the absence of any needed participant functions, the degree of role flexibility of each member of the group, and the kind of role each took.

Figure 9.13 shows a simple rating form which can be completed and given to each participant by a critic-observer. The forms should be filled out toward the end of the discussion so the group does not have to wait while the observer completes them. This form was written by a group of students and has been used extensively to rate students engaged in practice discussions. Although only illustrative of many types of scales and forms which could be used, it has the virtue of being simple and brief, yet focuses on some of the most important aspects of participation. A somewhat more detailed rating scale for individual participants is shown in Figure 9.14. This form could be used by a critic-observer, or each participant in a small group might prepare one for each other member of the group.

All of the previously described observation forms and rating scales can be used to analyze and appraise functional leadership. However, because most discussion groups have a designated leader and because his or her participation is so vital to the group, many special forms have been developed for recording and evaluating the behaviors of designated leaders. The form shown in Figure 9.15 is one of the most comprehensive for evaluating designated leaders. The author adapted it from a form originally prepared for rating conference leaders in the Air Force.[3]

Observer-evaluators are not often available outside of the classroom. Designated discussion leaders, if they are to become more proficient should evaluate their own participation as a means to improvement. The questionnaire in Figure 9.16 may be used to evaluate one's own leadership. Many students of discussion and conference leadership have found it helpful to complete this form after practice discussions.

In this chapter we have examined the role of the nonparticipant observer as an aid to small groups in understanding and improving group discussions. The observer may function primarily as a "reminder" to the group of what it has overlooked, as a coach to the designated leader, or as a critic whose ratings are used to help discussants discover both their strengths and weaknesses. The student of small group communication is quite likely to learn even more when observing groups than when participating actively in the discussion.

3. Department of the Air Force, *Conference Leadership,* Air Force Manual No. 50-08 (Washington: Department of the Air Force, 1953), pp. 5-6.

BEHAVIORAL FUNCTIONS OF DISCUSSANTS

Date _____ Group _____

Time _____ Observer _____

	Participants' Names				
Behavioral Functions					
1. Initiating and orienting					
2. Information giving					
3. Information seeking					
4. Opinion giving					
5. Opinion seeking					
6. Clarifying and elaborating					
7. Dramatizing					
8. Coordinating					
9. Evaluating					
10. Consensus testing					
11. Suggesting procedure					
12. Recording					
13. Supporting					
14. Harmonizing					
15. Gatekeeping					
16. Tension relieving					
17. Norming					
18. Blocking					
19. Attacking					
20. Recognition seeking					
21. Horseplaying					
22. Dominating					
23. Advocating					
24. Withdrawing					

Figure 9.12.

PARTICIPANT RATING SCALE

for _____   Date _____

_____

(name)   Observer _____

1. Contributions to the *content of the discussion*? (well prepared, supplied information, adequate reasoning, etc.)

5	4	3	2	1

| Outstanding in | | Fair share | | Few or |
| quality and quantity | | | | none |

2. Contributions to *efficient group procedures*? (agenda planning, relevant comments, summaries, self-discipline)

5	4	3	2	1

| Always relevant, | | Relevant, no | | Sidetracked, |
| aided organization | | aid in order | | confused group |

3. Degree of *cooperativeness in attitude*? (listen to understand, responsible, agreeable, group centered, open-minded)

5	4	3	2	1

| Very responsible | | | | Self-centered, |
| and constructive | | | | stigmas |

4. *Speaking.* (clear, to group, one point at a time, concise)

5	4	3	2	1

| Brief, clear, | | | | Vague, indirect, |
| to group | | | | wordy |

5. *Value* to the group? (overall rating)

5	4	3	2	1

| Most valuable | | | | Least valuable |

Suggestions:

Figure 9.13.

DISCUSSION PARTICIPATION EVALUATION

For _____

Instructions: Circle the number which best reflects your evaluation of the discussant's participation on each scale.

Superior   Poor

1 2 3 4 5					1.	Was prepared and informed.

1 2 3 4 5   1.   Was prepared and informed.

1 2 3 4 5   2.   Contributions were brief and clear.

1 2 3 4 5   3.   Comments relevant and well timed.

1 2 3 4 5   4.   Spoke distinctly and audibly to all.

1 2 3 4 5   5.   Contributions made readily and voluntarily.

1 2 3 4 5   6.   Frequency of participation (if poor, too low ( )
or high ( ).

1 2 3 4 5   7.   Nonverbal responses were clear and constant.

1 2 3 4 5   8.   Listened to understand and follow discussion.

1 2 3 4 5   9.   Openminded.

1 2 3 4 5   10.   Cooperative and constructive.

1 2 3 4 5   11.   Helped keep discussion organized, following outline.

1 2 3 4 5   12.   Contributed to evaluation of information and ideas.

1 2 3 4 5   13.   Respectful and tactful with others.

1 2 3 4 5   14.   Encouraged others to participate.

1 2 3 4 5   15.   Assisted in leadership functions.

1 2 3 4 5   16.   Overall rating in relation to other discussants.

Comments:

Evaluator _____

Figure 9.14.

LEADER RATING SCALE

Date _____ Leader _____

Time _____ Observer _____

Instructions: Rate the leader on all items which are applicable; draw a line through all items which do not apply. Use the following scale to indicate how well you evaluate his or her performance:

> 5—superior
> 4—above average
> 3—average
> 2—below average
> 1—poor

Leadership Style and Personal Characteristics

To what degree did the leader:

_____ Show poise and confidence in speaking?

_____ Show enthusiasm and interest in the problem?

_____ Listen well to other participants?

_____ Manifest personal warmth and a sense of humor?

_____ Behave with objectivity, an open mind to all ideas?

_____ Create a supportive, cooperative atmosphere?

_____ Share functional leadership with other members?

_____ Behave democratically?

Preparation

To what degree:

_____ Were all physical arrangements cared for?

_____ Was the leader's preparation and grasp of the problem thorough?

_____ Were questions prepared to guide the discussion?

_____ Were members notified and given adequate guidance for preparing?

Figure 9.15.

Procedural and Interpersonal Leadership Techniques

To what degree did the leader:

_____ Put members at ease with each other?

_____ Introduce the problem so it was clear to all members?

_____ Guide the group to a thorough analysis of the problem before talking about solutions?

_____ Suggest an outline or pattern for group problem solving?

_____ Encourage members to modify the outline or agenda?

_____ State questions so they were clear to all members?

_____ Rebound questions to the group, especially if asking for an opinion?

_____ Facilitate mutual understanding?

_____ Keep the discussion on one point at a time?

_____ Provide the summaries needed to clarify, remind, and move forward?

_____ Encourage the group to evaluate all ideas and proposals?

_____ Equalize opportunity to participate?

_____ Stimulate imaginative and creative thinking?

_____ Control aggressive or dominant members with tact?

_____ Attempt to resolve misunderstandings and conflicts quickly but effectively?

_____ Test for consensus before moving to a new phase of problem solving?

_____ Keep complete and accurate records?

_____ See that plans were made to implement and follow-up on decisions?

Figure 9.15. (continued)

SELF-RATING SCALE FOR DISCUSSION LEADERS

Rate yourself on each item by putting a check mark in the "Yes" or "No" column. Score: five times the number of items marked "Yes"; 95, excellent; 85, good; 75, fair; below 75, poor.

		YES	NO
1.	I prepared all needed facilities.	___	___
2.	The meeting was started promptly and ended on time.	___	___
3.	I did all I could to establish an informal, permissive atmosphere.	___	___
4.	I had a plan for leading the group in an organized discussion of all major issues or phases of the problem.	___	___
5.	Everyone had equal opportunity to speak, and participation was widespread.	___	___
6.	I clearly oriented the group to its purpose and area of freedom.	___	___
7.	I listened well to understand all points of view, and encouraged all to do so.	___	___
8.	The discussion was focused on the problem before solutions were considered.	___	___
9.	All questions of judgment were rebounded to the group.	___	___
10.	My questions were clear and brief.	___	___
11.	Order and control were maintained throughout.	___	___
12.	All tangents were detected promptly and pointed out.	___	___
13.	Time was well distributed among all phases of the discussion.	___	___
14.	All important information, ideas, and decisions were promptly and accurately recorded.	___	___
15.	Summaries were used to clarify, test for agreement, and make transitions.	___	___
16.	Unclear statements were promptly clarified.	___	___
17.	I remained neutral during all constructive arguments.	___	___
18.	I did everything possible to stimulate creative thinking.	___	___
19.	Members were encouraged to evaluate evidence and ideas.	___	___
20.	The discussion was concluded well, with appropriate planning for action or subsequent meetings.	___	___

Figure 9.16.

A large number of forms have been provided to help you function as observer of discussion or to get responses from group members for improving future meetings of the group. You may want to practice using many of these forms, but I want to stress again that you may benefit most by using these as guides in preparing your own unique forms. After extensive experience as observer there may be times when you will prefer to use no forms, but only a note pad to keep a record of your observations.

Enough of reading! Only by getting in the fray as observer will you develop the insights and skills of the competent observer, whether you be called on to audit, coach, or critique small groups.

Bibliography

Beal, George M., Bohlen, Joe M., and Raudabaugh, J. Neil, *Leadership and Dynamic Group Action,* Ames, Iowa: Iowa State University Press, 1962.

Patton, Bobby R., and Giffin, Kim, *Problem-Solving Group Interaction,* New York: Harper & Row, Publishers, 1973; Part IV.

Potter, David, and Andersen, Martin P., *Discussion: A Guide to Effective Practice* 3rd ed., Belmont, Cal.: Wadsworth Publishing Company, Inc., 1976.

Smith, William S., *Group Problem-Solving Through Discussion* (rev. ed.), Indianapolis: The Bobbs-Merrill Co., Inc., 1965.

Key Concepts

Critic-observer—a nonparticipant observer of a small group discussion who evaluates the functioning of the members and the group as a whole; the critic may use any of a variety of observation forms and rating scales in order to provide feedback to the group.

Interaction diagram—a diagram showing seating arrangement of a discussion group, how often each member speaks, and to whom.

Postmeeting Reaction Sheet, or PMR—a form completed by group members following a discussion, on which they evaluate the discussion, the group, and/or the leader; the responses are usually tabulated and reported back to the group.

Rating scale—a pencil-and-paper instrument, usually completed by a critic-observer, to render an evaluation of some factor involved in the discussion.

Reminder-observer—a nonparticipant observer of a small group discussion who focuses on what is missing or has been overlooked by the group that would be helpful (information, roles, procedures, techniques, etc.), then interrupts to "remind" the group as a sort of advisor or coach.

Exercises

1. Divide your class at random into project groups of five to six members each. If there are both men and women in your class, draw them separately so that no group contains just one man or one woman.

    Each group should select a major term project which it will undertake. These can be limited to questions about small group communication and discussion, or your instructor may permit the groups to undertake any projects selected by the groups. For instance, groups from my classes have planned and held a party for the entire class, studied leadership in various campus groups and reported their findings in a panel discussion and paper, conducted studies of group counseling in area high schools, undertaken experiments in group interaction, participated in the National Contest in Public Discussion, evaluated learning discussion leadership in college classes, developed manuals, studied the jury system, and even written and produced short training films. The purpose and procedures for each project should be evaluated and approved by your instructor, who may be able to supply assistance with resources, ideas, and techniques.

The project groups will need a limited amount of time for meeting in regular class hours, but may need to conduct additional meetings outside of class.

The major purpose is to develop insights and skills as participant-observers. The project group exercise provides an opportunity to study how a group develops from a collection of people who at first lack any group goal, role structure, or norms. Each student should write a 10-15 page essay describing and evaluating the project group, using the questions at the end of this exercise as a guide.

Each group will need approximately 30 minutes of class time to report its findings near the end of the term. At this time the evaluation essays are collected and graded by the instructor. In my classes, all members of a group receive the same grades for the project report (written) and the oral presentation to the class. This is a minor grade, perhaps 5-10% of the course grade. Each evaluative essay is graded separately; this is a major grade, as much as 30% of the final grade for the course. If your class undertakes this exercise, it should begin not later than midterm so there are several weeks for the groups to develop, do their work, and prepare their reports.

Guidelines for Essay Evaluating Project Group

The questions below are only suggestive: there may be other issues of import in examining your particular group, some of these questions may be inappropriate or in need of modification for your essay, and you will need to decide what topics to raise in describing and evaluating your unique small group.

1.   What was the *goal* of the group? How did the group develop this as its objective? How adequately did this goal represent the interests and concerns of the members (individual goals)? What "hidden" agendas existed, and how did these contribute to or interfere with the surface agenda?

2.   What do you see as the structure of functional member *roles*? How did these emerge? What do you think was the impact of each member on the group, and the group on each member? Were any needed functions missing?

3.   What do you perceive as the *leadership* structure of the group? Is there a consensus leader? Who? How did this person emerge or become the acknowledged leader? What types of leadership behavior does she/he contribute? To what degree and in what ways is leadership shared in the group?

4. What *communication network* seems to exist in the group (i.e., who talks to whom)? What issues are talked about? How well do members listen to each other? Have there been problems in communicating such as ambiguity, bypassing, stoppers, or the mood of dismissal? How did the group handle these? Have adequate records been kept and reports made from meeting to meeting?

5. What *norms* governing individual and group behavior emerged? How did these come about? What effects do they have on group productivity and maintenance? If there were counterproductive norms, were these changed? How? Did you have any problem members? If so, who, and how were these persons handled?

6. What patterns were actually used in *problem solving*? How systematic and productive were these? How were decisions made? How well were all members' resources of knowledge, creativity, reasoning, and skill used? Were meetings adequately planned and organized?

7. What *climate* or atmosphere existed and now exists among the members? How have tensions been handled? Are members committed? Task oriented? Accepting and supportive of each other? Appropriately flexible?

8. *Overall*, how do you evaluate your group and your personal contribution to it? What changes would you make if you could? How, and why?

2. You may be given the opportunity to serve as a reminder-observer or critic-observer for small groups in other classes, such as fundamentals of speech communication, education, or social psychology. If so, plan carefully, then report your findings and outcomes of your interventions.

3. With one or more classmates you may be asked to serve as observer of small group discussions outside the university. Much can be learned by observing school boards, city councils, zoning commissions, or other groups whose meetings are open to the public. As a student you may even be granted permission to observe some meetings in private corporations. Tact, courtesy, unobtrusive observing, and disguising the names of those you observe will go a long way in gaining access and keeping the door open to other students who may want to follow you as observers.

Authors Index

Subject Index